Non-Drug Treatments
for ADHD

NON-DRUG TREATMENTS for ADHD

New Options for Kids, Adults & Clinicians

RICHARD P. BROWN, MD

PATRICIA L. GERBARG, MD

W. W. NORTON & COMPANY

New York · London

Cover photograph, courtesy of Petra Illig, MD President of Alaska Rhodiola Products Cooperative, shows 2-year old Rhodiola rosea growing in Bethel, Alaska on the Yukon— Koskoquim River delta. www.alaskarhodiolaproducts.com

For information about permission to reproduce selections from this book, write to Permissions, W. W. Norton & Company, Inc., 500 Fifth Avenue, New York, NY 10110

For information about special discounts for bulk purchases, please contact W. W. Norton Special Sales at specialsales@wwnorton.com or 800-233-4830

Manufacturing by Quad Graphics, Fairfield
Book design by Carole Desnoes
Production manager: Leeann Graham

Library of Congress Cataloging-in-Publication Data

Brown, Richard P.
Non-drug treatments for ADHD : new options for kids,
adults, and clinicians / Richard P. Brown, Patricia L. Gerbarg. — 1st ed.
p. ; cm.
Includes bibliographical references and index.
ISBN 978-0-393-70622-2 (hardcover)
1. Attention-deficit hyperactivity disorder—Diet therapy. I. Gerbarg, Patricia L. II. Title.
[DNLM: 1. Attention Deficit Disorder with Hyperactivity—therapy.
2. Complementary Therapies—methods. 3. Diet Therapy—methods. WS 350.8.A8]
RJ506.H9B764 2012
616.85'8906854—dc22

2011010952

ISBN: 978-0-393-70622-2

W. W. Norton & Company, Inc., 500 Fifth Avenue, New York, N.Y. 10110
www.wwnorton.com
W. W. Norton & Company Ltd., Castle House, 75/76 Wells Street, London W1T 3QT

1 2 3 4 5 6 7 8 9 0

To our family
and to yours.

CONTENTS

ACKNOWLEDGMENTS

Many people contributed to the writing of this book—professional colleagues, patients, consumer advocates, and people living with attention-deficit hyperactivity disorder (ADHD). We deeply appreciate those who allowed us to present material from their own treatment histories in the spirit of helping others to better understand and manage this multifaceted condition.

We set out to write a book that would not only be useful to clinicians and the general public, but one that would also be reader-friendly for those with ADHD. Writing in a manner that presents important scientific and medical information without being intimidating, dry, or boring was our challenge. To the extent that we succeeded, we are indebted to our manuscript readers and editors, in particular to Leslie Andrade, an elementary school teacher who deals with ADHD all day long because her husband, one of their children, and many of her students suffer from it.

We are especially grateful to Joy Bennett, IYT 500, founder of Joyful Breath Yoga Therapy, for describing the program she developed in working with boys with severe ADHD and co-existing conditions. Kim Sutherland, MEd, also shared her experiences as a special education teacher for children with severe ADHD.

We wish to thank the following colleagues who generously shared their expertise with us. Thanks to Dr. Stephen Larsen, Director of the Stone Mountain Center and Professor Emeritus, State University of

New York, for reviewing Chapter 6 and sharing his case material. Dr. Leslie Sherlin, Chief Science Officer at Neurotopia, Inc., past president of the International Society for Neurofeedback, and Adjunct Assistant Professor at Southwest College of Naturopathic Medicine, was instrumental in assuring the accuracy of the section on neurotherapy. Dr. Margaret D. Weiss, Clinic Head of the Provincial ADHD Program and Clinical Professor at the University of British Columbia, reviewed the manuscript and gave permission for us to publish some of the ADHD test measures she developed. Dr. Sat Bir Singh Khalsa, Assistant Professor of Medicine at Harvard Medical School, shared his current research on yoga in schools. We also appreciate the assistance of Dr. Charles Silberstein, attending psychiatrist at Martha's Vineyard Hospital; Dr. Pankaj Naram, Ayurvedic physician; Dr. Rollin McCraty, Director of Research, Institute of HeartMath; Dr. Larry Hirshberg, Director of the NeuroDevelopment Center and Clinical Assistant Professor at Brown University Medical Center; Naomi Gerbarg, MSW; and Judith Carrington, founder of Mental Health Resources.

Special thanks go to Dr. Petra Illeg, founder of and president of the not-for-profit Alaska Rhodiola Products Farmers Cooperative, who provided the photograph of Rhodiola rosea, a medicinal herb, that appears on the cover of our book.

This book would not have been possible without the support of our publisher, W. W. Norton & Company, particularly our editor, Andrea Costella Dawson, who was adept at helping navigate the book through the editorial and publication process while respecting the views of the authors. Her feedback, advice, encouragement, and responsiveness were invaluable. We also appreciate the work and support of Vani Kannan, associate managing editor, as well as the art department for working with us on the book cover.

Thanks are also due to our book shepherd, Wendy Jane Carrel, whose expertise and encouragement helped to shape our book and bring it to the attention of our readers.

We also want to thank one of our most candid critics, our son, David Braslow, MEd. David has always been a "math guy" who hopes to improve the way math is taught in public schools. What we didn't realize was that during his liberal arts education at Brown University he also became a skilled writer. We were the proud recipients of comments such as, "How can this be?" "Why does this matter?" "This is confusing." "If you're going to confuse me, at least tell me why it is important to be confused." As you read this book, you have our quixotic David to thank for insisting that we present material in a logical progression and for making us rewrite the unreadable prose.

Lastly, we wish to thank you, our readers, in advance for your interest in our work. We welcome your comments and questions; the notes sent to our HaveaHealthyMind.com Web site by those who read our last book, *How to Use Herbs, Nutrients, and Yoga in Mental Health Care*, assured us that we had succeeded in reaching beyond the walls of our offices and lecture halls to bring knowledge about the possibilities of integrative treatments to a global readership.

PREFACE

The impetus for this book came from the many questions we have been asked by people living with attention-deficit disorder (ADD) and attention-deficit/hyperactivity disorder (ADHD), and by the clinicians trying to help them overcome the multitude of challenges they face every day at school, in the workplace, and at home. We are both psychiatrists with over thirty years of experience. In addition, Dr. Brown is a psychopharmacologist, an herbal specialist, and a certified teacher of Akido (4th Dan), yoga, qigong, and meditation. We both practice and teach integrative approaches that combine the best of standard treatments with herbs, nutrients, cognitive enhancers, mind-body practices, and brain stimulation. Many talented clinicians, yoga therapists, and teachers have found creative methods to help those who struggle with attentional problems, and we present their work throughout this book. We would like to tell you a little more about two people in particular whose ideas enriched this book: Leslie Andrade and Joy Bennett.

In preparing this book, we wanted to be certain to address the questions that are important to people dealing with ADHD. The first three chapters provide information about diagnostic issues and the scientific foundation for understanding the known causes of ADHD as well as how different treatments may work. I (Dr. Gerbarg) was fortunate to meet Leslie Andrade, an elementary school teacher, in August, 2010 at the Brown University Summer Writer's Workshop.

The first session of the creative nonfiction group revealed that Leslie and I were both working on books about ADHD, but from different points of view. Leslie's book was based on her experiences living with a husband and a child with ADHD and dealing with ADHD in her students. It became evident that Leslie's irresistible humor and indomitable spirit had gotten her through the many crises that arise when raising and advocating for children with ADHD. Eager to learn about non-drug treatments that might help her family, Leslie agreed to critique a draft of our book. She pointed out what would make the text easier or harder for readers with ADHD to comprehend. Her observations were spot on and she sent just what we needed, a barrage of questions. Leslie also agreed to describe in her own words a little about her experience as the parent of a child with ADHD.

When my son was diagnosed with ADHD in fourth grade, I resisted the label. In the late 1990s many "busy boys" were given the diagnoses. It seemed all too easy to conclude that a boy who would not sit for a long period of time and stay focused on subject matter he was not interested in needed to be medicated to fit into the mold the educational system demanded. I searched for alternative treatments, pushed his teachers to the limits of their patience, worked hard to help him meet the state standards, and often fought to enforce the accommodations he needed to be successful both socially and academically. Most frustrating of all was his untapped potential. Many could not deny he was very capable, but only occasional glimpses of his intelligence were observable. Eventually, I realized that fighting a label was not helping my son. Although I was loath to give him medication, if it would help him fulfill his potential and relate better to other children, then so be it. He took the minimum necessary while we continued looking for alternative methods to improve his life.

When Dr. Gerbarg approached me to share my experience with ADHD as a parent, wife, and educator, I felt honored. I absorbed each chapter, learned many of the reasons behind the thoughts, feelings, and behaviors I knew to be true, and rejoiced in the fact that there will now be a comprehensive resource available with many alternative treatments for people with ADHD. This book inspired me with hope, and encouraged and helped me to capture

the joy of living with people with ADHD. I hope it does the same for
you and your unique, special loved one.

We met Joy Bennett, IYT 500, during a LifeForce Yoga training given by Amy Weintraub, MFA, E-RYT 500, at Kripalu Yoga Center. Joy studied with Amy, became one of her assistants, and is now a LifeForce Yoga mentor. Her understanding of children, her deep knowledge of yoga, her kindness of spirit, and her creativity provide an example for those who are searching for ways to help children whose symptoms of ADHD may range from mild to the most extreme. In Chapter 5 on mind–body practices you will read about some of the methods Joy developed to teach very troubled children and to make a difference in their lives and in the school where she worked.

Leslie and Joy exemplify the kinds of people who continue to inspire us to find new, alternative ADHD treatments. Indeed, the work of research scientists, clinicians, consumer advocacy groups, patients, and families all contributed to making this book a resource for anyone interested in looking beyond prescription medications for new approaches to the many challenges of ADHD.

Non-Drug Treatments
for ADHD

CHAPTER I OUTLINE

CHAPTER 1

A Many-Splendored Thing
*What Is Attention-Deficit/Hyperactivity
Disorder and Where Does
It Come From?*

For the child no one wants to play with, for the parent who is screaming inside with frustration, for the student who is locked in his or her room unable to finish an essay, and for the doctor who has run out of pills to prescribe, we hope this book makes a difference in your lives.

Consumers, families, and health care providers are all searching for better ways to treat attention-deficit/hyperactivity disorder (ADHD) because anyone who deals with this baffling condition knows that our current treatments do not work well enough. In this book you will find treatments *other than* stimulant medications, for which there is enough evidence of safety and effectiveness to justify their use in ADHD. The treatments we describe include special herbs, nutrients, mind–body practices, brain stimulation, and neurofeedback techniques—all of which can help millions of people live, love, and work more successfully.

The National Survey of Children's Health, under the aegis of the Centers for Disease Control and Prevention (CDC) randomly surveyed the parents of 70,000 children throughout the United States. In 2003–2004 7.8% of the children and adolescents of the parents interviewed had been diagnosed as having ADHD. In 2007–2008 the figures increased to 9.5% (Zoler, 2010). Estimates of the prevalence of ADHD in adults in the United States range from 1% to 5%. Given that ADHD impacts every facet of life, including psychosocial development, peer relationships, family dynamics, and academic and job performance, the need for better—that is, *safer* and *more effective*—treatments is urgent. Of even greater concern are studies showing that children with untreated ADHD are at greater risk for substance abuse, unemployment, accidents, and criminal behavior. These children also show a higher incidence of additional disorders such as learning disabilities, anxiety disorders, social phobia, depression, and bipolar disorder. On the upside, individuals with ADHD often bring a lot of energy, enthusiasm, and creativity to the tasks they undertake. They deserve the opportunity to fulfill their potential. This usually entails overcoming distraction, restlessness, and impulsivity in order to focus on learning, task completion, and understanding social cues.

Although we still have a great deal to learn about ADHD, we know that relying on only one approach will not solve all the problems. Because there are multiple contributing causes—genetic, nutritional, chemical, psychological, trauma-based, environmental—treatments must be strategically combined and tailored to the unique needs and sensitivities of each person. Andy's story shows how the best results come from combining multiple treatment approaches.

Eight-year-old Andy was in the emergency room for the fifth time with yet another broken bone. As usual, he was recklessly climbing something—a tree this time—and had taken another fall. By the age of 8, Andy believed he was a bad boy. If he wasn't climbing on and over things (often breaking a bone or two in the process), he was driving his family crazy asking questions, interrupting, and noisily banging about the house. Like most children, Andy believed what he was told by the grownups in his life. Now an adult, Andy reflected back on those trying times: "Adults told me I needed too much attention. I felt there was something wrong with me—that I was not very smart, that I was lazy. These are things I was told. Sometimes my parents or my teachers got impatient with me—and I got impatient with *myself*. As I got older, I learned to deal better with the ADHD feelings and symptoms, but they never went entirely away."

In fact, Andy is extremely intelligent. Considering how difficult it was for Andy to sit still or read a book, people were shocked when they heard he was accepted to medical school. While studying medicine, he realized that his lifelong problems were due to ADHD. He used prescription stimulant medication to study, but he never liked the way it made him feel speeded up. Over the years he figured out ways to manage his symptoms without medication by trying many different treatments, including herbs, supplements, exercise, and mind–body practices to focus his mind, enhance his information-processing abilities, quell his constant worries about people disliking him, and relieve his restlessness. Now a successful orthopedic surgeon, Andy has a wide circle of close friends and a family he adores. Two of his four children have ADHD. Based on his own experience, Andy has provided them with the treatments they need. More importantly, he and his wife are giving them love, understanding, and support to develop their many talents and to feel good about themselves.

In the coming chapters you will read about many of the non-drug treatments that have helped Andy. In the final chapter, we go into more detail about how each treatment helped with the specific symptoms Andy experienced.

Stimulant medications have become a mainstay of treatment. They often improve some symptoms, but not others, and they can cause unacceptable side effects. You may be feeling pressure from others to use medication or you may be a veteran of medication trials, in which case you are already familiar with the side effects and therapeutic limitations of taking drugs for ADHD. We briefly review medicines commonly used to treat ADHD and compare them with non-drug approaches.

The relatively new field of complementary and alternative medicine (CAM) covers a wide range of biological, psychological, and mind–body treatments that can augment the benefits of prescription drugs and sometimes reduce or obviate the need for those drugs. CAM therapies should be considered in every treatment because, overall, they have fewer side effects than drugs, and many actually have additional health benefits. Concern about drug side effects is one of the major issues driving consumers and clinicians to explore these promising new nonpharmacological treatments.

THE EVER-CHANGING IMAGE OF ADHD

There are many answers to the question "What is ADHD?" It has many facets and it can be seen in many different ways. Here we consider ADHD from several points of view. The official description of the condition by the American Psychiatric Association evolved from the "hyperkinetic child" in the 1968 *Diagnostic and Statistical Manual of Mental Disorders* (DSM-II) to attention-deficit/hyperactivity disorder in the DSM-III (1980), DSM-IV (1994), and DSM-IV-TR (text revised; 2000). Updates of the diagnostic criteria, which we describe later in this chapter in detail, should appear in the DSM-V due out in May 2013.

During the early years following the recognition of ADHD, children with a wide spectrum of learning and behavioral problems were given the diagnosis. This meant that instead of being seen as "naughty", "disobedient," "disruptive," "irresponsible," "lazy," or "unmotivated," they could be viewed as having a disorder that needed to be *understood* and *treated*. However, this paradigm shift did not change the predominant perception that the traits of people with ADHD were at best, undesirable, and at worst, disastrous.

Eventually, people began questioning the negative view of ADHD. Parents realized that although their inattentive, hyperactive children were more difficult to manage, they were also highly creative, kind, and generous. Understanding the strengths and weaknesses involved in a disorder such as ADHD is important when it comes time to choose a career. For example, many adults who recognized that they had undiagnosed ADHD knew that they had achieved more success by working as independent entrepreneurs than they would have by working in someone else's businesses. Others have become famous by channeling their energy and creativity into the performance arts.

With the explosion of stimulant medication prescriptions—and the selling, trading, and misuse of these pills by adults and school children who do not have ADHD but who want to improve focus and test performance—the perception of ADHD swung again from stigma to diluted generalization. One parent complained that when she tells other parents that her child has ADHD, they think nothing of it because they don't realize the vast difference between mildly overactive children and those with serious or even disabling ADHD symptoms.

More recently another facet has been added to public perceptions of ADHD as magazines have begun publishing stories about highly successful people with this disorder. Websites collected lists of hundreds of famous people whose biographies suggest that they might have had ADHD. Prominent names on such lists include Christopher Columbus, Thomas Edison, Gen. George Patton, Theodor Roosevelt, the Wright brothers, Samuel Clemens (i.e., Mark Twain), Ernest Hemingway, and Elvis Presley. Today, ADHD has "come out of the closet." Interviews of celebrities, business executives, performing artists, and athletes who overcame the challenges of ADHD to achieve success are appearing in the media. Here are a few representing a wide range of talent: billionaire Charles Schwab; David Neeleman, founder of JetBlue Airways; Paul Orfalea, founder of Kinko's; political pundit James Carville; Karina Smirnoff of *Dancing with the Stars*; Olympic gold medalist Michael Phelps; Olympic decathlon gold medal winner Bruce Jenner; NFL quarterback Terry Bradshaw; baseball's Pete Rose; golf prodigy Luke Kohl; Grammy-winning singer Justin Timberlake; comedian Jim Carrey; comedian/actor Howie Mandel; and starlet Paris Hilton. Many of their interviews appear in *ADDitude Magazine*, *Parenting*, and *Attention* (published by CHADD).

By scanning these names, we get a sense of the qualities that contribute to success in people with ADHD: their thirst for novelty and adventure, the capacity to channel tremendous energy in pursuing a goal, ability to think outside the box, creativity, disregard of conventional attitudes, belief in their own talents, willingness to take risks, courage, altruism, determination, and commitment to their ideas and values. While these traits are also found in people without ADHD, the point is to recognize that the very qualities that can cause problems in ADHD can also be used in positive ways. For example, rather than struggling to contain and suppress excess energy, direct it toward increased work productivity or sports performance. Think of outlets for creative energy, such as art projects, theater, dance, music, and community service. Finding ways to help yourself and your children engage in positive activities can be the best antidote for self-doubt and low self-esteem.

Consumer Activists Are Making It Better

Like many parents, Jane and Allen have overcome enormous obstacles in diagnosing, treating, and educating their son Brad, who was born in 1969, before ADHD was recognized as a diagnosis. Through their struggle, they pursued every possible avenue to learn more about the disorder, to find knowledgeable professional guidance, and to address their son's educational and vocational needs. Beyond this, they organized with other consumers to make the information they gathered available to everyone dealing with ADHD.

No crib, no playpen could contain Brad, the perpetual motion child. He could climb out of anything and tended to run continuously around whatever room he occupied. No meal could be completed without dishes on the floor. Terrified that he might climb out a window or up onto the stove, his mother watched him every minute and bolted his door shut when he slept at night—her only chance for peace. Yet she described him as "the sunniest, funniest, sweetest, most upbeat child."

In the early 1970s, when Jane and Allen took Brad, then 3 years old, to a pediatric neurologist for evaluation of his "mushy language," neither they nor their health care providers knew much about the "hyperkinetic child," and the diagnosis of ADHD had not yet been created. The first pediatric neurologist glared at them and made them feel that their child's problems were their fault. The second pediatric neurologist was kind and supportive, suggesting a trial of a stimulant medication, methylphenidate (Ritalin). The drug turned Brad into an expressionless zombie and had to be stopped. The doctor did not know what else to try and just suggested retesting the child at intervals.

Although Brad seemed to be a little better as he got older, kindergarten was a disaster. Brad was in perpetual motion, unable to focus or follow instructions, requiring constant attention. The school insisted that he enter therapy. A series of therapists ended with a psychiatrist who advised major tranquilizers. The parents refused to tranquilize their son.

They read about special schools that were successfully educating children with ADHD using an environmental approach, creating an atmosphere that contained their behavior and addressed their special needs. A long search led them to the Eagle Hill School where Brad blossomed in a noncritical, supportive, customized, multi-sensory environment. Unfortunately the family could afford the tuition ($36,000/year) for only 2 years. From 9th to 12th grade, Brad attended a highly structured, value-based school with a peer-behavioral approach that stressed personal responsibility and integrity. In addition to ADHD, he was found to have serious problems with cognition (processing information) and decoding (e.g., understanding the meaning of verbal information). Without any medication to help control the ADHD, Brad tried extremely hard to do his best. Jane recalls, "He'd scrunch up his eyes and say over and over, 'I have to control myself.'"

Learning about ADHD and working with professionals, Jane and Allen provided a consistent, structured, supportive, and loving home environment that brought out Brad's most endearing qualities. His mother describes their 6-feet 2- inches-tall son as "a gentle giant" because he is very kind and empathic.

Like many students with ADHD who leave home for the first time, Brad lost his bearings in the unstructured life at college. His impulsivity and low self-esteem got him into more and more trouble as he tried to impress the wrong set of friends. Experimentation with drugs led to multiple arrests. Yet, his sunny, outgoing, positive personality convinced judges not to incarcerate him. Eventually, Brad left college to try to settle into a job. Unable to sit still at a desk for even a few minutes, Brad worked as a salesman, but never managed to last a year in any job. His mother encouraged him to try to get a degree in substance abuse counseling, and he began the torture of trying to study for classes.

After hearing Dr. Brown lecture about CAM treatments, including a medicinal herb called *Rhodiola rosea* (R. rosea see Chapter 3), at an ADHD resource center, Mrs. Allen decided to give Brad a trial of the herb. His response was immediate. Taking 150 mg of

Rhodiola rosea in the morning enabled him to focus his mind, stop fidgeting, follow through on tasks, become productive, understand and retain material, and slowly complete his counseling degree with the help of an ADHD coach. His writing, which had previously been unintelligible, improved to the point where he could write clear clinical notes. Eager to succeed, he readily accepted and implemented advice. In his customarily sunny way, Brad is full of gratitude for the help he received and for all that he has finally achieved. In Chapter 3, we provide an update on how Brad is doing now.

Jane and Allen searched for all the knowledge they could find about ADHD to help their son. They joined with other parents to disseminate information so that other families might not have to run the gauntlet of getting services for their children. This led to the formation of a consumer support group: Children and Adults with Attention-Deficit/Hyperactivity Disorder (CHADD), a nonprofit organization founded in 1987 that promotes education, advocacy, and support for individuals with ADHD. Today CHADD represents 20,000 members, mostly families of children and adults with ADHD. About 2,000 members are professionals providing clinical and other services to persons with ADHD. The websites for CHADD and other educational organizations are listed in the Resources section at the end of this chapter.

The need for information and resources to help individuals and families living with ADHD is being recognized by professional and academic groups throughout the country. For example, the Center for Children and Families at the University of Buffalo maintains a website rich in information for individuals as well as for the professionals who work with them. Anyone can visit their website—http://ccf.buffalo.edu—and find detailed descriptions of parent training, classroom interventions, treatment plans, home behavior management plans, daily and weekly reports, and many other practical tools. At the end of this chapter you will find a list of resources to support your efforts.

EVOLUTION AND ADHD

Sociologists, geneticists, and psychologists wondered about why the traits of ADHD evolved and whether they helped humans adapt and survive. Thom Hartmann, founder of the Hunter School for children with ADHD, coined the phrase, "the Edison gene." This phrase is shorthand for a presumed set of genes that conveys traits associated with ADHD: enthusiasm, creativity, disorganization, nonlinear thinking, innovativeness, distractibility, hyperfocus, determination, eccentricity, prone to boredom, impulsivity, energetic. These characteristics can be seen to enhance the work of explorers, inventors, discoverers, and leaders in a variety of fields. Hartmann (2003) explains that in hunter-gatherer societies, people with ADHD-like traits would have made terrific hunters because they would scan their environment, react quickly and fearlessly, happily keep moving, and excel in the pursuit of quarry. Unfortunately, the postindustrial structure of our school systems and many work settings does not favor these qualities. Having to sit in a chair for long periods of time studying and memorizing facts can be excruciating for a child whose nature is to move, explore, and notice all the distracting stimuli in the world around him or her.

PROFESSIONAL DEFINITION OF ADHD

As noted above, the current standard definition of ADHD used by most health care professions is provided in the DSM-IV-TR (American Psychiatric Association, 2000). This descriptive approach relies upon lists of symptoms or characteristics, rather than underlying causes, to establish the presence of absence of ADHD. In other words, it does not attempt to explain what is different about the brain or what factors might influence the occurrence of ADHD. We briefly review the DSM criteria and some of the current discoveries and theories that may help us develop better treatments. Understanding some of the underlying causes will help you decide whether certain treatments make sense based on how likely they are to correct imbalances associated with ADHD.

Table 1.1 lists the criteria for ADHD based upon three subtypes:

1. Predominantly inattentive

   —Six or more symptoms are in the inattention category

   —Fewer than six symptoms of hyperactivity/impulsivity

2. Predominantly hyperactive/impulsive

   —Six or more symptoms are in the hyperactivity–impulsivity categories

   —Fewer than six symptoms of inattention

3. Combined hyperactive/impulsive and inattentive

   —Six or more symptoms of inattention and 6 or more symptoms of hyperactivity-impulsivity

For the sake of simplicity, we use *ADHD* to include all three subtypes. When we are limiting the discussion to only the inattentive form, we call it *ADD*.

How Do I Know If Either I or My Child Has ADHD?

The best way to address this crucial question is to start gathering information from reliable sources. These "sources" include your own behavior—for example, what you are doing right now—as well as reading books by experts, and going for consultations or evaluations from professionals who are experienced in diagnosing and treating ADHD. Although reading will give you valuable information and insights about both the diagnosis and management of ADHD, it is always wise to consult professionals because they will help you put your situation into perspective, objectively evaluate your symptoms, help you overcome any obstacles to treatment, and discuss with you a range of treatment options.

Table 1.1 ADHD Symptoms List

Inattention may appear in any of the following ways:
- Often fails to pay attention to details or makes careless mistakes at school, work, or other activities.
- Often has difficulty sustaining attention on tasks or play activities
- Often does not seem to listen when spoken to directly
- Often does not follow instructions or complete schoolwork, chores, or work. (This is not due to oppositional behavior or inability to understand directions.)
- Often has difficulty organizing tasks and activities
- Often avoids or dislikes tasks that require sustained mental effort (schoolwork)
- Often loses things needed to complete tasks (pencils, toys, school assignments, tools)
- Often is easily distracted by external stimuli
- Often is forgetful in daily activities

Hyperactivity can manifest in the following ways:
- Often squirms or fidgets with hands or feet
- Often leaves seat in classroom or other settings
- Often runs about or climbs excessively. Adolescents and adults may feel restless.
- Often has difficulty playing quietly
- Often is "on the go" as if "driven by a motor"
- Often talks excessively

Impulsivity can appear in the following ways:
- Often blurts out answers before questions have been completed
- Often has difficulty waiting turn
- Often interrupts or intrudes on others (butts into conversations or games)

Q&A

Q: What are ADHD symptoms?

A: The core symptoms of ADHD are inattention, hyperactivity, and impulsivity. All children have these qualities to some degree. Watch any 3-year-old. What makes children with ADHD different is that they have these traits to a greater degree compared to other children of the same age and that these symptoms cause impairments in two or more settings (i.e., school, work, and/or at home). There must be evidence of significant impairment in social, academic, or occupational functioning. Some symptoms must be evident by 7 years of age. Although ADHD may not be recognized until a child is older, particularly the inattentive type, careful exploration of the history usually reveals some symptoms before the age of 7 years. Furthermore, the symptoms cannot be explained by some other physical or mental disorder, such as anxiety, depression, or schizophrenia (see Table 1.1).

Q: Can I use a symptoms list to diagnose ADHD?

A: As you read this list of symptoms in Table 1.1, you may be wondering whether you or a family member has ADHD and, if so, is it severe enough to warrant treatment. You can use this list to determine whether ADHD is a *possibility*, but it will not give you a definite diagnosis.

Q: What is meant by "often"?

A: If the behavior or symptom occurs every day in at least two settings (home, school, and/or work), then it is considered "often."

Q: What is evidence of significant impairment?

A: Significant impairments in school include difficulty learning at a level commensurate with the person's IQ when that difficulty in learning is due to inattention, inability to focus, disorganization, distractibility, or disruptive classroom behaviors. Social impairments involve difficulty in making or keeping friends or in engaging in age-appropriate activities. These difficulties may be due to aggressive–impulsive behavior, inattention to what others are saying, or problems focusing and following social communications, to note a few possibilities. Examples of work impairments include low productivity due to inattention and disorganization; inability to focus on what is being said by coworkers, supervisors, or clients; and inability to sit at a desk for required periods of time.

Q: I checked off only five symptoms of inattention and three symptoms of hyperactivity/impulsivity. Does that mean that I don't have ADHD?

A: It sounds like you are concerned about some problems you have with inattention and perhaps a little hyperactivity/impulsivity. Based on your checklist score, we cannot say that you do or do not have the diagnosis of ADHD. However, you have enough difficulties in this area that you could have an attention disorder that does not meet all of the criteria for the full diagnosis of ADHD. If you feel that these symptoms may be interfering with your achievement, happiness, relationships, or fulfillment in life, then you might want to consult a professional to help you decide if you could benefit from the many options available, including coaching, counseling, cognitive therapy, non-drug complementary treatments, or medication.

STEPS FOR ASSESSING ADHD

There are both similarities and differences in assessing ADHD in adults versus children. One of the challenges in evaluating adults for this disorder has been the absence of appropriate diagnostic instruments; most of these tools were primarily designed for assessing children. In an adult, some of the symptoms may be less obvious because the person may have learned how to control or mask the behaviors. For example, by the time a squirmy, restless, overactive child reaches adulthood, he or she may have developed enough self-control to sit still in a chair, rather than running around the room, or he or she may have learned how to burn off excess energy through vigorous exercise. Another common coping mechanism is to pursue physically active jobs and avoid situations requiring long periods of attentive stillness. For these reasons it can be harder to identify the number of symptoms required to qualify for the full ADHD diagnosis. Yet, such individuals may struggle with symptoms that adversely affect their relationships, such as interrupting other people's conversations or talking too long without awareness of the interest (or disinterest) of others.

Professional Advice

Although there are many ADHD scales, there is no single standardized test that can definitely establish, by itself, the ADHD diagnosis. Additional information is always required, and tests must be interpreted in the context of the individual's history, including social and educational influences. Professional advice is needed for a thorough evaluation, interpretation of test results, and discussion of treatment options. The following components should be included in the diagnostic process (Weisler & Goodman, 2008; Weiss, 2010):

1. Assess core ADHD symptoms: inattention, hyperactivity, and impulsivity.

2. Take developmental history of symptoms, including prior to age 7.

3. Elicit family history of similar behaviors in parents, siblings, and other relatives.

4. Ask about social history of problems in relationships.

5. Elicit educational history of difficulties in academic achievement.

6. Ask about the extent to which symptoms significantly impair functioning at home, school/work, or in relationships.

7. Assess character strengths and positive qualities that may contribute to a better prognosis (future outcome). This information will provide material for building positive self-esteem as well as for career counseling. The Strengths and Difficulties Questionnaire (www.sdqinfo. org) includes assessment of positive qualities.

8. In assessing children, obtain information from parents and teachers. In assessing adults, it is helpful to get information from close relatives who know the person well.

9. Use psychiatric history and assessment to identify comorbid (coexisting) disorders of anxiety, mood, learning disabilities, personality, or substance abuse.

10. The person should undergo a complete physical examination to identify possible medical causes of symptoms, such as head injury, seizures, thyroid disorders, diabetes, vitamin deficiencies, or cardiovascular disease.

ADHD Rating Scales

Different standardized measures are designed to be completed by a clinician (*clinician-administered*), a patient, a parent, or a teacher. Scales that are completed by the patient are called *self-administered* or *self-reported*. Table 1.2 lists some of the commonly used ADHD assessment tools. Brief tests are used for screening, whereas more detailed tests help to identify more specific areas of impairment.

Table 1.2 Sample of ADHD Rating Scales

Clinician Administered Scales
Conners Adult ADHD Diagnostic Interview (Conners, 1997)
Brown ADD Scale Diagnostic Form
    http://www.drthomasebrown.com/assess_tools/index.html
Test of Variables of Attention (TOVA; Greenberg & Kindischi, 1999)

Self-Administered ADHD Scales
WHO Adult Self-Report Scale (ASRS) (World Health Organization)
    www.hcp.med.harvard.edu/ncs/ast.php.
Barkley's Current Symptoms Scale (Berkley & Murphy, 2005)
Weiss Functional Impairment Rating Scale Self-Report (WFIRS-S)
    (www.caddra.ca/cms4/pdfs/caddraGuidelines2011WFIRS_S.pdf)

Parent Rating Scales
Conners Parent Rating Scale (CPRS; Conners, 1997)
Weiss Functional Impairment Rating Scale for Parents (WFIRS-P)
    (www.caddra.ca/cms4/pdfs/caddraGuidelines2011WFIRS_P.pdf)

Teacher Rating Scales
Conners Teacher Rating Scale (CTRS; Conners, 1997)

These tests can also be used to evaluate progress over time and in response to treatments.

The World Health Organization maintains a widely used simple screening tool, the Adult ADHD Self-Report Scale—Version 1.1 (ASRS-v1.1) screener. You can check the boxes that best describe how you have felt and behaved over the past 6 months. If you check four or more boxes in the gray area, there may be reason for you to seek further evaluation for ADHD (see Table 1.3 Adler & Weiss, 2004).

The six questions in this table were found to be the most predictive of symptoms consistent with ADHD.

If four or more marks occur in the darkly shaded boxes, then the symptoms are highly consistent with ADHD in adults and further evaluation is warranted. To pursue the evaluation consult your health care provider.

Your doctor or other care provider may review the screener and evaluate the level of impairment associated with each symptom as it occurs in work/school, social, and family settings.

If symptoms are frequent, you will be asked to describe how these

Table 1.3 Adult ADHD Self-Report Scale (ASRS-v1.1) Screener

Please answer the questions below, rating yourself on each of the criteria shown using the scale on the right side of the page. As you answer each question, place an X in the box that best describes how you have felt and conducted yourself over the past 6 months. Please give this completed checklist to your healthcare professional to discuss during today's appointment.	Never	Rarely	Sometimes	Often	Very Often
1. How often do you have trouble wrapping up the final details of a project, once the challenging parts have been done?					
2. How often do you have difficulty getting things in order when you have to do a task that requires organization?					
3. How often do you have problems remembering appointments or obligations?					
4. When you have a task that requires a lot of thought, how often do you avoid or delay getting started?					
5. How often do you fidget or squirm with your hands or feet when you have to sit down for a long time?					
6. How often do you feel overly active and compelled to do things, like you were driven by a motor?					

problems have affected the ability to work, take care of things at home, or get along with other people such as your spouse/significant other.

The next step is to assess the history, the presence of these symptoms or similar symptoms in childhood. Adults who have ADHD need not have been formally diagnosed in childhood. There may be evidence of early-appearing and longstanding problems with attention or self-control. Some significant symptoms should have been present in childhood, but full symptomatology is not necessary.

Dr. Margaret D. Weiss (2010) of the Canadian ADHD Resource Alliance points out that although the DSM-IV helps identify symptoms and diagnostic criteria, it is just as important to evaluate the individual's difficulties in specific functions within six domains: home, self-concept, learning and school, activities of daily living, social activities, and risky activities. The Weiss scales can also help pinpoint the main problems that continue to affect the person's life in each of the six domains after medications have been stabilized. This information is useful in choosing non-drug treatments to target the remaining ADHD symptoms. These scales can also be used to evaluate how ADHD continues to affect the person's life. Table 1.4 reproduces the Weiss Functional Impairment Rating Scale—Self-Report (WFIRS-S) for adults and adolescents; Table 1.5 reproduces the Weiss Functional Impairment Rating Scale—Parent Report (WFIRS-P) for evaluating children.

Visitors to the website of the Canadian ADHD Resource Alliance (see www.caddra.ca) will find a wealth of information on diagnosis, treatment, and resources for consumers and clinicians. The website offers detailed treatment plans as well as copies of assessment scales. A membership fee may be required for access to all documents.

For each item on these scales, a score of 2 or 3 is considered clinically significant. A child or adult is considered to have significant impairment in an area (domain) if at least two items are rated 2 or one item is rated 3. To calculate the total scores, add up all the numbers circled in each domain and divide by the number of items in that domain to get the mean (average) score. Omit any items rated n/a (not applicable). At the end of the test, fill in the mean score for each domain (A–G on the self-report scale; A–F on the parent-report scale). This scale is well validated and available in 14 languages.

WHAT ARE THE CAUSES OF ADHD?

The many contributing causes of ADHD are roughly divided into those that are genetic and those that are due to environmental influences. However, in some cases genetic variants affect susceptibility to environmental effects. Conversely, environmental factors can influence the expression of genes. Here you will be introduced to the role of genetics in ADHD symptoms and the influence of major envi-

Table 1.4 Weiss Functional Impairment
Rating Scale—Self Report (WFIRS-S)

Circle the number for the rating that best describes how your emotional or behavioural problems have affected each item in the last month.

		Never or not at all	Sometimes or somewhat	Often or much	Very often or very much	n/a
A	**Family**					
1	Having problems with family	0	1	2	3	n/a
2	Having problems with spouse/ partner	0	1	2	3	n/a
3	Relying on others to do things for you	0	1	2	3	n/a
4	Causing fighting in the family	0	1	2	3	n/a
5	Makes it hard for the family to have fun together	0	1	2	3	n/a
6	Problems taking care of your family	0	1	2	3	n/a
7	Problems balancing your needs against those of your family	0	1	2	3	n/
8	Problems losing control with family	0	1	2	3	n/a
B	**Work**					
1	Problems performing required duties	0	1	2	3	n/a
2	Problems with getting your work done efficiently	0	1	2	3	n/a
3	Problems with your supervisor	0	1	2	3	n/a
4	Problems keeping a job	0	1	2	3	n/a
5	Getting fired from work	0	1	2	3	n/a
6	Problems working in a team	0	1	2	3	n/a
7	Problems with your attendance	0	1	2	3	n/a
8	Problems with being late	0	1	2	3	n/a
9	Problems taking on new tasks	0	1	2	3	n/a
10	Problems working to your potential	0	1	2	3	n/a
11	Poor performance evaluations	0	1	2	3	n/a

		Never or not at all	Sometimes or somewhat	Often or much	Very often or very much	n/a
C	**School**					
1	Problems taking notes	0	1	2	3	n/a
2	Problems completing assignments	0	1	2	3	n/a
3	Problems getting your work done efficiently	0	1	2	3	n/a
4	Problems with teachers	0	1	2	3	n/a
5	Problems with school administrators	0	1	2	3	n/a
6	Problems meeting minimum requirements to stay in school	0	1	2	3	n/a
7	Problems with attendance	0	1	2	3	n/a
8	Problems with being late	0	1	2	3	n/a
9	Problems with working to your potential	0	1	2	3	n/a
10	Problems with inconsistent grades	0	1	2	3	n/a
D	**Life Skills**					
1	Excessive or inappropriate use of internet, video games or TV	0	1	2	3	n/a
2	Problems keeping an acceptable appearance	0	1	2	3	n/a
3	Problems getting ready to leave the house	0	1	2	3	n/a
4	Problems getting to bed	0	1	2	3	n/a
5	Problems with nutrition	0	1	2	3	n/a
6	Problems with sex	0	1	2	3	n/a
7	Problems with sleeping	0	1	2	3	n/a
8	Getting hurt or injured	0	1	2	3	n/a
9	Avoiding exercise	0	1	2	3	n/a
10	Problems keeping regular appointments with doctor/dentist	0	1	2	3	n/a
11	Problems keeping up with household chores	0	1	2	3	n/a
12	Problems managing money	0	1	2	3	n/a
E	**Self-Concept**					
1	Feeling bad about yourself	0	1	2	3	n/a

		Never or not at all	Sometimes or somewhat	Often or much	Very often or very much	n/a
2	Feeling frustrated with yourself	0	1	2	3	n/a
3	Feeling discouraged	0	1	2	3	n/a
4	Not feeling happy with your life	0	1	2	3	n/a
5	Feeling incompetent	0	1	2	3	n/a
F	**Social**					
1	Getting into arguments	0	1	2	3	n/a
2	Trouble cooperating	0	1	2	3	n/a
3	Trouble getting along with people	0	1	2	3	n/a
4	Problems having fun with other people	0	1	2	3	n/a
5	Problems participating in hobbies	0	1	2	3	n/a
6	Problems making friends	0	1	2	3	n/a
7	Problems keeping friends	0	1	2	3	n/a
8	Saying inappropriate things	0	1	2	3	n/a
9	Complaints from neighbours	0	1	2	3	n/a
G	**Risk**					
1	Aggressive driving	0	1	2	3	n/a
2	Doing other things while driving	0	1	2	3	n/a
3	Road rage	0	1	2	3	n/a
4	Breaking or damaging things	0	1	2	3	n/a
5	Doing things that are illegal	0	1	2	3	n/a
6	Being involved with the police	0	1	2	3	n/a
7	Smoking cigarettes	0	1	2	3	n/a
8	Smoking marijuana	0	1	2	3	n/a
9	Drinking alcohol	0	1	2	3	n/a
10	Taking "street" drugs	0	1	2	3	n/a
11	Sex without protection (birth control, condom)	0	1	2	3	n/a
12	Sexually inappropriate behaviour	0	1	2	3	n/a
13	Being physically aggressive	0	1	2	3	n/a
14	Being verbally aggressive	0	1	2	3	n/a

ronmental factors including maternal health, nutrition, exposure to neuro-toxic substances, media exposure, and the family milieu.

Genetics and Heredity

Although it is well-known that genetics play a role in the inheritance of ADHD, only a few of the specific gene variants have been identified. ADHD is not 100% inheritable. In many families, one child may develop ADHD whereas his or her brothers and sisters do not. However, most people with ADHD have at least one first-degree relative with ADHD. Only 30% of men who had ADHD during childhood will have children with ADHD. Studies of twins suggest that heredity may account for about 75% of the etiology (the assignment of causes) of ADHD (Blum et al., 2008).

The variations that can occur in a single gene are called *polymorphisms*. Researchers are finding that polymorphisms in some children with ADHD are associated with reduced brain tissue volume in areas involved in attention, the activity of neurotransmitters, and the patterns of electrical activity (Cubillo et al., 2010; Konrad et al., 2010; Monastra, 2008; Wang et al., 2007). Already, studies are finding that some of these variations improve naturally with time, while others respond to specific treatments.

Environmental Effects

In contrast to genetic effects that stem from the body's DNA code, environmental effects associated with ADHD include dietary, physical, chemical, and psychological influences from outside the body. This traditional division between genes and environment, however, is becoming less distinct because, as you will see in Chapter 2, scientists are finding that environmental factors can affect the function and expression of genes involved in ADHD.

We know that nutrition affects brain development in infants and children. Researchers are trying to understand why some people with ADHD are sensitive to certain foods whereas others are not, why some people with ADHD have specific micronutrient deficiencies

CANADIAN ADHD RESOURCE ALLIANCE

Table 1.5 Weiss Functional Impairment
Rating Scale—Parent Report (WFIRS-P)

Circle the number for the rating that best describes how your child's emotional or behavioural problems have affected each item in the last month.

		Never or not at all	Sometimes or somewhat	Often or much	Very often or very much	n/a
A	**Family**					
1	Having problems with brothers & sisters	0	1	2	3	n/a
2	Causing problems between parents	0	1	2	3	n/a
3	Takes time away from family members' work or activities	0	1	2	3	n/a
4	Causing fighting in the family	0	1	2	3	n/a
5	Isolating the family from friends and social activities	0	1	2	3	n/a
6	Makes it hard for the family to have fun together	0	1	2	3	n/a
7	Makes parenting difficult	0	1	2	3	n/a
8	Makes it hard to give fair attention to all family members	0	1	2	3	n/a
9	Provokes others to hit or scream at him/her	0	1	2	3	n/a
10	Costs the family more money	0	1	2	3	n/a
B	**Learning and School**					
1	Makes it difficult to keep up with schoolwork	0	1	2	3	n/a
2	Needs extra help at school	0	1	2	3	n/a
3	Needs tutoring	0	1	2	3	n/a
4	Causes problems for the teacher in the classroom	0	1	2	3	n/a
5	Receives "time-out" or removal from the classroom	0	1	2	3	n/a
6	Having problems in the school yard	0	1	2	3	n/a
7	Receives detentions (during or after school)	0	1	2	3	n/a

		Never or not at all	Sometimes or somewhat	Often or much	Very often or very much	n/a
8	Suspended or expelled from school	0	1	2	3	n/a
9	Misses classes or is late for school	0	1	2	3	n/a
10	Receives grades that are not as good as his/her ability	0	1	2	3	n/a
C	**Life Skills**					
1	Excessive use of TV, computer, or video games	0	1	2	3	n/a
2	Keeping clean, brushing teeth, brushing hair, bathing, etc.	0	1	2	3	n/a
3	Problems getting ready for school	0	1	2	3	n/a
4	Problems getting ready for bed	0	1	2	3	n/a
5	Problems with eating (picky eater, junk food)	0	1	2	3	n/a
6	Problems with sleeping	0	1	2	3	n/a
7	Gets hurt or injured	0	1	2	3	n/a
8	Avoids exercise	0	1	2	3	n/a
9	Needs more medical care	0	1	2	3	n/a
10	Has trouble taking medication, getting needles or visiting the doctor/dentist	0	1	2	3	n/a
D	**Child's Self-Concept**					
1	My child feels bad about himself/herself	0	1	2	3	n/a
2	My child does not have enough fun	0	1	2	3	n/a
3	My child is not happy with his/her life	0	1	2	3	n/a
E	**Social Activities**					
1	Being teased or bullied by other children	0	1	2	3	n/a
2	Teases or bullies other children	0	1	2	3	n/a
3	Problems getting along with other children	0	1	2	3	n/a

		Never or not at all	Sometimes or somewhat	Often or much	Very often or very much	n/a
4	Problems participating in after-school activities (sports, music, clubs)	0	1	2	3	n/a
5	Problems making new friends	0	1	2	3	n/a
6	Problems keeping friends	0	1	2	3	n/a
7	Difficulty with parties (not invited, avoids them, misbehaves)	0	1	2	3	n/a
F	**Risky Activities**					
1	Easily led by other children (peer pressure)	0	1	2	3	n/a
2	Breaking or damaging things	0	1	2	3	n/a
3	Doing things that are illegal	0	1	2	3	n/a
4	Being involved with the police	0	1	2	3	n/a
5	Smoking cigarettes	0	1	2	3	n/a
6	Taking illegal drugs	0	1	2	3	n/a
7	Doing dangerous things	0	1	2	3	n/a
8	Causes injury to others	0	1	2	3	n/a
9	Says mean or inappropriate things	0	1	2	3	n/a
10	Sexually inappropriate behaviour	0	1	2	3	n/a

whereas others do not, and how certain nutrients can improve symptoms. These issues are explored in Chapter 2 on scientific developments and Chapter 4 on food issues.

Some studies suggest associations between maternal health during pregnancy and the risk of developing ADHD. We know that a mother's nutrition affects the rapidly developing brain of her child, and poor oxygenation in utero may also affect brain development. Similarly, toxic substances such as cigarette smoke, alcohol, and legal or illegal drugs can adversely affect neuronal development. Following head injury, some children show behaviors similar to those seen in ADHD. In children, exposure to high levels of toxic metals, such as lead or cadmium (in old plumbing fixtures or paint) or organic pesticides in food, also increases the risk of developing ADHD. A recent study of

1,139 children by the Department of Environmental Health, School of Public Health, Harvard University found that children with higher concentrations of organophosphate pesticides (dialkyl phosphate concentrations, especially dimethyl alkylphosphate (DMAP) in their urine were more likely to be diagnosed as having ADHD. Children with levels higher than the median for the pesticide DMAP metabolite, dimethyl thiophosphate, were twice as likely to have ADHD compared with children whose levels were undetectable. Most of the pesticides found in children come from food. These results support the theory that organophosphate exposure, at levels common among American children, may contribute to ADHD prevalence. The authors indicate that further studies are needed to firmly establish a causal association between pesticides and ADHD (Bouchard, Bellinger, Wright, & Weisskopf, 2010).

We don't usually think of television or computers as having environmental effects, but research is indicating that they do. Dr. Mary G. Burke, associate professor in child and adolescent psychiatry at the University of California (2010), points out that screen media provide neurologically arousing input to the developing brain.Their adverse effects are mediated by sensory organs. When used wisely, televisions and computers can enhance learning, deliver educational material, and provide social resources. However, excess exposure, particularly to media violence, can adversely affect language development, attention, and behavior. Screen media are the most detrimental during the first 5 years of life. The risk of being diagnosed with ADHD at age 7 increased with every hour of television viewed per day at ages 1 and 3 (Christakis, Zimmerman, DiGiuseppe, & McCarty, 2004). Although the American Academy of Pediatrics recommends no screen media use for children under age 2, in the United State the average baby is exposed to 2 hours daily. While limiting and monitoring television and video-game exposure makes sense for all children, particularly young children, it is even more crucial in those who are vulnerable due to ADHD. Overly stimulating and violent media content can delay development of language and reading skills and exacerbate core ADHD symptoms of inattention, impulsivity, and aggressive behavior. Furthermore, when television substitutes for interaction with family and peers, it can impair development of interpersonal and communication skills.

The home environment can also affect the expression of ADHD symptoms. Homes in which the family is able to provide stability, consistency, calmness, and structure enable the child with ADHD to function at his or her best capacity. Furthermore, the family's cooperation in creating and maintaining treatment plans is critical for the success of treatment (Bussing & Lall, 2010). Children with ADHD naturally have greater difficulties when there is a lot of conflict or instability in the home. They tend to react to conflict, anger, and uncertainty with anxiety, which further impairs their ability to focus and worsens many of their symptoms. Being susceptible to overstimulation from intense emotions, they may react to anger by becoming even more excited, hyperactive, and impulsive. If children with ADHD are subjected to abuse, they may develop dissociative symptoms that make them even more distractible, unfocused, disorganized, and forgetful.

Most families benefit from professional guidance regarding how to better understand their child's behavior, set appropriate limits (including effective rewards and punishments), provide consistent love and patient reinforcement, and shepherd their child through the school years toward appropriate, achievable vocational goals. Being able to talk with health care providers, other people with ADHD, and other parents about the struggles and mixed feelings that occur while living with ADHD can help to dispel fears and misinformation, put things in perspective, relieve feelings of guilt or inadequacy, and clear the path for learning new and better ways to handle the situation.

BENEFITS AND LIMITATIONS OF MEDICATION AND NON-DRUG TREATMENTS

The main differences between medication and non-drug treatments are their mechanisms of action, potential side effects, and additional health benefits. The most widely used and well-known treatments are prescription medications and behavioral therapy. Although behavioral therapies are an important component in ADHD treatment, they are not discussed in detail in this book. Our focus is on new and less familiar approaches such as the use of herbs and nutrients, mind–body practices, neurofeedback, and brain stimulation techniques.

Synthetic Prescription Medications

Medication classes commonly used to treat ADHD are stimulants and antidepressants. The three main forms of stimulants are Ritalin (methylphenidate), amphetamines, and alpha-adrenergic stimulating agents. The Ritalin group contains different forms of methylphenidate in commonly used brands: Concerta, Metadate, and Focalin. The amphetamine group includes Dexadrine (dextroamphetamine), Adderall (mixed amphetamine salts), and Vyvanse (lisdexamfetamine). The adrenergic stimulanting agents, clonidine (Catapres) and guanfacine (short-acting Tenex and long-acting Intuniv), reduce the flow of messages from the stress response system that lead to the physical expressions of stress reactions, for example, increased heart rate, shaking, or stomach pain.

The Ritalin group has stronger effects in stimulating the neurotransmitter norepinephrine, and lesser, but still significant, effects on dopamine. In contrast, amphetamines have greater effects on dopamine and lesser, but significant, effects on norepinephrine. The alpha-adrenergic stimulators increase levels of norepinephrine. In Chapter 2 we explain how increasing these key neurotransmitters improves attention, mental focus, and behavior in ADHD.

Although many people are able to take stimulant medications without serious adverse effects, the Ritalin and amphetamine groups can cause overstimulation, difficulty sleeping, agitation, loss of appetite, rapid heart rate, increased blood pressure, and other problems. While they are in the body, stimulant medications can have powerful effects on reducing ADHD symptoms, but they have the disadvantage of wearing off. It is necessary to allow them to wear off at night to enable sleep, but when the wearing off occurs too abruptly, the result can be a crash into irritability, bad mood, tantrums, and insomnia.

Several classes of antidepressants can be beneficial for ADHD, particularly the tricyclics (imipramine, nortriptyline, and desipramine) and bupropion (Wellbutrin), an atypical antidepressant that is the only one in its class. Another class of antidepressants are the monoamine oxidase inhibitors (MAOIs) including selegiline (Deprenyl), phenelzine (Nardil), and tranylcypromine (Parnate). Tricyclics act mainly by increasing levels of norepinephrine and sometimes serotonin. Unfortunately, they have many side effects, such as dry mouth, constipation, and heart palpitations. Nevertheless, they can be useful, often in low doses. A newer drug, Strattera (atomoxetine), was designed to increase norephinephrine, but it is also prone to cause side effects including agitation, manic reactions, and difficulty urinating.

Bupropion (Wellbutrin) is not as effective as Ritalin, but it can be a useful alternative way to affect norepinephrine and dopamine. Generally well tolerated, bupropion can cause insomnia, rash, and other side effects. Until recently, MAOIs were avoided because they could trigger serious adverse reactions if the patient ate the wrong foods or took certain medications. However, one of the MAOIs, Emsam (selegiline), now available in a skin patch, does not require a special diet when used in low doses. However, the patient must avoid certain over-the-counter and prescription medications to use it safely.

Natural, Complementary, Alternative, and Integrative Treatments

Complementary and alternative treatments have a vast array of mechanisms of action that can treat specific ADHD symptoms by improving overall brain function, cellular metabolism and repair, energy production, autonomic nervous system activity, and stress response system balance. Mind–body practices help by calming down the over-reactive stress response system and by improving mental focus, body awareness, and emotional regulation. Overactivity of the stress response system burns a lot of energy, generates free radicals that damage tissues, and increases inflammation. Mild brain stimulation techniques and neurofeedback (a form of biofeedback using signals from the brain's electrical activity as feedback)can correct brain-wave imbalances, thereby improving brain-wave patterns and facilitating calmer mental states and better communication among the different parts of the brain. Over time, mind–body and brain stimulation techniques can potentially induce brain development through neuroplasticity. Furthermore, because many CAM treatments improve cellular health and reduce excess wear and tear on our systems, they provide health benefits such as slowing disease progression and improving cardiovascular and immune function. Although there are possible side effects with any intervention, in general, the adverse reactions to properly used CAM treatments are far fewer and less severe than those that can occur with prescription medications.

Limitations of Medications and Behavioral Therapy

Although prescription medications and behavioral therapy can be very helpful, they do not cure many of the problems of ADHD, as was demonstrated by the Multimodal Treatment Study of Children with ADHD (MTA). This large randomized study by the National Institute of Mental Health (NIMH) evaluated the effects of stimulant medications and behavioral therapies on 579 children with ADHD between the ages of 7 and 10 (Swanson et al., 2008a, 2008b). In a nutshell, this is what they did and what they found after about two years: All of the students with ADHD were divided into four groups. One group received routine community care from their local doctors. The other three groups were treated by the research staff: the second group got stimulant medication; the third group was given intensive behavioral treatment; and the fourth group received combined behavioral and medication treatments. How did the groups compare after 2 years of treatment?

- Children receiving both medication and behavioral treatments improved the most.
- Stimulant medications brought greater improvements in attention, hyperactivity, and impulsivity compared to behavioral treatments.
- Stimulant medications were no better than behavioral treatments for oppositional behavior, peer relations, and academic achievement.

How did the children, who were treated between ages 7 and 10, do when they reached adolescence? Eight years after the first testing, the outcomes for 436 of the original group of children with ADHD were compared with those of 261 children of the same ages who did not have ADHD (Molina et al., 2009)

- The children who responded well to treatment during the first 3 years continued to do better in adolescence.
- Despite initial symptom improvement during the first 3 years of treatment (and maintenance of treatment in most cases), children with the combined-type of ADHD (inattention plus hyperactivity/ impulsivity) showed significant impairment in adolescence and performed worse on 91% of measures of academic, behavioral, and social functioning than their peers who did not have ADHD (Molina et al., 2009).

Would children treated in a regular community do as well as children treated in a research study? Probably not. Analysts of this study point out that the success of the medications depended on closer monitoring and dosage adjustments than most children receive in community treatment. Many doctors providing treatment in community settings do not optimize the medication regimens and therefore do not get as much improvement in the ADHD symptoms. Similarly, the magnitude of the benefits of the behavioral interventions used in the study would be unlikely to occur in most community treatment settings (Murray et al., 2008). Even though better treatments have been developed, it can take years for new information to be absorbed by the medical community. What does this study mean and what can we do about it?

- Combining both medication and behavioral treatments is likely to be more effective than either alone.
- It is best not to rely only on medication and behavior treatments. Although they are beneficial, they fall short of solving many of the long-term problems of ADHD. Additional innovative treatments are needed. That's what this book is all about.
- You or your child may not be getting the most out of your current treatments because your doctor may not have the training to determine the type of medication and the dose that would work best in your case. If you are concerned about this, it might be

worth getting a consultation with a specialist who could help fine-tune your medication regimen.

• The same may be true for behavioral treatments. Health care providers in community settings do not have all the resources of a research facility. Although they are doing their best within the constraints of their time, if you feel that more could be achieved for you or your child, then you could request a consultation and take time to look into new and additional approaches that might lead to better results.

Q&A

Q: If non-drug treatments are so good, why don't more doctors use them?

A: Only a minority of doctors knows about the benefits of complementary treatments. At the time these doctors went to medical school, there were no courses in CAM. Although many younger doctors are interested in innovative, non-drug treatments, only a few medical schools have added CAM to their curriculum. Consumers can play a major role in bringing this information to the attention of their health care professionals.

THE GOOD NEWS

On the positive side, in the past 30 years since ADHD has been accepted as a diagnosis, a great deal has been learned and numerous treatments have been developed. Studies of behavioral and family therapy are improving treatment outcomes, and studies of genetic variants may someday enable us to predict who is more likely to respond to particular treatments (see Chapter 2). Research using brain-imaging techniques is increasing our understanding of the biological basis of ADHD. The possibility that the brain of a child or adult with ADHD is different from the brain of other children or other adults can be frightening. No one wants to feel that something is "wrong" with their brain or the brain of their child. Yet, if we are to understand the underlying causes and possible cures for ADHD, researchers must intently scrutinize the brain structures that mediate our mental and emotional responses to daily activities, events, and interactions. More and more sophisticated brain-imaging studies are focusing on the neuroanatomical and neurophysiological variations found in people with ADHD.

Modern research is showing us that the brain is capable of changing, growing, and healing. *Plasticity* is the term used to describe the ability of cells to grow and develop new neural connections that can change the way the brain functions. Just as physical exercise can enlarge the size and efficiency of muscles, so, too, areas of the brain that may be underdeveloped can be strengthened and even enlarged. Although discoveries that specific areas of the brain may be thinner or less developed in people with ADHD may be disturbing, remember that this area of research is also finding ways to stimulate and improve functioning where it will make the greatest difference. Rather than fear such discoveries, we can take this information and use it to fuel hope, future research, and our determination to help ourselves and our children find even better solutions to ADHD. Many of the treatments discussed in this book are aimed at increasing the brain's plasticity and growth.

For those interested in learning the basic scientific explanations for understanding and treating ADHD, we provide essential concepts in Chapter 2. We encourage you to read Chapter 2 because it will provide you with the vocabulary and foundation to understand the symptoms and treatments that are available now and that will become available in the future. You will need this knowledge to make good decisions about your health and your family's health. In Chapters 3 through 7, you will learn about innovative treatments using herbs, brain boosters, dietary changes, vitamins, nutrients, supplements, mind–body practices, and brain stimulation techniques to help relieve many of the symptoms of ADHD so that you can improve relationships with the people you love and pursue your personal goals in life, whatever they may be. This is such a rapidly changing field that by the time our book is published, there will be new discoveries for you to learn about. We want to prepare you to keep seeking new information, to understand and evaluate what you are hearing and reading, and to be able to make the most of the many new treatment approaches as they emerge.

In addition, many people with ADHD have discovered their own strategies for overcoming the challenges they face due to distractibility, disorganization, forgetfulness, inability to complete tasks, social anxiety, relationship issues, hyperactivity, and impulsive behaviors. They are sharing their solutions through websites such as ADDitude. com, organizations such as CHADD, and publications including blogs, magazines, and books. For example, bridging the doctor–patient gap, Dr. Ed Hallowell highlights the positive aspects of ADHD in *Driven to Distraction* (Hallowell & Ratey, 1995) and *Delivered from Distraction* (Hallowell & Ratey, 2006). Writing about his own struggles with ADHD, he demonstrates that people with this condition have a great deal to contribute to their families and their work, but that they also need understanding and patience from those who are close to them. Dr. Hallowell shows how a sense of humor, honesty, nondefensiveness, and determination enable him and many of his patients to achieve joyful, fulfilling lives—which is what we hope for all our readers.

RESOURCES

In this last section of the chapter we provide various sources of information and support for assessing, treating, and living with ADHD.

Websites and Organizations

Attention Deficit Disorder Association (ADDA): www.add.org.
Provides information and networking to help adults with ADHD. Active in raising awareness, advocacy, outreach and education.

Canadian ADHD Resource Alliance: www.caddra.ca.
Information on diagnosis, treatment, and resources for consumers and clinicians, detailed treatment plans, assessment scales.

Center for Children and Families at the University of Buffalo: www.ccf.buffalo.edu.
Information on diagnosis, treatment, and resources for consumers and clinicians, and detailed treatment plans.

Children and Adults with Attention-Deficit/Hyperactivity Disorder (CHADD): www.chadd.org (800.233.4050).
Provides education, advocacy, and support for children and adults with ADHD.

Books

Hallowell, E. M., & Ratey, J. J. (2006). *Delivered from Distraction: Getting the Most out of Life with Attention Deficit Disorder*. New York: Ballantine Books.
Provides practical advice and lists of additional resources, including state by state. Empowers people with ADHD to leave negative thinking behind and provides many creative ways to move forward.

Hallowell, E. M., & Ratey, J. J. (2010). *Answers to Distraction*: New York: Ballantine Books.
Provides extremely helpful practical advice for many aspects of life. Helps people with ADHD understand and deal more effectively with the challenges they face.

Journals and Magazines

ADDitude: www.additudemag.com.
This excellent newsletter covers many topics relevant to home, school, work, parenting, and relationships.

The ADHD Report: www.guildford.com.
Provides expert coverage of current developments.

CHAPTER 2 OUTLINE

CHAPTER 2

Why Sweat the Science?
Getting to Know Three New Faces of ADHD

You may be one of those people who just wants a quick solution to your problem and who would rather eat worms than have to slug through reading about the science behind treatments for ADHD. If you have ADHD, it may be particularly difficult for you to slow down and focus on this material, but it will be worth the effort because a little science can go a long way in helping you to understand the many causes of ADHD and how to use multiple viewpoints and treatments to overcome symptoms. Knowing the science behind the behaviors that drive you and your loved ones crazy can help to reduce guilt, blame, and anger. Also, this knowledge will help you to evaluate new treatments you might hear about or read about on the Internet and to decide if they are really worth trying and are likely to apply to your particular situation. A lot of time, money, and disappointment can be avoided if you know how to assess product claims and even so-called "research evidence" that may be used to boost sales.

JUST A TASTING OF SCIENCE SOUP

We are going to ease you in with an overview—just the most important highlights—to give you a sense of where the science of ADHD is now and where it is going. If this whets your appetite for more, you may continue to feast on the chapters that follow.

The Who's Who of Neurotransmitters

Neurotransmitters are the molecules that move between neurons (brain cells) and enable them to communicate and transmit information. These molecules deliver messages by first attaching to receptor sites on the surface of the neurons. Small shifts in the balance of neurotransmitters dancing on receptor sites can make all the difference in how smoothly the mind functions.

The problem with studying neurotransmitters is that there are too many of them and they are everywhere in the nervous system, slipping through cell membranes, hugging and releasing surface receptors, swimming across synaptic clefts, fending off attacks by enzymes, exciting some nerves while squelching others. Tracking these chemical acrobats is like watching a circus with thousands of rings in which the performers keep jumping into each others' acts. Imagine that you are the catcher swinging on a high trapeze and that

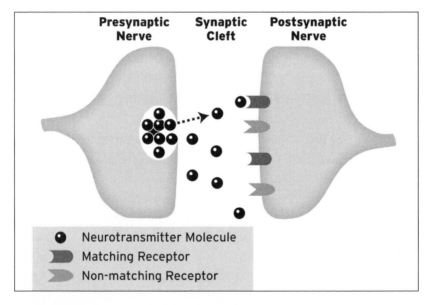

Figure 2.1 *Neurotransmitters at a Synapse*

Neurotransmitter molecules released from the presynaptic neuron traverse the synaptic cleft, attach to a matching receptor on the postsynaptic neuron and are taken up into the postsynaptic neuron to participate in cell processes.

just as your flying partner is about to seize your wrists, another aerialist dives from above to snatch your hands away while your partner tumbles helplessly into the net. That's what it's like all the time in the wacky world of neurotransmitters. (See Figure 2.1.)

Another maddening aspect of neurotransmitters is that just when we think we know all of the major players, somebody discovers a new one. Unfortunately, our brains can't function without the little devils, so we do need to know who they are, what they do, and how to help them work better.

The neurotransmitters involved in ADHD include catecholamines and non-catecholamines. The easiest way to remember the catecholamines is to think of three cats. For definitions of neurotransmitters, see Sidebar 2.1. While each transmitter has many functions throughout the brain, here are some of their major actions that affect ADHD:

Catecholamines

Dopamine—activation for pleasure and reward

Norepinephrine —attention and alertness

Epinephrine—arousal and alertness

Non-catecholamine neurotransmitters

Serotonin—mood regulation, inhibition of action, and balancing dopamine activity

Sidebar 2.1.
Neurotransmitter Definitions

Acetylcholine—important for learning and short-term memory. Recent studies indicate that it also has a role in attentional effort (voluntary directing of attention) and the detection of important stimuli (Klinkenberg, Sambeth, & Blokland, 2010). Acetylcholine modulates the allocation of visual attention—for example, the selection of which visual cue to focus on when there are many things going on in the environment (Rokem, Landau, Garg, Prinzmetal, & Silver, 2010; Dalley et al., 2004).

Dopamine—important for activation and processing of reward and pleasure. Its activity is affected by the other neurotransmitters, including serotonin, epinephrine, and GABA.

Epinephrine—involved in arousal and alertness.

Gamma-aminobutyric acid (GABA)—inhibits and reduces excessive activation and is essential for feelings of calmness.

Glutamate—an excitatory transmitter crucial for memory (through long-term potentiation).

Histamine—necessary for learning to inhibit behaviors.

Norepinephrine—essential for attention, alertness, overall arousal, mood, and sexual behavior; it supports and amplifies the effects of serotonin and probably dopamine.

Serotonin—important for the regulation of mood and the inhibition of actions that would cause pain. Insufficient serotonergic* (i.e., involving serotonin) activity is associated with depression. Serotonin affects sleep, cognitive functions, anxiety regulation, and sexual activity, and it balances the activity of dopamine.

*-ergic—Adding the suffix -ergic to a neurotransmitter name means activated by, or involving, that transmitter. For example, cholinergic transmission is the activation of a sequence of nerves that utilizes choline (from *acetylcholine*). Similarly, dopaminergic refers to nerve cells that contain dopamine, substances that cause nerves to release dopamine, or nerve cells that respond to dopamine.

Gamma-aminobutyric acid (GABA)— calms and quiets the brain
Acetylcholine—learning, memory, and attention
Histamine—learning to inhibit behaviors

THREE NEW FACES OF ADHD: HYPOAROUSAL, REWARD DEFICIENCY, AND EMOTIONAL DYSREGULATION

Although the DSM diagnostic categories have provided more consistency in the diagnosis of ADHD, they have created a somewhat limited view of the disorder as a collection of observable behaviors, the "core symptoms" of inattention, hyperactivity, and impulsivity. We want to go beyond the DSM-IV surface description of symptoms by delving a little deeper into three areas of dysfunction that are based on neurophysiology, neuroanatomy, and genetic research: (1) hypoarousal and impulse control, (2) reward deficiency, and (3) emotional dysregulation. These categories are important because they enrich our understanding of the causes of ADHD behaviors and help us to home in on treatments that may better target the underlying dysfunctions in brain systems. We're going to use a case example to first give you a sense of the ways in which these categories can be expressed in behaviors and interactions.

> Although she had never been formally diagnosed with or treated for ADHD, I suspected that Mrs. L. had this disorder. Despite being highly intelligent, she had dropped out of high school and become the black sheep of her family, the only one without a college education. As a teenager, she drank, experimented with drugs, and had her first child at age 17. Determined to be a good mother, she stopped drinking and began a small landscaping business. By working long hours 7 days a week, she gained customers and soon she had five people working for her. What she lacked in organizational skills, she made up for in energy.
>
> Mrs. L. understood that yelling and arguing with her husband was hurting their relationship and setting a terrible example for their four children, but she was unable to control herself. Any neg-

ative comment, such as his complaining about the house clutter, would set her off on a torrent of accusations. In all fairness, hubby was very critical. When her son entered adolescence and began talking back, Mrs. L.'s yelling got out of control. As the family fights escalated and her son became more provocative, Mr. L. began losing control, either becoming physically violent or running out of the house to avoid hitting someone. Mrs. L. came to therapy asking for help with the family turmoil.

Mrs. L. refused to take any prescription medications because, to her, that would confirm that something was wrong with her brain. Her low self-esteem made it even more difficult for her to accept even the idea of medication. One day she brought her 15- year-old son, Lamar, to the office and told him to sit in the waiting room and read a book during her session. Within 5 minutes, we began to hear noises, banging, stomping, and finally knocking on my office door. Lamar stood there grinning, saying, "I'm bored. When will my mother be finished?" I gave Lamar a sketch pad and asked him to stay quietly in the waiting room, reminding him that it would be another 40 minutes. No sooner had I sat down, than the noises began again, thumping and shrieking. The phone rang. The other therapists in my suite were complaining about the noise and the mess in the waiting room. What mess? Opening the door, we saw Lamar laughing and splashing water from the fountain all over the carpet. Mrs. L. let out a grunt of rage through clenched teeth. The Three Faces of ADHD had struck again: hypoarousal with poor impulse control, reward deficiency, and lack of emotional regulation.

A DISORDER OF HYPOAROUSAL AND IMPULSE CONTROL

ADHD has been called a disorder of hypoarousal, meaning that part of the brain is under-aroused or not active enough (Kuntsi, McLoughlin, & Asherson, 2006). How can we say that the brain is underactive in a person who is overactive and hardly seems to sleep? How can a stimulant calm down a system that seems to be in overdrive? The key to making sense of this puzzle lies in the particular parts of the brain that are under- aroused: brain circuits in the command-and-control centers that are supposed to regulate attention, impulse control, and pleasure-seeking behaviors. When dopamine levels are low, these control circuits are sluggish, slow to respond, and less effective. Stimulants such as methylphenidate (Ritalin) are believed to work in part by increasing neurotransmitter levels, particularly of dopamine and norepinephrine (Kuntsi et al., 2006).

If we think of our impulses as mice scurrying around our emotion centers just waiting for a chance to run amuck, and imagine the neurotransmitters as cats, then we can understand why having drowsy cats doesn't work very well. Underactive neurotransmitters (sleepy cats), particularly norepinephrine and serotonin, compromise the ability of the brain circuits to control impulsive behavior (trouble-making mice). So, for instance, when Lamar feels an impulse to knock on the door and interrupt his mother's therapy session, his centers of judgment and control fail to remind him that he should sit quietly and not disturb anyone. In a sense, his inhibitory circuits are asleep at the wheel, failing to put on the behavioral brakes as he careens out of control. Stimulants such as methylphenidate (Ritalin) increase norepinephrine activity in the impulse control circuits. Norepinephrine also enhances the inhibitory effects of serotonin. As a result of the increased norepinephrine, the impulse control centers (combined with serotonin inhibition) are better able to maintain more appropriate behavior. Furthermore, by increasing levels of norepinephrine, stimulants improve arousal and alertness. We tend to be less alert when norepinephrine levels are low. Alertness is a necessary part of paying attention.

Complementary treatments, such as stimulating herbs and mind–body practices, can also improve hypoarousal and the balance of neurotransmitters (more on that topic later).

REWARD DEFICIENCY SYNDROME—
CAN'T GET NO SATISFACTION

Many people with ADHD complain of feeling bored, just like Lamar sitting in the waiting room. How did he get so bored so quickly? Why couldn't he read a book or draw pictures? He didn't feel like reading or drawing. These activities did not give him pleasure or satisfaction. Reward deficiency syndrome (RDS) is a condition in which the person is unable to experience pleasure or a sense of reward in ordinary activities that others enjoy. This inability is thought to be due to dysfunction in the neurotransmitter systems involved in feelings of reward, such as pleasure, excitement, and satisfaction. As a result, there is a tendency to feel bored, restless, impatient, and a need to stir up trouble or provoke intense emotional reactions.

In order to have fun, Lamar needed to do something more exciting or dangerous, something that would get him into trouble—better yet, something that would get everyone upset and angry. His mother would be embarrassed. Maybe everyone would start yelling. For Lamar, that would be exciting enough to stimulate his pleasure centers. That would really be fun.

The problem is that without the usual everyday "feel good" experiences, people with reward deficiency syndrome tend to feel bored, unhappy, discontented. They are prone to engage in activities that will stimulate their system intensely enough to produce some pleasurable experiences. This puts them at increased risk for engaging in dangerous, addictive, impulsive, or compulsive behaviors. Reward deficiency syndrome can be found in people being treated for substance abuse and addictions. Studies are also finding that a subset of people with ADHD may also have genetic variants that lead to imbalances in the neurotransmitter systems in brain areas involved in reward processing.

Dopamine and Reward Processing

Dopamine plays the largest role in reward processing. The release and activity of dopamine is affected by other neurotransmitters such as serotonin, norepinephrine, and gamma-aminobutyric acid (GABA). GABA, in particular, controls or inhibits the amount of dopamine released in brain reward areas. If there is too little dopamine reaching the reward centers, then it is more difficult for the person to experience pleasure (Blum et al., 2008). For example, increasing dopamine levels improves the ability to enjoy social rewards such as praise and approval. It is easier to teach a child appropriate behavior when the child is able to enjoy pleasing his or her parent or teacher.

The identification of gene variants that affect dopamine is consistent with the idea that inheritance of ADHD is *polygenetic* (i.e., involves multiple genes). Specific gene variants that have been linked to ADHD include the dopamine receptor gene *DRD4*, a transporter gene (*DAT1*), and a B-hydroxylase gene (*DBH*). In one study, the number of variants in genes affecting dopamine correlated with the severity of ADHD symptoms. In other words, people with three gene variants had more severe ADHD than those with two, and people with two gene variants had worse ADHD than those with only one.

The ability of stimulants such as methylphenidate (Ritalin) and Dexedrine to improve symptoms of ADHD has been attributed in part to their increasing the level of dopamine in synapses (the spaces between neurons) in the frontal lobes. In Chapter 3 you will find a discussion of an herb that has been shown to increase levels of dopamine. This may be an alternative way to enhance feelings of pleasure and well-being without needing excessive stimulation.

Recognizing Reward Deficiency Syndrome

Many people with ADHD complain of feeling bored, just like Lamar. Why did he get bored so quickly? Why couldn't he just sit quietly reading a book or drawing pictures like most boys his age? Being unable to enjoy quiet pleasures left him feeling unsatisfied. In an attempt to have fun, Lamar tried more exciting activities, doing things he knew were wrong and that would put him in danger of getting into trouble. Better yet, he did things that would get everyone angry and upset to create more excitement and stimulate his sluggish pleasure centers.

Recognizing problems in reward processing can help us understand some of the behaviors that occur in ADHD and thereby help us develop more effective treatment approaches. For example, it is known that many children with ADHD respond differently to rewards than other children, and they cannot tolerate the usual delays involved in being rewarded for finishing or accomplishing something. In general, children with ADHD prefer small immediate rewards rather than larger delayed rewards. Therefore, if rewards are being used as part of a behavioral treatment plan, they should be structured in a way that will elicit responses more effectively in these children. See the Resources section at the end of Chapter 1 for help with specific behavior management strategies.

Helping children and adolescents learn how to enjoy healthy activities may also reduce their risk-taking behaviors. Teaching mind–body practices that induce feelings of well-being can compensate for symptoms of reward deficiency syndrome; Chapter 5 describes some of these techniques.

DEFICIENT EMOTIONAL SELF-REGULATION— BEING OUT OF CONTROL

One of the more recent concepts in understanding ADHD is that of *deficient emotional self-regulation* (DESR). Deficient emotional self-regulation can be seen as a politically correct way of describing people who tend to lose control of their emotional reactions so frequently and to such an extent that this lack of self-control causes significant problems in their academic, professional, and personal lives. Deficient emotional self-regulation may contribute to the following problems:

- Inability to inhibit inappropriate behavior associated with strong emotions.
- Inability to self-soothe physiological responses aroused by strong emotions (e.g., once the person becomes upset, it is very difficult for him or her to calm down); this includes physiological responses such as adrenaline release, heart pounding, rapid breathing, shaking, or muscle tensing.
- Inability to refocus attention.
- Inability to organize coordinated behaviors to accomplish a goal.

People with ADHD are often impaired in their ability to control their emotions, particularly frustration, impatience, and anger. Lapses in inhibition of these emotions result in emotional impulsivity—that is, rapid negative reactions (e.g., anger) and responses (e.g., shouting, hitting, or attacking). This response pattern erupted over and over again whenever Mrs. L. felt insulted or unappreciated. Her anger rushed in, her control circuits failed, and within seconds she was yelling uncontrollably. She was at the mercy of her hurt and angry feelings, unable to soothe or calm herself.

Russell Barkley explains the relationship between emotional impulsivity and emotional self-regulation in this way: "One cannot self-soothe or otherwise moderate one's initial emotional reactions to events if one has not first inhibited the impulsive expression of those initial reactions. EI [emotional impulsivity], therefore, will interfere with subsequent efforts to engage in emotional self-regulation" (p. 6). Dr. Barkley recommends including *emotional impulsivity–deficient emotional self-regulation* (EI-DESR) as a core symptom of ADHD because it is an underlying factor in low frustration tolerance, impatience, quickness to anger, and easy excitability to emotional reactions. EI-DESR contributes to serious impairments in social interactions, work, driving, marriage/cohabitation, and parenting (Barkley, 2009).

Understanding emotional self-regulation is central to dealing with ADHD. In Chapters 5 and 6 we focus on mind–body treatments and neurostimulatory techniques that can improve emotional self-regulation, which is critical for controlling anxiety, over- reactivity, anger, aggression, and other impulsive behaviors.

SUBTYPES, GENES, POLYMORPHISMS, AND FOOD ADDITIVES—'THE TIMES THEY ARE A-CHANGIN'

At the moment, and as noted above, ADHD is divided into three subtypes based on symptom clusters:

1. Predominantly hyperactive/impulsive
2. Predominantly inattentive
3. Combined hyperactive/impulsive and inattentive

In the not-too-distant future, however, genetic research is going to change the way we diagnose and treat ADHD. In fact, the change has already begun. The various symptoms seen among the subtypes of ADHD may reflect differences in the absolute and relative levels of neurotransmitters. There are genes within our DNA that code for the manufacturing of not only neurotransmitters, but also substances that affect their transportation and how they function. For example, genetic variants (*polymorphisms*) can affect the levels of the major catecholamines—norepinephrine and dopamine. Looking at the ADHD subtypes and genetic variants may ultimately help us design more effective treatments (Blum et al., 2008). Let's look into our crystal microscope to see what the polymorphisms are telling us about the future of ADHD treatment.

> *"Eenie, meenie, chili beanie! The spirits are about to speak"*
> —Rocky & Bullwinkle, 1961

Polymorphisms are found in specific genes. To get a clearer picture of polymorphism codings, imagine a gene that is capable of designing a shoe. We'll call it gene *SH1*. This gene comes in different forms, or polymorphisms, which can produce different styles of shoes. So, the polymorphism *SH1B* produces blue shoes, and the polymorphism *SH1R* makes red shoes. To be more specific, *SH1B2* makes blue shoes with 2-inch heels, whereas *SH1B6* makes blue shoes with 6-inch heels. *SH1B6L* makes leather blue shoes with 6-inch heels, and *SH1B6S* makes blue suede shoes with 6-inch heels. Transfer this concept into thinking about your genetic code, and you can see how scientists create code names for polymorphisms based on the specific traits or actions they produce. For example, just for fun, let's decipher a gene:

• DR is a dopamine receptor.
• *DRD4* is the gene that codes for the D4 type of dopamine receptor.

> *Are they friendly spirits?* —Rocky & Bullwinkle, 1961

Polymorphisms of the genes that affect dopamine levels have been found in ADHD, especially in the hyperactive/impulsive subtype. Sim-

ilarly, variants in genes that affect norepinephrine have been identified in the inattentive subtype of ADHD. In addition, polymorphisms
in genes involved in cholinergic transmission have been noted in
ADHD with both inattention and hyperactivity/impulsivity.

Each gene is a segment of DNA that carries the code for a specific
trait. Chromosomes come in pairs, and each pair of chromosomes is a
double helix that contains pairs of matched genes, one set from each
parent. Different genes code for at least five types of dopamine receptors: D_1, D_2, D_3, D_4, and D_5.

The *DRD4* gene is located on the 11th human chromosome in
a segment called 11p15.5. *DRD4* contains the code for making the
dopamine receptor D4. During dopaminergic transmission, the neurotransmitter dopamine attaches to and activates the D4 receptors
on the nerve cell membranes. One polymorphism of the "*DRD4* long"
variant, with 7-repeat (7R) base pairs, has been linked to ADHD.
The 7R polymorphism reacts less strongly to dopamine molecules.
This means that the neurons in people with the 7R variant are not
as easily activated when dopamine attaches to their receptors as in
people without the 7R variant. The dopamine transmission is less in
these individuals, and this decrease could contribute to symptoms of
ADHD. (See Figure 2.2.)

Nomad or Couch Potato?

How did the *DRD4* 7R long variant evolve? The 7R allele appeared
about 40,000 years ago (Chen, Burton, Greenberger, & Dmitrieva,
1999), and it occurred more frequently in populations who migrated
long distances in the past 1,000–30,000 years. In short, nomadic populations had higher frequencies of 7R alleles than sedentary ones.
In two studies scientists found that people whose personality testing showed them to be exploratory and excitable—two hallmarks of
novelty-seeking behavior—also possessed a 7R version of *DRD4* compared with those who are more reserved and reflective (Ebstein et al.,
1996; Benjamin et al., 1996).

In the section on reward deficiency syndrome we discussed evidence for the link between polymorphisms in the dopamine receptor

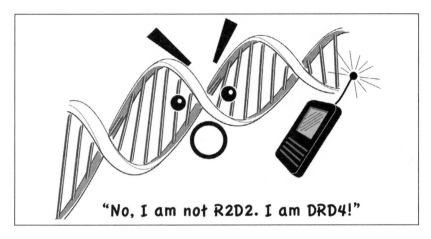

"No, I am not R2D2. I am DRD4!"

Figure 2.2

(*DRD4*) and dopamine transporter (*DAT1*) genes and the severity of ADHD symptoms. Because these genes have been identified as playing a role in ADHD, they are considered to be candidates for research directed toward creating new treatments (Stergiakouli & Thaper, 2010). The race is on to discover treatments that could correct, modify, or compensate for the effects of polymorphisms. However, these dopamine polymorphisms account for only a small portion of the genetic effects on ADHD symptoms. So far, other genomic studies have not been able to demonstrate more significant effects for specific polymorphisms, perhaps because of confounding factors such as environmental, dietary, and psychosocial effects.

The Mystery of Food Additives May Soon Be Solved by Genomic Sleuths

The role of food additives in ADHD has been hotly contested since 1975 when Benjamin Feingold, M.D., popularized the notion that artificial food colors, flavors, and preservatives caused hyperactivity and learning disabilities (Feingold, 1975). These issues are discussed in greater detail in Chapter 4. Over the past 35 years, studies have yielded inconsistent results. Now geneticists are figuring out why.

At the University of Southamptom School of Medicine in Hamp-

shire, England, Dr. Jim Stevenson and colleagues (2010) discovered
a connection between the effects of food additives and histamine
degradation gene polymorphisms on ADHD symptoms in children.
An enzyme produced by the histamine degradation gene is responsible for breaking down histamine molecules. Certain variants in the
histamine degradation gene result in diminished capacity to degrade
histamine molecules. If a child has an allergic reaction to food additives, histamine may be released. Normally, the excess histamine is
degraded. However, if the child has certain polymorphisms, then there
is less capacity to degrade the histamine such that it accumulates
and interferes with neurotransmission. This could result in increased
symptoms of ADHD. In a well designed study of 153 children ages
3 and 4 and 144 children ages 8 and 9, researchers simply rubbed a
small swab on the inside of each child's cheek to obtain a sample of
tissue for genetic testing. Children who had the histamine degradation polymorphisms of *HNMT* showed greater overall hyperactivity
and were more vulnerable to the effects of food additives on their
behavior. The fact that in some children food additives exacerbate
ADHD symptoms, whereas in others they do not, could be explained
by these polymorphisms. Although the scientists caution that more
studies are needed to confirm these findings, nevertheless, this is a
milestone in the quest for new ways to determine who is more likely
to benefit from specific treatment approaches.

Q&A

*Q: What does histamine have to do with food additives and
ADHD?*

A: Histamine may be the missing link in our understanding of why
some food additives exacerbate ADHD symptoms in some people but
not in others. Histamine receptors are found throughout the brains
of mammals (including humans). When it was discovered that causing histamine levels to rise in mice adversely affected their ability to
learn to inhibit certain behaviors and increased their hyperactivity,
the histamine neurotransmitter system became a new candidate for

ADHD researchers. Histamine is more commonly known for its role in allergic reactions. When allergens provoke basophil cells to release histamine, it can produce a skin rash. Certain food additives, such as Azo dyes (i.e., dyes with a particular synthetic chemical structure), can cause histamine release. This can occur even in the absence of a skin rash. In people with certain polymorphisms of the histamine degradation gene (*HNMT*), there is a reduced capacity to degrade and clear histamine out of the cells. So, if such a person eats something that causes histamine release, such as food containing an Azo coloring, then he or she will not be able to clear the histamine as rapidly. The histamine will accumulate and could then increase hyperactivity and interfere with the person's ability to inhibit behaviors. This was the hypothesis that was tested by Dr. Stevenson's group. Although their study does not absolutely prove this theory, it certainly provides strong support for pursuing this line of research.

Q: How can I use this information now?

A: We can do what the researchers did. Although we cannot yet get cheek swabs to identify histamine receptor polymorphisms, we can still use this information. In their study, they gave a standardized test to assess the level of ADHD symptoms (the Abbreviated ADHD Rating Scale–IV) before and after a 6-week period of eliminating the following artificial colors and preservatives in the children's diets:

- Tartrazine (Yellow 5)
- Sunset yellow (Yellow 6)
- Quinoline yellow, carmosine (Red 3)
- Allura red AC (Red 40)
- Ponceau 4R
- A preservative called sodium benzoate

It should be possible for you to get a standard ADHD symptom test, eliminate or reduce as much as possible (does not have to be 100%) the same food colorings for 6 weeks, and then repeat the testing. In addition to the testing, you and your family may observe changes. If you see significant improvements in ADHD symptoms, then it is possible that you have a histamine receptor polymorphism and that you would continue to benefit by restricting your consumption of foods containing color additives. On the other hand, if you don't notice much change, then this approach is not worth pursuing unless you wish to reduce artificial additives for general health reasons. In Chapter 4 we go into more detail on the effects of food and dietary treatments on symptoms of ADHD.

Q: What do you see in the future regarding the use of genetics to identify and treat ADHD?

A: Someday, you will be able to get a cheek swab to check for polymorphisms related to ADHD. Then, based on the profile of your particular polymorphisms, you will be able to select from a menu of treatment options those that are most likely to be beneficial for you.

EVIDENCE-BASED TREATMENTS

When we read about scientific studies, it is important to assess the quality of the evidence. There are many ways to do a scientific study. Although there is no guarantee that the results of any one study will stand the test of time, some methods are believed to produce more solid, significant, and higher-quality evidence than others. In general, studies with larger numbers of participants and those that use a *randomized, double-blind, placebo-controlled* design are considered to be more convincing than smaller studies that do not use a control group, randomization, or double-blind conditions. In a randomized study, participants are randomly assigned to different groups. In a double-blind study, the participants do not know which group they are in (treatment vs. control group), and the researchers who administer the tests do not know which group participants are in. Placebo-controlled studies use an identical placebo tablet (a tablet that has no biological effect—a "sugar pill") for the control group to compare their response with the group given a tablet with the active ingredient being tested. Although these methods reduce the potential for bias, they do not guarantee accurate results. Treatments that are supported by more than one study and by studies of better design are considered to have a more solid evidence base.

Q&A

Q: Why aren't there more randomized, double-blind, placebo-controlled studies of non-drug treatments for ADHD?

A: It is very costly to do randomized, double-blind, placebo-controlled studies. The pharmaceutical industry is able to finance studies of prescription medications because they can make a good profit through high drug prices. In contrast, small herbal companies and businesses developing alternative treatments find it extremely difficult to raise enough money to do such studies. Although there are some grants for CAM research, they are often for small amounts of money, and the granting agencies tend to fund the same old familiar herbs rather than the "new kids" on the block.

Q: If there are fewer studies, how do you decide that a non-drug treatment is worth trying?

A: We wrote this book to help you, your doctor, and your other health care providers make those decisions. Also, we have tried many of these treatments in our practices over the years. This book emphasizes treatments we have used successfully in our patients and which are supported by credible scientific evidence. When we describe the studies, we will indicate the study methods, the limitations of the study, and the rationale for our recommendations.

Now that you understand more about the underlying causes of ADHD, we can explore some non-drug treatments that can help reduce symptoms and improve the quality of every day of your life. The next chapters introduce you to nutrients, herbs, mind–body practices, and brain stimulation methods. For some people these approaches will make it possible to reduce the amount of prescription medication needed, whereas for others these treatments will build on the benefits of medication, leading to even more improvements in attention, mood, productivity, relationships, and enjoyment of life.

CHAPTER 3 OUTLINE

From Mother Nature

Herbs, Melatonin, and Nootropics (Brain Boosters)

Stimulant medications are used to treat ADHD because, in many cases, they improve mental focus and reduce distractibility, hyperactivity, and impulsivity. But not all stimulants are manufactured in pharmaceutical laboratories. Many naturally growing plants contain compounds that have stimulant activity—such as the caffeine in your morning coffee or the nicotine in cigarettes. In fact, many ADHD folks become addicted to coffee and cigarettes because they temporarily improve the ability to focus. Eventually, the ADHD brain habituates (becomes accustomed to) these stimulants and stops responding unless the person keeps increasing the amounts. We have found that some people drink gallons of coffee and smoke cigarettes non-stop trying to maintain their mental focus. Unfortunately, this approach can have disastrous side effects, including ulcers, obstructive lung disease, heart disease, stroke, and cancer.

Fortunately, Mother Nature has also provided us with many plants whose stimulating compounds do not cause as many side effects or addictions. And, being the master chemist, she has enriched many of her herbs with antioxidants and other compounds that provide a cornucopia of health benefits. Thus, humankind may live long and prosper on the roots, berries, and leaves of Mother Nature's medicinal plants.

Although scientific studies have shown that certain plants improve attention and learning, only a few studies have been conducted using people with ADHD. When we have tried these herbs in clinical practice with patients who have ADHD, many of them have had excellent responses. It is possible to combine herbs with other substances and complementary and alternative medicine (CAM) treatments to further enhance learning. Here we introduce you to some of the most useful herbs and show you how to combine them with other treatments.

In addition to herbs, this chapter covers the use of melatonin to aid sleep and a group of nootropics, or brain boosters, called *racetams*. Melatonin is a natural sleep hormone produced by a small brain structure, the pineal gland, to regulate sleep and other natural body rhythms. Melatonin is safe and effective for treating sleep problems that are commonly found with ADHD. Nootropics are synthetic compounds that enhance brain function through a variety of mechanisms. In general, they are very low in side effects. Nootropics have been studied and used in clinical practice in Europe and Russia for decades, but they are not well known in the United States.

At the end of this chapter you will find lists of all the treatments we presented in Tables 3.1 and 3.2. Table 3.1 reviews *how to use each treatment* including dosage guidelines and side effects, and Table 3.2 provides information on *where to buy good quality brands*. We want to assure you that we do not sell any of these products. Also, we have no financial relationship with any company that grows, processes, or markets these supplements. For additional information, you will find websites, organizations, books, and journals in the Resources sections at the end of this chapter.

SILVER BULLET OR KITCHEN SINK?

Before getting into specifics about these various substances, let's consider an often-asked question of why certain treatments work in some of the people some of the time, but not in all of the people all of the time. This is a very important question to keep in mind while pursuing solutions to symptoms of ADHD. In Chapter 2 we introduced you to some of the genetic and neurological differences among people with ADHD, which may account for the wide spectrum of symptoms that can be present. Through scientific research, we are learning more about the neuroanatomy, brain functions, neurotransmitters, and genetics that may determine why some people respond better to certain treatments than others. ADHD comes in many forms with many genetic variations affecting how the symptoms emerge and how various brain areas are affected. The bottom line is: *it can be difficult to predict the extent to which an individual will to respond to different therapies*. It is often necessary to do a treatment trial.

There is no one magic *silver bullet* that will fix ADHD. If you go trawling on the Internet, you will find websites touting hundreds of treatment regimens. While we *do* advocate using more than one kind of treatment, we *do not* advocate a kitchen-sink approach. From a seemingly infinite menu of options, we have selected only those therapies that have a sound scientific basis and that we have found to be effective in our work with patients. Our approach is to use multiple treatments that target specific aspects of brain dysfunction and behavior found in ADHD in order to accomplish the following:

- Improve overall brain growth and development.
- Optimize the health of neurons.
- Strengthen cellular maintenance and repair systems.
- Protect against further injury.
- Improve neurotransmitter function.
- Improve brain-wave patterns.
- Strengthen compensatory systems, such as the autonomic nervous system.
- Balance the stress response systems.

By enhancing these aspects of brain function, we can help improve many symptoms of ADHD, such as attention, memory, planning, organization, impulse control, emotion regulation, hyperactivity, academic and work performance, and behavior.

QUALITY OF HERBAL PRODUCTS

The safety and effectiveness of any product, whether it is a supplement or a prescription medication, depend upon its quality. This is especially true for herbs because the quality and potency (strength) can be affected by numerous factors, including where it was grown, whether the soil was certified free of contaminants, when it was harvested, the method used to dry and extract the medicinal compounds, what percentage of the product is in an active versus an inactive form, whether the herbal extract was tested for contaminants, the process of standardization, and the stability of the medicinal components. It is difficult for consumers to get all the information needed to be certain that they are buying a good-quality product. However, there are things that you can do to help identify the best brands.

1. Read the labels on each supplement bottle. Check to see if the product is certified organic and free of contaminants. Read the full name of the herb to be sure you are buying the correct species. Look for evidence of standardization. Some herbs are standardized by the percent of "marker compounds." Markers are specific components used to identify an herb as genuine and help assure that it contains the minimum amount of pure herb to be effective. So, on the label you may see "standardized extract" and then the percent of the marker compound.
2. Check the number of milligrams (mg) of the herb in each capsule so that you will know how many capsules to take for therapeutic effects.
3. If a specific herbal preparation has been used in a research study and shown to be effective, then it is a good choice. Untested brands of the same herb may not be as effective.

You may wish to visit websites showing the results of impartial evaluations of many supplements. Although these sites do not present every possible aspect of product quality, they do cover important basics such as whether the product in the bottle is exactly what it is claims to be on the label, what percent of the product is in an active form, and whether it contains contaminants:

- www.consumerlab.com
- www.supplementwatch.com
- www.fda.gov/medwatch

We have done a good deal of your homework for you by checking out supplements for quality and efficacy. Remember, you may take a shortcut by simply consulting the tables at the end of this chapter. There you will find lists of supplement brands that we have found to be consistently effective. This is not a comprehensive list, but it will provide you with some reliable choices for each of the supplements discussed in this book.

RHODIOLA ROSEA (GOLDEN ROOT/ARCTIC ROOT)

Rhodiola rosea (golden root, arctic root), an ancient medicinal herb, improves alertness, attention, and accuracy. It is especially effective in reducing the number of errors during tedious tasks such as computer work or homework that require many hours of attention. Rhodiola grows in extremely cold environments at high altitudes, above 8,000 feet, in the Caucusus Mountains of the Republic of Georgia, the Altai Range in the former Soviet Union, Scandinavia, Alaska and northern Canada. Large farms are cultivating *R. rosea* in Scandinavia and the former Soviet Union. In the last five years, as the demand for this versatile herb have soared *R. rosea* farms have been started in Canada and Alaska. Dr. Petra Illig initiated the Alaska Rhodiola Products, a non-profit farmer's co-op by growing 90,000 R. rosea seedlings in her front yard (http://www.alaskarhodiolaproducts.com). After two years of growth the plants were distributed to Alaskan farms. The picture on the cover of this book shows a stunning three-year old *R. rosea* plant blooming in Bethel on the Yukon–Koskoquim River delta on the southwest coast of Alaska. The flowers are bright yellow at their peak, turning to rose, purple, and rust colors as fall approaches. Rhodiola rosea (R. rosea) is the perfect example of an herb that has long- term health benefits rather than health risks. Here is an example of how this herb helped a student with ADHD get better grades naturally.

Joseph was a highly intelligent 16-year-old. Despite having an IQ in the superior range, he maintained only a B average in school. He got by on whatever he picked up in class, spent no time studying, and dashed off assignments while riding the bus or eating lunch in a noisy cafeteria. His parents chalked it up to immaturity and assumed he would get serious about his studies as college approached. Instead, as the high school courses became harder, his grades slipped to C's and then D's. Talking, offering rewards, arguing, shouting, punishing, or confinement—nothing worked. Joseph became resentful and frustrated. He was getting to the point of giving up rather than repeatedly trying and failing.

Joseph's high school guidance counselor called a meeting because he had begun skipping classes, and his English teacher was alarmed by an essay in which he wrote, "I wish I was dead." The parents immediately made an appointment with a child psychiatrist, who concluded that Joseph had the inattentive form of attention-deficit disorder (ADD)—that is, without hyperactivity. He also had depression secondary to all of the negative effects of ADD on his life. The psychiatrist recommended individual therapy and a stimulant medication, Ritalin, for Joseph, as well as family therapy. Joseph adamantly refused. Like many teenagers, he did not want to be labeled or seen as abnormal, different, or "crazy." However, he did agree to meet with the psychiatrist alone to see if anything else could be worked out. During these sessions, the psychiatrist listened to Joseph's frustrations and engaged him in trying to find some solution other than medication. When he suggested an herb, Joseph got interested because, to him, herbs, unlike medicine, were natural. Once the doctor explained that Rhodiola rosea had been shown to improve both mental and physical performance in athletes, military cadets, and cosmonauts (Russian astronauts), Joseph was eager to try it. The fact that Rhodiola rosea had been used by the Vikings for strength and endurance added to its appeal.

The next day, Joseph began taking R. rosea (Rosavin Plus brand) 150 mg in the morning on an empty stomach. Each week he increased the dose by one capsule until he was up to 300 mg twice a day. This dosage enabled him to sit and study, complete writing assignments on time, and prepare for exams. His average rose to a B+ with A's in math and science. Although he was no longer at odds with his parents, he still couldn't wait to leave home, especially with the chance of going to a great college.

Joseph was lucky to have such a good response to R. rosea. In other people, the herb may help, but to a lesser degree. Yet, even a smaller improvement can make a big difference in the quality of life, particularly when added to other treatments. In our practices, we find a range of responses to this herb. We use it often, because most people report improvements in energy, mood, mental clarity, and focus. For some people, like Joseph and Brad (the Gentle Giant from Chapter 1), this herb can make an enormous difference.

Let us update you on what happened to Brad. Taking 150 mg a day of Rosavin Plus, Brad was able to finish school and get a job as a counselor. Although he loved working with clients, it was difficult for him to communicate with his superiors. He was often criticized for how he spoke to the clients and after about 5 months, when he did not show enough improvement, he lost the job. When I (Dr. Gerbarg) spoke with Brad, it was apparent that he was so caught up in his own circular thoughts about what had gone wrong at work, he could not listen to or respond to my questions.

I suggested that he increase his Rosavin to take two 150 mg capsules in the morning and one mid-day. The increased dose helped him to think more clearly and the effects lasted longer. Six weeks later he found a new job with higher pay. So far he is getting along well there. The supervisors are satisfied with his work, and the staff enjoys and appreciates him.

Before moving on to the next herb, we review the scientific evidence, risks, benefits, and dosage details that you and your doctor will need in deciding whether to try R. rosea.

The Science of *Rhodiola rosea*—What Went on Behind the Iron Curtain?

Most of the research on *Rhodiola rosea* (R. rosea), done by the Soviet Union and the Swedish Herbal Institute, was hidden in classified documents and kept from publication until the late 1990s (after the collapse of the former Soviet Union). The Soviet Ministry of

Defense tested *Rhodiola rosea* and other herbs to increase the intellectual productivity of scientists and the performance of military personnel, Olympic athletes, and cosmonauts (Baranov, 1994; Panossian & Wikman, 2009). In numerous studies their researchers found that R. rosea root enhanced learning, memory, intellectual work capacity, speed, and accuracy. Tests run for many hours showed that over time, under the stress of fatigue and boredom, this herb significantly reduced the rate of errors, for example, in a tedious symbol correction test, compared to placebo (Brown & Gerbarg, 2004).

Rhodiola rosea is one of an elite class of medicinal herbs called *adaptogens*, based on their ability to protect living organisms from multiple stressors—infections, toxins, free radicals, radiation, heat, cold, low oxygen, physical strain or injury, and psychological stress (Brekhman & Dardymov, 1969). The following list describes some of the most useful adaptogens and their benefits:

1. *Eleutherococcus senticosus* (Siberian ginseng)—antistress, strength, endurance, intellectual productivity, immune cell response

2. *Panax ginseng* (Asian ginseng, Korean ginseng)—antistress, antifatigue, muscle strength, reaction time, alertness, intellectual performance, immune function, anticancer

3. *Rhodiola rosea* (Arctic Root, Golden Root)—anti-stress, antifatigue, physical and mental energy, physical and mental performance and endurance, alertness, memory, accuracy, learning, strength, recovery time, depression, anxiety, PTSD, menopausal symptoms, sexual function, high altitude sickness, liver protection and detoxification, anticancer, recovery from stroke or other brain injury

4. *Rhaponticum carthemoides* (luzea)—antistress, strength, endurance, work capacity, recovery following illness, liver health, antibiotic, blocks absorption of carcinogens

5. *Schizandra chinensis* (Schizandra)—antistress, antianxiety, energy, sleep, memory, physical strength and endurance, liver health

6. *Withania somnifera* (Ashwaganda)—antistress, physical strength and endurance

Other medicinal herbs that are used in combination with adaptogens to enhance their benefits include:

1. *Aralia mandshurica* (Manchurian thorn tree) –physical performance, energy, antiradiation

2. *Ginkgo biloba* (Ginkgo) –antioxidant, mental performance, erectile function, stroke prevention, vascular disease, macular degeneration

3. *Rhododendron caucasicum* (Georgian snow rose) –antistress, antifatigue, physical and mental performance, strength, recovery time, work capacity, alertness, memory

4. *Ribes nigrum* or *Rives nibrum* (black currant) –anti-inflammatory, atopic dermatitis, essential nutrients

One of the main differences between the contents of a prescription medication and the root of a plant is that most synthetic medications contain only one biologically active compound designed to have one specific effect, whereas the root of the *Rhodiola rosea* plant contains hundreds of bioactive compounds with countless effects on organ systems throughout the body. For example, studies have shown that extracts of R. rosea can increase the ability of chemotherapy drugs to kill many kinds of cancer cells, while at the same time protecting normal cells of the liver, breast, and bone marrow from the toxic effects of the chemotherapy (Brown, Gerbarg, & Muskin, 2009).

Rhodiola rosea improves brain functions through a number of different mechanisms. At the cellular level, its arsenal of antioxidants prevents free radical damage to energy-producing mitochondria, DNA, and cell membranes. Studies suggest that it also increases production of creatine phosphate (CP) and adenosine triphosphate (ATP)—the high-energy molecules that transport energy wherever it is needed to keep brain cells running and to fuel cellular repair mechanisms (Furmanowa, Skopinska-Rozewska, Rogala, & Malgorzata, 1998; Kurkin & Zapesochnaya, 1986). In brain cells, this prevents mental fatigue, maintains focus, and enhances intellectual functioning.

Rhodiola rosea stimulates a network of nerves in the brainstem, called the reticular activating system, which literally wakes up the brain, increases attention and alertness, and raises the level of neurotransmitters such as dopamine, serotonin, and norepinephrine (Petkov et al., 1986). These neurotransmitters are essential for intellectual activity, regulation of mood and emotion, organization and planning, and inhibition of impulsivity. Furthermore, *Rhodiola rosea* helps balance the stress-response system, preventing the excess release of stress hormones (e.g., cortisol) and excitatory neurotransmitters, which can damage brain cells (Panossian & Wikman, 2009).

One unexpected finding was that although *Rhodiola rosea* was mentally stimulating, at the same time it was emotionally calming. As a result, people given the herb not only performed better on tests, but they also did not get frustrated, even after 12 or 18 hours of testing. In contrast, those given an inactive placebo became crabby, tired, and negative after so many hours of repeated testing. This unintended benefit was attributed in part to the herb's effects on the stress response system as well as on neurotransmitters—serotonin, norepinephrine, and dopamine.

How to Use *Rhodiola rosea*: Timing, Dosing, and Side Effects

The following information provides guidelines for using Rhodiola rosea as a complementary treatment for people with ADHD. This herb is not intended to replace medication. Be sure to check with your doctor and to ask him or her to monitor your response (or the response of your child) before using this or any of the other treatments we describe.

Sidebar 3.1
Scientific Studies of *Rhodiola rosea*

In double-blind, placebo-controlled studies, *Rhodiola rosea* prevented mental fatigue, reduced errors, enhanced learning, and improved the quality of work. Here are examples of a few of these studies.

- Sixty Indian medical students studying in Russia were randomly assigned to groups given 100 mg/day of *Rhodiola rosea* extract (SRH-5 Swedish Herbal Institute), placebo, or nothing. Those given R. rosea had less mental fatigue, higher final exam grades, better physical fitness and coordination, and a greater sense of well-being compared to those who didn't take the herb (Spasov, Wikman, Mandrikov, Mironova, & Neumoin, 2000).

- Out of 60 foreign seniors at Russian high schools, 20 were given 660 mg/day of a *Rhodiola rosea* preparation with vitamin C, called *Rodaxin*; 20 got a placebo; and 20 got no treatment. The group given Rodaxin had less mental fatigue and anxiety as well as better work performance, higher final exam grades, improved coordination and well-being, and a 60.7% increase in their language-learning ability compared to the students who didn't take the extract (Spasov, Mandrikov, & Mironova, 2000).

- The Russian Ministry of Health evaluated two different doses of standardized *Rhodiola rosea* extract on mental functioning under conditions of stress and fatigue. In a randomized, double-blind, placebo-controlled study of healthy military cadets, ages 19–21, *Rhodiola rosea* showed a pronounced anti-fatigue effect as well as significant improvements in pulse and blood pressure. The cadets also reported greater feelings of general well-being (Shevstov et al., 2003).

Children 8–12 Years Old

Although very small doses of R. rosea can be helpful in children, it can also cause overstimulation and difficulty sleeping and therefore should be used cautiously. If agitation or insomnia occurs, the dose should be reduced or the herb discontinued. Soviet research on R. rosea in children was never published in any detail. However, among the people living at 8,000–10,000 feet in the Caucasus Mountains, where the herb grows wild, families brew a tea from the herb and drink it daily. It is given to children there without harm.

One way to try R. rosea in young children is to use a brand that comes in capsule form—for example, Rosavin (Ameriden International) containing 100 mg *Rhodiola rosea*. Open the capsule and dissolve the contents in one 8-ounce cup of any drink, such as juice, milk, tea, or cocoa. Stir thoroughly and give 1/16 cup (that is ½ ounce or 6.25 mg of herb) for the first dose. Store the rest in the refrigerator with a cover and a label so no one else drinks it by mistake. *Rhodiola rosea* should be given in the morning. See what effect it has that day. If that does not cause agitation or difficulty sleeping, increase to 1/8 cup (i.e., 1 ounce or 12.5 mg of herb) the next morning. The next day, increase to 1/4 cup (2 ounces or 25 mg of herb). Repeat this same dose for 3 or 4 days to determine the effect. If there are no problems, use 3/8 cup (3 ounces or 37.5 mg of herb) for 3 or 4 days. Then try ½ cup (4 ounces or 50 mg of herb).

Continue this for 1 week to evaluate the results. After this trial, you may increase by ¼ cup or 25 mg of herb every 5–7 days as long as there are no problems. When you get up to a full capsule, continue that same dose for 2 weeks before increasing further. The idea is to allow enough time to evaluate the effects before increasing the dose further. If significant side effects occur, then the dose should not be increased. Depending on the size of the child and his or her sensitivity to the herb, the final dose could range from ¼ of a capsule (25 mg) up to a maximum of 4 capsules (400 mg) per day for an older child.

Adolescents 12–18 Years Old

R. rosea 50 mg/day; increase by 50 mg every 5–7 days, up to a maximum of 500 mg/day, as long as this dose does not cause anxiety, agitation, or insomnia. It is best taken about 30 minutes before breakfast on an empty stomach. To start with a 50 mg dose, get the 100 mg capsules. Open the capsule and pour the contents into a cup containing 8 ounces of juice, milk, or a hot drink. Drink half of the liquid and store the rest in the refrigerator for use the next morning.

Adults over 18 Years of Age

Rhodiola rosea 150 mg capsules: Start with one capsule 30 minutes before breakfast on an empty stomach for 1 week. Then add one capsule 30 minutes before lunch for 1 week. As long as you are comfortable and experience no agitation, irritability, or sleep disturbance, add a second capsule before breakfast for 1 week for a total of 450 mg a day. Wait several weeks to see the effects. If you feel you need more, add a second capsule before lunch for a total of four capsules (600 mg) daily.

Doses above 600 mg a day are not generally recommended because they have not been adequately studied. At higher doses (above 600 mg), the herb may have some effect on the function of blood platelets (as do many antidepressants), leading to bruising or increased bleeding, especially when combined with aspirin or other anticoagulants (e.g., heparin). Rarely, we find a patient who has a better response on higher doses.

In Good Company

Like many herbs, R. rosea is highly sociable. It works even better when teamed up with other herbs. In traditional folk medicine, herbs are often used in combinations rather than as solo treatments because they work best in good company. One limitation of research studies, with a few exceptions, is that they test one herb at a time. Other herbs that may be added to R. rosea to improve cognitive stimulation, learning, and productivity include ginkgo, Asian ginseng, American ginseng, passionflower, *Schizandra chinensis*, acanthopanax (*Eleutherococcus senticosus*), and ashwaganda (*Withania somnifera*).

GINKGO AND GINSENG

Studies have shown that ginkgo and ginseng can improve learning in animals and humans. These herbs affect neurotransmitter systems and are known to be natural cognitive activators. A few studies of ginkgo and ginseng in people with ADHD have shown weak or mixed results. This is probably because the majority of people with ADHD do not benefit from these herbs. However, we find that a small number of individuals improve considerably. In situations where the person has not responded well to standard treatments or does not want prescription medications, it is reasonable to try these herbs. Using good products with high potency in adequate doses and combinations can make all the difference in response.

At the age of 31, Angie came across as a tense, critical, mistrustful, no-nonsense woman with a Pollyanna smile plastered on her face. She had held numerous secretarial and administrative jobs for short periods of time, but had been unemployed for 5 years. As a mother, she had been incompetent and custody was assigned to her husband during their divorce. In the middle of a sentence, she would abruptly stop talking, glance away, and then look back asking, "Where was I?" Lost, confused, unable to make decisions, she required constant oversight from her mother, who worried about whether she would ever become independent and self-supporting. A psychologist told her that she had ADHD and processing problems that needed treatment. Angie was afraid to take any medication because in the past she had experienced allergic reactions to many of them.

She finally agreed to see me (Dr. Brown), hoping for a non-medication treatment that would enable her to pursue a career. Angie's mother brought her to the first appointment. Her conversation was so disjointed that it was difficult to follow her meaning. After the first visit, she was unable to find my office. Month after month she would go to the wrong entrance, wander the halls, and finally get the doorman to lead her to my door.

She agreed to try *Rhodiola rosea*. The first improvement was that her conversation became clearer and easier to follow. However, the effect was lost after a few days, possibly because she was inconsistent in taking the herb. Biofeedback (see Chapter 6) never had a chance because she missed most of the sessions. Aniracetam, a nootropic compound (see below) that improves language-related functions, did help her process better by enabling her to listen and retain more when people were talking (see Chapter 4 for more information on aniracetam). A second trial of Rhodiola rosea (Rosavin Plus) at 300 mg twice a day somewhat improved her mental focus and clarity. Angie's mother finally convinced her to try Adderall. After 3 days she sounded calmer, but she did not like the feeling of being quieted down, preferring to feel energized and bubbly. She refused to continue the medication.

I decided to treat her with a combination of ginkgo plus ginseng: Ginkgold 120 mg twice a day, plus a mixture of Korean, Chinese, American, and Siberian ginseng (Action Labs PowerMax 4X) taken once a day. One month later she found her way to my office alone, without the doorman. The big, natural smile on her face told me that the herbs were working and that they helped her feel the way she wanted to feel.

Angie was not totally cured, but with the ginkgo and ginseng her focus and attention improved enough that she became able to go on the Internet, read and retain better, complete household chores more consistently, and go places without getting hopelessly lost.

Ginkgo biloba—The Devil's in the Details

Ginkgo biloba, extracted from leaves of the maidenhair tree, has been used for centuries in traditional Chinese medicine to treat cognitive and memory impairment. The mechanisms of action believed to be responsible for the effects of various components of the extract include:

- Increasing blood supply to brain tissues by dilating blood vessels and reducing blood viscosity (thickness).

- Stimulating the activity of neurotransmitter systems, including dopamine.
- Stimulating the brain's "wakeup" pathways in the reticular activating system.
- Counteracting oxygen free radicals.
- Improving cell membrane fluidity.

Research on the effects of ginkgo on memory has shown mixed results, possibly due to the use of unproven products, variations in the populations studied, or other factors. Ginkgo was used in a small pilot study of six adolescents (17–19 years old) who had ADHD with additional diagnoses: three with oppositional defiant disorder; two with conduct disorder; and one with learning disabilities. All were given 200 mg a day of ginkgo extract EGb 761, a product that has proven to be clinically effective in many studies for other conditions. Significant benefits were found in arousal, hyperactivity, calming, anxiety, frustration tolerance, affect regulation, irritability, cognitive aspects of selective attention and processing, and discriminant attention. Adolescents with higher levels of arousal, irritability, and hyperactivity obtained the most benefit (Niederhofer, 2010). Although this was a small, uncontrolled study, the use of a ginkgo product with proven potency led to significant improvements in these complex cases.

In contrast, a 6-week randomized, double-blind, placebo-controlled study of 50 children with ADHD compared the effects of 80–120 mg per day of *G. biloba* (Ginkgo T.D., Tolidaru, Iran) to 20–30 mg per day of methylphenidate. Although it caused more side effects, methylphenidate was far more effective than Ginkgo T.D. for ADHD (Salehi et al., 2010). We could not find previous published studies using this Ginkgo T.D. preparation. This study is an example of the difficulty of interpreting research studies. We have seen a number of studies of herbs reporting negative or weak results. Looking more deeply into the details, we usually find that the researchers either used an untested product or they gave too low a dose. When interpreting new research studies, particularly when they are inconsistent with previous information, we have to get the details before accepting the results.

Ginkgo rarely causes side effects, but when it does, these can be minimized by starting with 60 mg/day and gradually increasing to 120 mg twice daily. Side effects may include nausea, headaches, and skin rashes. Although ginkgo somewhat decreases platelet aggregation (i.e., ability of blood cells to clump together to form clots), it does not appear to affect other measures of coagulation (clotting). Nevertheless, caution is needed when using ginkgo in patients who are also taking anticoagulants such as heparin, warfarin, or aspirin. Gingko should be discontinued 2 weeks prior to surgery. Ginkgo works well with nootropics, special substances that improve brain function, which are discussed below.

Q&A

Q: Who should take gingko?

A: Although ginkgo is not the first herb we would recommend for ADHD, it does have a place because it is less stimulating than some of the other treatments. Gingko can be useful for:

- People who are overly sensitive to, and overly stimulated by, prescription stimulants, Rhodiola rosea, or other treatments.
- People with ADHD who also have anxiety—they may find that gingko is calming.
- People who want to enhance their alertness and attention—gingko can be added to any other herb or nootropic.

American Ginseng (*Panax quinquefolius*)

Compared to Asian ginseng (*Panax ginseng*), American ginseng (*Panax quinquefolius*) is gentler, less stimulating, and less likely to cause agitation or headaches. So, although there is less research on American ginseng compared with Asian ginseng, it may be less likely to cause overstimulation in children. American ginseng also can improve immune function. A 4-week open study of 36 children with ADHD given American ginseng 400 mg per day, plus gingko 100 mg per day, found that 74% improved significantly on the Conner's ADHD scale and 44% improved on a social problems measure. Only two children experienced mild side effects (agitation) (Lyon et al., 2001). Interpretation of the impact of ginkgo on improving test scores in this study is limited because 25 of the children were also taking methylphenidate and there was no comparison control group.

Q&A

Q: Who could benefit from American ginseng?

A: American ginseng should be considered for:

- Young children under the supervision of a physician
- People who want to avoid overstimulation
- People with ADHD who also want to improve their immune response.

FRENCH MARITIME PINE BARK (*PINUS PINASTER*)—PYCNOGENOL

Pycnogenol® is the brand name for an herb that is made from an extract of French maritime pine bark (*Pinus pinaster*). Extracts from boiled tree barks used in traditional medicines in many countries may contain polyphenols and other antioxidants whose modes of action may include:

- Reducing oxidative stress.
- Increasing blood flow to areas of the brain that are impaired in ADHD by dilatation of cerebral blood vessels.
- Regulation of catecholamine metabolism.
- Regeneration and protection of vitamins C and E.

In a 1-month double-blind, placebo-controlled study 61 children with ADHD were randomly assigned to receive either Pycnogenol or a placebo. Standardized measures and teacher and parent ratings showed that the students given Pycnogenol had significantly greater improvements in hyperactivity, attention, concentration, and visual–motor coordination (Trebaticka et al., 2006).

A smaller study of 24 adults with ADHD randomized to receive Pycnogenol, methylphenidate, or placebo showed no differences among the three groups. This negative result may have been caused by usage of too low a dose of Pycnogenol, too short a trial period (3 weeks), or lack of herbal effect. However, some of the subjects given Pycnogenol had significant improvements and continued to take it after the study (Tenenbaum, Paul, Sparrow, Dodd, & Green, 2002). Larger randomized controlled trials (RCTs) are needed to validate these interesting findings and to determine whether people with certain polymorphisms are more likely to benefit from Pycnogenol.

There may be an association between increased levels of copper and decreased levels of zinc with hyperactivity, learning disabilities, and depression. (See Chapter 3 for a discussion of the importance of trace minerals in the diet.) Pycnogenol contains polyphenols, natural compounds with antioxidant properties. Polyphenols modulate antioxidant enzyme activities and have the ability to chelate (bind to and remove) metal ions such as copper and iron. Copper tends to increase oxidative stress whereas zinc tends to reduce it. A 1-month randomized double-blind study compared 65 children with ADHD, ages 6–14, with 54 healthy children of the same ages. At the beginning of the study, children with ADHD had significantly lower zinc levels and higher copper-to-zinc ratios than the children who did not have ADHD. In other words, they had an imbalance of trace minerals that would be associated with increased oxidative damage. Copper levels were higher in the ADHD group. Children with ADHD given Pycnogenol (1mg/kg body weight/day) showed significant decreases in copper levels and decreases in copper-to-zinc ratios, although zinc levels did not change significantly. There were no significant changes in copper, zinc, or copper-to-zinc ratios in the children who did not have ADHD. This study supports the theory that Pycnogenol may modify levels of trace minerals, normalizing antioxidant status by decreasing copper and copper-to-zinc ratios. The study also found a correlation between reduced iron levels and response to Pycnogenol with improvements in ADHD in children (Viktorinova et al., 2009).

Q&A

Q: Who could benefit from Pycnogenol?

A:
- People who need a gentler, less stimulating treatment.
- People with low ferritin (iron) levels.

LEMON BALM (*MELISSA OFFICIANALIS*), VALERIAN (*VALERIANA OFFICIANALIS*), AND PASSIONFLOWER (*PASSIFLORA INCARNATE*)

Lemon balm and passionflower, common ingredients in over-the-counter preparations, have modest benefits, such as reducing anxiety and restlessness (Akhondzadeh et al., 2001; Kennedy, Little, & Scholey, 2004). Studies show that valerian may improve sleep (Krystal & Ressler, 2002). Although no studies have been done in people formally diagnosed with ADHD, one trial of a combination of valerian and lemon balm (Euvegal forte) was tested in an uncontrolled (meaning, no placebo comparison group) study of 918 children under the age of 12 who had restlessness and difficulty sleeping. Substantial improvements occurred in 80.9% of the children with sleep problems and 70.4 % of those with restlessness (Muller & Klement, 2006). It is likely that some of the children in this study had ADHD. Overall, studies have reported few side effects. Side effects and toxicity have not been investigated. These mild herbs may be tried, starting with lemon balm first for:

- People with ADHD and anxiety.
- People who need a mild, less powerful effect.

ST. JOHN'S WORT (*HYPERICUM PERFORATUM*)

While St. John's wort may be helpful in mild-to-moderate depression, there is no indication that this herb is useful for ADHD alone. The activity of St. John's wort is similar to the antidepressants called *serotonin reuptake inhibitors* (SRIs). Since SRI antidepressants are not beneficial in ADHD, we would not expect St. John's wort to be. One study of 54 children with ADHD, ages 6–17, did not find any effect from St. John's wort (Weber et al., 2008). However, for people with ADHD who also suffer from mild depression, it can be useful to improve mood. St. John's wort can interfere with the activity of many medications. Nevertheless, in 17 studies, the herb was well tolerated. Among these studies, at most, 5.7% of participants dropped out because of side effects, and these side effects were not serious. Before trying this herb, check with your doctor to be sure it is safe to take with your medications.

Q&A

Q: Who might benefit from St. John's wort?

A:
- People with ADHD and mild depression.
- People with a history of improving on a serotonin reuptake inhibitor (SSRI) antidepressant (such as Zoloft, Paxil, or Prozac), but who could not tolerate the side effects of the prescription medications. People with ADHD and symptoms of Obsessive Compulsive Disorder such as repeatedly checking things, perfectionism, repeating certain actions (for example hand washing) or rituals to control their anxiety.

BRAHMI (*BACOPA MONNIERA*)

Brahmi has been used in Ayurvedic medicine for thousands of years to enhance stress resilience, reduce anxiety, and improve cognitive function. Antioxidant effects on brain areas *involved in ADHD* (hippocampus, frontal cortex, and striatum) have been demonstrated in animal studies. Clinical trials of brahmi in healthy adults as well as in children with ADHD have found it can mildly enhance certain aspects of learning. For example, in a small but well-done 12-week (randomized, double-blind, placebo-controlled) study of 36 children with ADHD, those given brahmi performed better on tests of sentence repetition, logical memory, and paired associate learning (Negi, Singh, Kushwaha, et al., 2000).

Brahmi shows mild cognitive enhancing effects, anti-stress effects, and other health benefits in asthma, gastric ulcers, hypothyroidism, and cardiovascular disease. In our practices, we have found it to have relatively weak benefits for ADHD. Side effects from brahmi are negligible.

COMPOUND HERBAL PREPARATIONS

We tend to customize combination treatments based upon the needs and responses of the individual. Many of these treatments are described in examples throughout the book. However, studies are being pursued to develop preparations containing many herbs, vitamins, and other nutrients believed to be of benefit for most people with ADHD. Although this may sound like a shotgun approach, it has some merits. For example, if subgroups of patients with ADHD show responses to different supplements, then preparations containing combinations of herbs and nutrients might help a fair number of people. If such combination products prove to be effective, they would provide an option for people who do not have access to health care professionals who are willing or able to administer customized complementary treatment combinations.

EASTERN MEDICINE: AYURVEDIC HERBS AND MARMA

Many systems of medicine, developed over thousands of years throughout the world, have understood and included the essential elements we use in treating ADHD today. One of the most elaborate, Ayurvedic medicine, began in India, spread throughout Asia, and is now practiced worldwide. While it is based on the science available thousands of years ago, each generation of master practitioners has expanded and refined the techniques. Just as we are trying to understand Eastern therapies in terms of Western science, modern-day Ayurvedic specialists are using Western scientific discoveries to enrich their work. For example, both Western integrative medicine and Ayurveda prescribe dietary and lifestyle changes in the treatment of ADHD: elimination of artificial food additives; supplementation with herbs containing antioxidant, calming, energizing, and cognitive-enhancing compounds, family involvement in treatment, and personal development. Although we cannot review the myriad of herbal and mind–body therapies developed in other countries, we would like to introduce you to the work of Dr. Pankaj Naram, an Indian physician who uses Siddha Veda, a system of Himalayan medicine that predates Ayurveda and that has been passed down through a lineage of clinical practitioners. Based on texts written 2,500 years ago, and the guidance of his master teacher, Dr. Naram developed protocols for treating ADHD, autism, and other developmental disorders.

Before describing Dr. Naram's work, we will tell you how we met him. It began with the September 11 terrorist attacks on the World Trade Center in 2001. A small group of volunteers formed an organization called Serving Those Who Serve (STWS). Their mission was to provide support, yoga, mind–body treatments, and herbal medicines to help first responders, Ground Zero workers, and area residents recover from the physical and psychological effects of the disaster. The staff of STWS asked Dr. Brown to teach his Breath~Body~Mind© practices to members of the 9/11 community to relieve severe respiratory problems as well as symptoms of anxiety, depression, and PTSD.

(In Chapter 5 we discuss the Breath~Body~Mind program, which includes movement, breathing, and meditation.) We (Drs. Brown and Gerbarg) heard that they were also distributing packets of Dr. Naram's herbs to the first responders and others exposed to the toxins from Ground Zero. Over time the combination of Breath~Body~Mind and Dr. Naram's herbs produced major improvements in both psychological and respiratory symptoms. Eventually we were able to meet Dr. Naram and learn more about how he developed his formulas as well as the treatments he found to be effective for ADHD. Following is an interview with Dr. Naram.

Dr. Naram's Story

Dr. Naram: Thirty years ago, my master sent me to work in one of the largest slums in India, Dharavi, near Mumbai. You know, the one in that movie.

Dr. Gerbarg: *Slum Dog Millionaire*?

Dr. Naram: Yes, that one. There were extremely bad health problems. So many children had chronic coughs, heart problems, and skin diseases. Regular medicines did not help them. So I asked my master what to do. He told me to find out where the children were working. I could not believe that these children, 12, 13, 14 years old were working. But it was true. The children took me to their workplace, a chemical plant where they spent all day, stripped down to their underwear, walking around inside the vats of chemicals in order to stir and mix the sludge. It was cheaper to pay children 10 rupees a day, about 10 pennies, than to use a machine. The vats contained industrial chemicals including lead, arsenic, and cadmium—serious toxins. I had to create a formula to detoxify them. In one of our ancient texts I read about an army of warriors who poisoned the tips of their arrows with lead and arsenic. Exposure to these toxic metals would have made them sick if they had not been treated regularly with herbs to detoxify (eliminate the toxins) from their bodies. They had to be strong, healthy, and battle ready. I created a new formula, based on those same herbs, to heal the children of Dharavi.

Years later, on the night of December 2, 1984, the world's worst industrial accident occurred at a pesticide manufacturing plant in Bhopal, India. Hundreds of thousands of people were exposed to a cloud of toxic gases. Government agencies estimate 15,000 deaths and over 500,000 injuries. I was able to help many recover with herbal formulas. Then, in 2001, I saw on television two planes strike the World Trade Center and set the towers on fire. I knew there would be deadly toxic exposure and a cloud of toxic gases, so I went to New York to help. There I met the volunteers of STWS and gave them the herbs. They had to take three formulas every day for 6–24 months.

Dr. Gerbarg: We met people who were very sick after working at Ground Zero and they told us how much your herbs had helped them.

Q&A

Q: Are there scientific studies of Dr. Naram's herbs?

A: There have been very few controlled studies of Ayurvedic therapies, in general. Although there are many case reports, overall, we find that Indian doctors are reluctant to do placebo-controlled studies because they do not want to withhold treatment from people who would be assigned to the control groups. However, 18 people affected by the 9/11 attacks participated in a small pilot study of Dr. Naram's herbs (Dahl & Falk, 2008). Participants were given the following compounds, made up of herbs grown and prepared in India and certified by the U.S. Food and Drug Administration (FDA) as over-the-counter herbal supplements marketable here:

Pulmo—respiration support
Herbal Detox—multilevel toxin formula
Mento—mind-nourishing formula
Immuno—strengthens immune system

Participants reported significant improvements during Ayurvedic treatment for symptoms that had not improved during 7 years of conventional medical treatment. The symptoms included cough, difficulty breathing, fatigue, exhaustion, depression, not feeling well, difficulty sleeping, among others. The only side effect, stomach upset during the first few weeks of treatment, was reported by 15% of the respondents.

Q&A

Q: Do Dr. Naram's herbs have contaminants such as heavy metals?

A: No. Dr. Naram's herbs were independently tested in a laboratory and found to be free of contaminants.

Dr. Naram's Treatment of an Italian Boy with ADHD

Dr. Naram treats people in many countries. While in Italy, he was asked to evaluate Ricardo, a 14-year-old boy who was so hyperactive, impulsive, and violent that his father developed anxiety, high blood pressure, heart problems, and diabetes from the stress of being his parent. An eminent psychiatrist in Rome had diagnosed Ricky as having extreme ADHD. He never slept and never stopped moving. When he watched television, he changed the channels every second, driving everyone crazy. His attention and memory were so impaired that whatever he did would be forgotten 2 minutes later. Lacking impulse control, he hit and punched his parents, teachers, and classmates.

When Ricky first visited Dr. Naram's office, he punched the secretary in the face, breaking her glasses. The boy was being treated with nine medications, including stimulants, sedatives, major tranquilizers (antipsychotics), and mood stabilizers. Nothing worked. Dr. Naram concluded that Ricky's mind was in a state of extreme turmoil and that the different parts of his mind had to be brought into balance. He started Ricky on an ADHD regimen that included (1) dietary changes, (2) herbal formulas, (3) special juices, and (4) a mind–body technique called Marma.

1. Dietary changes involved the elimination of dairy products, wheat products, sugar, pesticides, and artificial food colorings and preservatives (we discuss these in Chapter 4).

2. The herbal formulas were Calm Mind, Healthy Mind, Healthy Brain, Herbal Antioxidants, Heart Health, Cough and Cold formula, Ghee Treatments.

3. The special juices were white pumpkin, ginger, and holy basil.

4. Dr. Naram taught Ricky's parents to give him a set of Marma treatments. The basic Marma sequence is done nine times a day:

   a. Apply gentle pressure while moving the hands on the head, repeated six times.

   b. Press the right earlobe gently between two fingers six times.

   c. Use the tip of one index (pointer) finger to gently press the center of the area between the upper lip and the bottom of the nose six times.

   d. Use the tip of the left index finger to gently press the tip of the right index finger just under the top edge of the nail.

After 3 weeks of these treatments, Ricky showed marked improvements in sleep, mood, hyperactivity, anger, violence, speech clarity, memory, and learning. Over the next 6 months he got even better. Ricky secured a job in a pizza and gelato (ice cream) shop and later joined the army. His mental focus was sharp enough for him to win second prize in an army marksmanship competition.

Ricky visits Dr. Naram once a year when he is in Italy. Whenever he comes, the secretary takes her broken glasses out of the drawer to remind him. Now 21 years old, Ricky offers to fix them for her, but she always says, "You fixed yourself. That is enough."

Once a year Dr. Naram breaks his very strict Ayurvedic diet to enjoy pizza and gelato made especially for him by Ricky. Dr. Naram explains that the pizza and gelato are good for his "emotional mind," but, afterward, he takes mung soup and Healthy Detox formula to restore the clarity of his "intellectual mind."\CASE\

How does Marma work? According to Vedic medicine, Marma helps remove blocks to the blood circulation and the natural flow of metabolites (body chemicals), nutrients, hormones, and neurotransmitters. The use of tapping and pressure points can be found in many medical systems, including modern treatments such as Emotional Freedom Technique (EFT; Church, Hawk, Books, et al., in press). EFT is becoming widely used to relieve symptoms of military trauma in veterans and others. According to Eastern medicine, the tapping affects certain meridians (energy channels) in the body. We think that Marma techniques activate the parasympathetic nervous system, the soothing, recharging, healing, calming, anti-inflammatory part of the nervous system. This may be one among many physiological mechanisms that could account for the therapeutic effects. We hope that future research will enable us to understand these fascinating treatments more completely.

SLEEP PROBLEMS

Sleep problems occur in about 50% of children with ADHD and may persist into adulthood. These include difficulty falling asleep, resistance to sleep at bedtime, morning tiredness, and daytime sleepiness. An analysis of sleep studies in children with ADHD found a greater risk for sleep onset latency (difficulty falling asleep), decreased sleep efficiency, reduced sleep time, and increased daytime sleepiness (Cortese, Faraone, Konofal, & Lecendreux, 2009). Furthermore, the sleep problems of a child can affect the parents, who may have to stay up to make sure that their child is safe. Parents whose children sleep less than 8 hours a night are at higher risk to develop anxiety, depression, exhaustion, and loss of the patience that is so important in dealing with a child who has ADHD. Dr. Margaret Weiss and Dr. Jay Salpekar (2010) stress the importance of careful diagnosis to determine the causes of sleep problems associated with ADHD.

Common Causes of Sleep Problems with ADHD

1. *Stimulant medication.* If the effects of stimulant medications used to treat ADHD persist into nighttime, they can delay sleep. Another effect of stimulant medications is loss of appetite. When appetite suppression reduces daytime eating, hunger may not be felt until the medication wears off at night. In this situation, it is better to eat some healthy food at night and go to bed on a full stomach (Weiss & Salpekar, 2010).
2. *Restless leg syndrome* (RLS). This syndrome is characterized by frequent leg movements that can interfere with sleep. We mentioned earlier that iron deficiency, one of the causes of RLS, can be treated easily

with iron supplements. However, in some cases, medications that affect the dopamine system, such as levodopa-carbidopa, ropinirole (Requip), or pergolide (Permax), are needed.

3. *Sleep-disordered breathing.* Obstructive sleep apnea (OSA) in adults, and less commonly, sleep-disordered breathing in children can lead to daytime tiredness, inattention, hyperactivity, and irritability.

4. *Chronic sleep onset insomnia.* Chronic sleep onset insomnia—that is, delay in falling asleep—accounts for up to half of these sleep difficulties (Bendz & Scates, 2010). Difficulty sleeping can lead to reduced academic performance as well as increased hyperactivity, irritability, impulsivity, and accidental injuries.

5. *Other psychiatric conditions.* Other conditions that may occur along with ADHD can contribute to sleep problems. Insomnia is often part of the picture in people who suffer from depression, anxiety disorders, PTSD, bipolar disorder, tic disorder, or substance abuse.

6. *Poor sleep hygiene.* The term *sleep hygiene* refers to all the things you do during the evening before sleep (and once you get into bed) that influence how well you sleep. It includes bedtime routines, activities leading up to bedtime, and substances ingested within a few hours of bedtime. Some adults have irregular sleep habits, and they may have difficulty establishing the consistent sleep routines that they and their children need. This problem can be addressed by educational counseling and behavior therapy. The American Academy of Sleep Medicine (AASM) publishes best practices for good sleep hygiene, including specific behavioral treatments for ADHD-related sleep problems.

Evaluating Sleep Disorders

Weiss and Salpekar (2010) explain a comprehensive process used by health care professionals to accurately diagnose sleep disorders that includes the use of parent–child questionnaires, sleep questionnaires, sleep diaries, and clinical interviews. If the results of these measures suggest a sleep disorder, the next step would be either an overnight sleep study such as *polysomnography* (monitoring electrical activity on the scalp with electroencephalogram [EEG] and other body function measures in a sleep laboratory) or *actinography* (wearing a small device on the wrist to record movements over several days and nights in the patient's normal environment). Your doctor will be able to arrange sleep studies for you in a nearby hospital.

Solving Sleep Problems

Establish Good Sleep Hygiene

Whatever is conducive to sleep for an individual constitutes good sleep hygiene. Typically good sleep hygiene includes establishing a regular bedtime and avoiding stimulating activities during the hour before sleep, such as playing computer games, watching suspenseful television shows, or listening to loud music. The hour before bedtime should be used for quiet activities such as reading (not emotionally disturbing material), taking a warm bath, or doing calming breathing and relaxation practices (see chapter 5).

Try Melatonin for Chronic Sleep Onset Insomnia

Melatonin is a natural hormone produced primarily in the pineal gland, a small anatomical structure at the base of the brain. Melatonin binds to receptors in the hypothalamus, which synchronize melatonin secretion with the 24-hour day–night cycle. Prior to sleep, melatonin levels rise and help induce sleep onset. Children and adults with ADHD can have a delay in the rise of melatonin that should occur in the evening to facilitate sleep (Van Veen, Kooij, Boonstra, Gordijn, & Van Someren, 2010). The result is that it takes longer to fall asleep.

If sleep onset delay persists despite good sleep hygiene, then it may be time to discuss a trial of melatonin with your doctor. Good sleep hygiene is necessary for melatonin to be effective. For example, if you stay up until 2:00 A.M. playing *Lara Croft Tomb Raider*, *Call of Duty*, or *World of Warcraft* on your computer and drinking caffeinated soda, it is unlikely that melatonin will put you to sleep. Bright light from computer screens tends to suppress melatonin and may interfere with the action of melatonin supplements. Once the melatonin is effective, it should be taken for a month or two and then discontinued just to see if it is still needed. If sleep difficulties return, then it should be resumed. Every few months, discontinuation can be tried to check on whether the melatonin is still necessary. It is reassuring that at least one study found the hormone to be safe for 3 years. Many of our patients have used melatonin every night for decades without any problems. Additional, long-term studies in larger numbers of people would further confirm its safety.

Melatonin supplements have been shown to increase melatonin levels and shorten the time needed to fall asleep. In a rigorous (double-blind, randomized, placebo- controlled) 4-week study of 105 children (ages 6–12) with sleep onset insomnia and ADHD, those given melatonin showed significant improvements in sleep (Van der Heijden, Smits, Van Someren, Ridderinkhof, & Gunning, 2007). A 3-year follow-up study of these children found that 65% continued to use melatonin every evening, and 12% used it occasionally (Hoebert, van der Heijden., van Geijlswijk, & Smits, 2009). Melatonin was safe and effective for long-term use in children ages 6–12.

How to Use Melatonin for Sleep

Overall, melatonin is beneficial for sleep in children and adults. Melatonin supplements cause very few side effects. Rarely, it can cause headache or activation instead of sedation. Doses range from 1 to 3 mg for children weighing 100 pounds (40 kg) or less, 3–6 mg for those over 100 pounds (40 kg), and 3–9 mg for adults. Melatonin comes in short-acting and long-acting forms. The short-acting form helps you fall asleep, whereas the long-acting form helps you stay asleep. For sleep onset insomnia, short-acting melatonin is preferable. However, for problems falling and staying asleep, a 50–50 mix of short- and long-acting forms may work better. This mix can be achieved either by taking two pills (one short- and one long-acting) or by finding a product that contains both forms. The quality of melatonin used in different products varies. You can check the chart on Quality Products at the end of this book to be sure you are buying a high quality product that will be effective.

Taking One Step at a Time in Treating Sleep Disorders Associated with ADHD

After careful evaluation, as described above, and depending on the cause of the sleep disorder, there are numerous approaches to treatment:

1. Stimulant medication doses and timing can be adjusted.

2. Specific behavioral treatments, including sleep hygiene education, can be combined with other approaches.

3. Melatonin can be added.

4. Relaxation techniques such as paced breathing (see Chapter 5) and relaxation CDs can be used.

5. Biofeedback or brain stimulation (see Chapter 6) sessions can be tried.

6. When stimulant medication cannot be reduced and causes sleep problems that do not respond to the natural treatments described above, it may be necessary for your doctor to prescribe either clonidine or guanfacine for sleep onset insomnia and nighttime agitation.

For more information on the diagnosis and management of sleep disorders, see the Resources section at the end of this chapter.

NOOTROPICS

Nootropics (pronounced *no-o-tró-pics*) improve how the brain functions and protect neurons from damage. How do they work? There are numerous ways in which nootropics may improve brain functions:

1. Scavenging of free radicals and preventing them from damaging delicate cell structures.

2. Increasing antioxidants and thereby raising the levels of other free radical fighters.

3. Improving membrane fluidity enhancing electrical conduction in nerve pathways.

4. Increasing neurotransmitter levels improving the communication between neurons and among the neural networks that coordinate thinking, problem solving, and behavior.

5. Improving mitochondrial function increases and maintains energy supplies needed to fuel cellular functions, including cellular repair.

6. Stimulating messenger ribonucleic acid (mRNA) protein synthesis helps the cell produce all the compounds necessary for the brain to function properly.

7. Enhancing/increasing cerebral blood flow by slightly increasing the diameter of the small blood vessels in areas of the brain that are underactive can enhance functioning by transporting more oxygen and nutrients to brain structures.

The nootropics we find most useful for ADHD are meclofenoxate (centrophenoxine), picamilon, and the racetams (pyrrolidones). Meclofenoxate and picamilon are discussed in Chapter 4.

Racetams for Learning Disabilities, ADHD, and Oppositional Defiant Disorder

Racetams (pyrrolidones) bind to and modulate the activity of glutamate alpha-amino-3-hydroxy-5-methyl-4-isoxazole-propionic acid (AMPA) receptors involved in excitatory neurotransmission, learning, and memory (Ahmed & Oswald, 2010; Gouliaev & Senning, 1994; Mizuno et al., 2005). Whether this activity contributes to the clinical effects is not yet known. Racetams may contribute to neuroprotection and improved function through the release of brain-derived neurotrophic factor (BDNF), essential for neuroplasticity (Iulu et al., 2009; Wu et al., 2004). Furthermore, they improve interhemispheric transmission, thereby improving communication between the right and left sides of the brain. While racetams such as piracetam, aniracetam, and pramiracetam are useful, in general, for learning disabilities, they are especially effective for language disabilities, including reading, listening, and speaking disabilities (Tallal, Chase, Russell, & Schmitt, 1986). In people with dyslexia (reading disability), racetams activate the verbal processing areas in the left hemisphere. One double-blind, randomized, placebo-controlled multicenter study of 225 children with dyslexia (ages 7–12 years) found that those given 3,600 mg/day of piracetam had significant improvements in reading and comprehension. The improvements were evident after 12 weeks and were maintained through the full 36 weeks of the trial. There were no adverse reactions to the piracetam (Wilsher et al., 1987).

Pramiracetam tends to be more calming, whereas aniracetam is more stimulating. In our patients, we find 750 mg twice a day of aniracetam to be particularly effective, well tolerated, and unlikely to cause agitation or other side effects. In one of our cases, aniracetam cleared up stuttering.

Because racetams are so low in side effects, they are easy to try. Although they may work within a few weeks, it is worth giving them a full 12-week trial to determine whether or not they will make a difference in verbal processing, other learning disabilities, and symptoms related to ADHD.

Oppositional Defiant Disorder

Oppositional defiant disorder is the DSM term used to describe children who are extremely uncooperative to the degree that their behavior significantly impairs their ability to function. This disorder can occur alone or in combination with other disorders, including ADHD. Technically, it is supposed to be separate from ADHD, but sometimes when the ADHD is treated, the oppositional behavior also remits. Although there are no formal studies of the use of racetams for oppositional behavior, we would like to report one case in which piracetam transformed a child's life.

> Marlene was the child who always said no. Whatever she was asked or told or expected to do, Marlene was sure to oppose. Explaining, coaxing, bribing, threatening—all the usual tactics failed. And if any physical force was applied, the child went wild—kicking, screaming, biting. By the age of 10, Marlene had been evaluated many times by specialists who diagnosed her as having ADHD, oppositional defiant disorder, dyslexia, anxiety, and obsessive–compulsive disorder. Treatments included numerous medications, neurofeedback (see Chapter 6), cognitive–behavior therapy, and family therapy—and all failed. Sertraline (Zoloft) reduced her anxiety and OCD symptoms, but nothing more. Finally, her parents brought her to me (Dr. Brown) for a consultation. Intending to improve her brain function and dyslexia, I gave Marlene a trial of piracetam 1300 mg twice a day. The results exceeded all expectations. The next time Marlene came to see me she did not have to be dragged. Her parents said, "She's transformed . . . a different child. Marlene is calmer, happier.

She smiles and sings all the time. She still loses her temper about once a day when she doesn't get her way, but it only lasts a minute and then she's fine. She remembers to use the breathing you taught her (see Chapter 5) and it calms her down quickly. Before, she hated books. Now she reads all the time."

Q&A

Q: When should racetams be tried?

A:

1. When the person with ADHD also has problems reading and other language-related disabilities. Racetams are even more effective when combined with remediation or rehabilitation.

2. Other learning disabilities such as slow processing.

3. In cases of learning disabilities where there is a history of brain injury, due to trauma or cerebrovascular disease (e.g. stroke) racetams can improve recovery.

TAKING ONE TREATMENT STEP AT A TIME

You may be eager to try some of the treatments described in this chapter, but where should you begin? Begin with your doctor by discussing your interest in trying non-drug treatments. If your doctor does not know about them, give the doctor a copy of this book or a copy of the relevant pages. Ask your doctor to review the material and look up whatever references are needed. There should be enough material for your doctor to integrate this information with his or her medical background. The principles for doing safe trials of complementary treatments are the same as for standard treatments. If your doctor still feels uncomfortable overseeing your use of complementary treatments, you can either ask for a referral to someone experienced in integrative medicine or suggest that your doctor contact us (Dr. Brown and Dr. Gerbarg) for guidance.

How to Choose Treatments

The treatments you and your doctor choose should depend on the following considerations:

1. Age: With children less than 12 years of age, start with the mildest treatments that have the fewest side effects, such as Pycnogenol, picamilon, centrophenoxine, or aniracetam. Adolescents and adults may want to start with one of the stronger treatments such as Rhodiola rosea and add the other treatments to enhance benefits. People over the age of 60 may also benefit from improving brain circulation with picamilon.

2. Presence of other concurrent diagnoses, such as insomnia, learning disabilities, developmental disorders, brain injury, stroke, seizures, anxiety, or mood disorders. Focus on treatments that are particularly helpful in these disorders; for example, melatonin for sleep or racetams for learning disabilities.

3. ADHD subtype and whether the treatment is more effective for ADHD of the inattentive, hyperactive/impulsive, or mixed type (inattentive with hyperactive/impulsive).

We Recommend These Treatment Steps

1. Obtain a careful evaluation for ADHD and other possible concurrent diagnoses from your doctor and whatever specialists may be needed, such as a psychiatrist, a pediatric psychiatrist, a psychologist, a sleep specialist, or a neurologist.

2. Consult with your health care professionals to develop a plan for treatment trials and monitoring. Monitoring is important in order to evaluate changes over time as well as to watch for side effects.

   • Decide how you will evaluate the effects over time. This may include observing changes in target symptoms, getting feedback from those who know you well, and repeating brief symptom questionnaires. Getting feedback is important because other people may notice improvements before you do.

   • Start only one new treatment at a time so that you can clearly evaluate the effects.

3. Begin with moderate doses for treatments that have potential side effects and increase gradually every 3–7 days until you reach

a maximum dose, see clear benefits, or encounter side effects. When side effects occur, back off a bit by returning to the previous lower dose, wait another week to see if the side effects clear, and then proceed. If the side effects are severe or there is an allergic reaction, discontinue the treatment. The trial period for most of these treatments should be between 6 and 12 weeks once you have attained the maximum dose. However, if you see results sooner and these appear stable, then it may not be necessary to increase the dose further. Maintain that dose and move on to the next supplement trial. If you see no results after a full trial, then discontinue it and start the next supplement trial. If you see partial benefits that plateau, then continue at that dose and add the next treatment for further improvements.

Table 3.1 Supplement Guidelines for Herbs, Melatonin, and Nootropics

Supplement	Clinical Uses	Dose (mg/d[a])		Side Effects and Interactions[b]
		over 12 years	8–12 years	
		Adults and children over age 12 years	Children ages 8–12 years	
Arctic Root *Rhodiola rosea*	Mental clarity, focus, attention, memory, stress, mood, cognitive function	50–600 mg/d	25 mg/day; increase gradually as needed	Activation, agitation, insomnia, jitteriness, mania. Rare: ↑BP, angina, can cause bruising or bleeding in doses above 800 mg/day or if combined with aspirin or other blood thinners. Avoid in bipolar I; caution in bipolar II
Ayurvedic herbs	ADHD	Consult an Ayurvedic doctor		Mild
Brahmi (*Bacopa monniera*)	ADHD; mild benefits	280 mg b.i.d. (higher doses for more severe cases)	140 mg b.i.d. (but preparations vary)	Minimal

Supplement	Clinical Uses	Dose (mg/d[a]) over 12 years	8–12 years	Side Effects and Interactions[b]
Chamomile (*Matricareia recutita*)	Mild; for sleep	Depends on the preparation		Ragweed family— if allergic reactions or pregnant, D/C
Ginkgo (*Ginkgo biloba*)	Alertness, attention, memory, learning; combine with ginseng	120–240 mg/d	60 mg/d	Minimal: headache, ↓ platelet aggregation, anticoagulants, agitation (rare); D/C prior to surgery
Ginseng (*Panax ginseng*)	Adult ADHD	300–800 mg/d		Activation, anxiety, insomnia, headache, GI symptoms, tachycardia, ↓ platelet aggregation anticoagulants
Ginseng (*American Ginseng*)	Child ADHD	450–900 mg/d	Depends on age/ weight 225–450 mg/d	
Lemon balm (*Melissa officianalis*)	Mild; for sleep, anxiety	Adult: 60–100 mg/d or b.i.d. Child 13–16 years: 30–50 mg b.i.d.	15–30 mg/d or b.i.d.	No serious side effects
Meclofenoxate (*Centrophenoxine*)	ADHD, brain injury	Adult: 500–2000 mg/d Child 13–16 years: 250–500 mg/d	250 mg/d	Minimal side effects when given alone. When combined with other cholinergic[c] agents: headache, muscle tension, insomnia, irritability, agitation, facial tics
Melatonin	Sleep	1–9 mg h.s.	1-3 mg h.s.	Occasional agitation, abdominal cramps, fatigue, dizziness, headache, vivid dreams. D/C: pregnancy
Passionflower (*Passiflora incarnata*)	Mild effect for sleep, anxiety	90 mg t.i.d.	45 mg t.i.d.	Minimal

Supplement	Clinical Uses	Dose (mg/d[a])		Side Effects and Interactions[b]
		over 12 years	8–12 years	
Pycnogenol®	ADHD with learning disabilities	100 mg b.i.d.	50 mg b.i.d.	Minimal
Racetams	ADD with learning disabilities; medication-related cognitive impairment			Minimal. Rarely: anxiety, insomnia, agitation, irritability, headache
Aniracetam		750 mg b.i.d.	750 mg b.i.d.	
Piracetam		1800–3600 mg/d	1800–3600 mg/d	
Pramiracetam		600 mg b.i.d.	600 mg b.i.d.	
St. John's wort (*Hypericum perforatum*)	Depression, mild to moderate	300–600 mg t.i.d.		Advise: Do not use in children; it can cause phototoxic reactions such as severe sun burn
Schizandra chinensis	Stress, anxiety, energy, sleep, memory, strength, liver health	100 mg b.i.d Can range up to 1000 mg b.i.d. depending on the preparation		Minimal. Rarely: anxiety, insomnia, agitation, irritability
Valerian (*Valerian officianalis*)	Sleep	450–900 mg h.s.		150–450 mg/h.s.
ADAPT-232 *R. rosea 4%* *E. senticosus* *S. chinensis*	Swedish Herbal Institute	2-4 tabs/d over age 12		Minimal: side effects Caution: Bipolar disorder can cause agitation or mania
Clear Mind™ *R. rosea 3%,* *Rhododendron caucasicum,* *Rives nigrum*	Ameriden	2–4 tabs/d	1 or 2 tabs/d	Minimal: side effects of component herbs Caution: Bipolar Disorder can cause agitation or mania
EZ Energy® *R. rosea 70 mg* *E. senticosus* *S. chinensis* *A. mandshurica* *R.carthamoides*	Mental clarity, focus, attention, memory, stress, mood, cognitive function; calms patients who become agitated on activating herbs	2–4 tabs/d	1 or 2 tabs/d	Minimal: side effects of component herbs Caution: Bipolar disorder can cause agitation or mania

Supplement	Clinical Uses	Dose (mg/d[a])		Side Effects and Interactions[b]
		over 12 years	8–12 years	
Energy Reserves *R. rosea* *E. senticosus* *S. chinensis*	Mental clarity, focus, attention, memory, mood, stress, cognitive function.	2-4 tabs/d	1-2 tabs/d	Minimal: side effects of component herbs Caution in Bipolar disorder
Kare-n-Liver® *S. chinensis* *100 mg E. senticosus 100 mg*	Combine with *R. rosea* for mental clarity, focus, attention, memory, mood, stress, cognitive function	2–4 tabs/d	1–2 tabs/d	Minimal: side effects of component herbs

Note. ADHD = Attention-deficit/hyperactivity disorder (includes all three subtypes); mg/d = milligrams per day; tabs = tablets; b.i.d. = twice a day; t.i.d. = three times a day; A.M. = in the morning; P.M. = in the evening; h.s. = at bedtime; g = grams; mg = milligrams; BP = blood pressure; GI = gastrointestinal side effects; D/C = discontinue.

[a] The dosages on this table are meant only as guidelines. People who are more sensitive may need to use lower doses. Readers should discuss the choice of supplements and the adjustment of doses with their personal physician.

[b] Common side effects are listed. There are additional rare side effects. Individuals with high blood pressure, diabetes, pregnancy (or during breastfeeding), or any chronic or serious medical condition should check with their physician before taking supplements. Patients taking anticoagulants should consult their physician before using supplements. Parents are advised to consult a qualified physician to prescribe and monitor all supplements given to children.

[c] Cholinergic = causes effects similar to acetylcholine such as reduced heart rate and vasodilation. Necessary for arousal, learning, and memory.

Table 3.2 Guide to Quality Products for Herbs, Melatonin, and Nootropics

Supplement	Company	Brand Name	Source	Cost/d[a]
Arctic Root (*Rhodiola rosea*)	Ameriden International	Rosavin™ 100mg Rosavin Plus™ 150mg	888-405-3336 www.ameriden. com	$0.50– 1.50
	Kare-n-Herbs	Energy Kare	www.karen herbs.com 800-774-9444	
	ProActive Bioproducts	Botanica Verde Mind Body & Spirit	www.proactive-bio.com 877-282-5366 x701	
	Swedish Herbal Institute	SHR-5	www.shi.se	
Ayurvedic herbs	Consult a certified Ayurvedic doctor			

Supplement	Company	Brand Name	Source	Cost/d[a]
"Brahmi" (*Bacopa monniera*)	Major brands[b]**		Health food stores	$1.50–3.00
Chamomile (*Matricareia recutita*)	Major brands		Health food stores	$0.25
Ginkgo (*Ginkgo biloba*)	Nature's Way	Gingold	Health food stores/ pharmacies	$0.35
	Pharmaton	Ginkoba		
Ginseng, Asian or Korean (*Panax ginseng*) Ginseng, American (*Panax quinquefolius*)	Hsu's Ginseng	Panax Ginseng	800-388-3818 www.hsuginseng.com	$0.20
	Action Labs	PowerMax-4x Ginseng	800-932-2953	
Ginseng, Siberian (*Eleuterococcus Senticosus* or *Acanthopanax senticosus*)	Hsu's Ginseng	Siberian ginseng Eleuthero	800-388-3818 www.hsuginseng.com	$0.20–0.40
Lemon balm (*Melissa officianalis*)	Major brands		Health food stores	$0.25
Meclofenoxate (*Centrophenoxine*)	IAS	Lucidril	www.antiaging-systems.com	$0.50–2.50
Melatonin	LEF		www.lef.com	$0.05–0.20
	IAS		www.antiaging-systems.com	
	Natrol Schiff, Solgar		Health food stores/ pharmacies	
Passionflower (*Passiflora incarnata*)	Major brands		Health food stores	$0.50–1.50
Pycnogenol®	Many brands Puritan's Pride	Pycnogenol®	www.pycnogenol.com www.puritan.com	$0.50–1.00
Racetams Aniracetam Piracetam				$1.50-$1.80
	IAS		www.antiaging-systems.com	
	Smart Nutrition		www.smartnutrition.com	
Schizandra chinensis (*Schizandra*)	Gaia Herbs NaturesWay	Schizandra	www.Gaiaherbs.com Health food stores	$1.80

Supplement	Company	Brand Name	Source	Cost/d[a]
St. John's wort (*Hypericum perforatum*)	Natures Way	Kira (LI-160) Perika	www.Nature-sway.com Health food stores	$0.75 –3.50
	Nature Made	St. Johns Wort	www.nature made.com 800-276-2878	
Valerian (*Valerian officianalis*)	Major brands		Health food stores	
ADAPT-232 *R. rosea* *E. senticosus* *S. chinensis*	Swedish Herbal Institute	ADAPT-232	www.shi.se	$0.50 –1.50
Clear Mind™ *R. rosea 3%, Rhododendron caucasicum, Rives nigrum*	Ameriden International	Clear Mind™	www.ameriden.com 877-282-5366 x701	$1.30 –3.60
EZ Energy® *R. rosea 70 mg* *E. senticosus* *S. chinensis* *A. mandshurica* *R. carthamoides*	Ameriden International	Easy Energy®	www.ameriden.com 877-282-5366 x701	$1.30
Energy Reserves *R. rosea* *E. senticosus* *S. chinensis*	Proactive Bioproducts Botanica Verde	Energy Reserves	www.proactive bio.com 877-282-5366	$0.70– 1.40
Kare-n-Liver® *S. chinensis* 100mg *E. senticosus* 100mg	Kare-n-Herbs	Kare-n-Liver®	www.kare-n-herbs.com 800-774-9444	$0.40

Note. Parents are advised to consult a qualified physician to prescribe and monitor supplements given to children. *R. rosea* = *Rhodiola rosea*; *E. senticocus* = *Eleutherococcus senticosus*; *S. chinensis* = *Schizandra chinensis*; *A. mandshurica* = *Aralia mandshurica*; *R. carthamoides* = *Rhaponticum carthamoides*. LEF = Life Extension Foundation; IAS = International Antiaging Systems.

[a] Costs of products may vary. This table lists approximate costs at the time of publication. Unless noted otherwise, all prices are costs per day based upon recommended treatment dosages. This is not a comprehensive list of all available products.

[b]Major brands: indicates that there is no one "best brand" and that as long as you purchase well known brands with good manufacturing standards, you are likely to get a good product. This is true of supplements that are more easily available and that do not require as much special care in processing.

RESOURCES

The following are resources for additional and updated information on herbs, melatonin, and nootropics.

Websites for Organizations

Alaska Rhodiola Products: http://www.alaskarhodiolaproducts.com
  A non-profit farmer's co-op growing Rhodiola rosea in Alaska.

American Academy of Sleep Medicine (AASM): www.aasmnet.org and www .Sleepeducation.com
  Information on diagnosis and treatment of sleep disorders.

American Psychiatric Association Caucus on Complementary, Alternative and Integrative medicine: www.APACAIM.org
  Information for health care providers seeking courses, workshops, references, and options for networking and advocacy.

ConsumerLab.com—www.consumerlab.com
  Rates many brands of herbs and supplements on some measures of quality and labeling accuracy. Does not assess shelf life, the length of time the product may sit on a shelf without losing potency.

Drugs.com—www.drugs.com
  Provides concise updated presentation of CAM, including risks and interactions.

National Center for Complementary and Alternative Medicine, National Institutes of Health, National Library of Health Complementary and Alternative Medicine Specialist Library (NeLCAM): www.library.nhs.uk/cam.
  Database for scientific publications.

Natural Medicines Comprehensive Database: www.naturaldatabase.com.
  Database of information on natural treatments. Descriptions of adverse reactions are often overstated and based on unsubstantiated cases.

Research Council for Complementary Medicine: www.rccm.org.uk/default.aspx ? m=o.
  Devloping database of references on CAM.

Serving Those Who Serve (STWS): www.stws.org.
  Non-profit organization providing complementary, herbal, and mind-body workshops to First Responders and others affected by the 9/11 World Trade Center Attacks.

Supplement Watch: www.supplementwatch.com.
  Undated information on quality and safety of supplements.

U.S. Food and Drug Administration: www.fda.gov/medwatch. Updated information on quality and safety of supplements.

Websites for Journals

BMC Complementary and Alternative Medicine: www.biomedcentral.com. Peer-reviewed journal publishes articles on CAM.

Evidence-Based Complementary and Alternative Medicine: www.hindawi.com. Peer-reviewed journal publishes articles on CAM.

Herbalgram: Journal of the American Botanical Council: www. Herbalgram.org. In depth, authoritative articles on herbs from around the world.

Journal of Complementary and Alternative Medicine: www.liebertpub.com. Peer-reviewed journal publishes articles on CAM.

Other Websites

Dr. Naram, information and videotapes: www.drnaram.com. Ayurvedic treatments

Emotional Freedom Techniques (EFT): www.eftuniverse.com/index.php?option= com_content&view=article&id=18. Used to relieve symptoms of military trauma in veterans and others.

Books

Blumenthal, M. (Ed.). (2003). *The ABC Clinical Guide to Herbs.* Austin, TX: American Botanical Council. Authoritative, comprehensive publication of non-profit research and education organization, clearly written overview of herbs including their uses, doses, contraindications, and adverse reactions.

Brown, R.P., Gerbarg, P.L., & Muskin, P.R. (2009). *How to Use Herbs, Nutrients, and Yoga in Mental Health Care.* New York: Norton. Synthesis of 30 years experience shows the reader how to integrate herbs, nutrients, and yoga with standard treatments for all categories of mental health and illness. Suitable for training health care practitioners as well as providing information for the general public.

Ernst, E., Pittler, M.H., & Wider, B. (Ed.). (2006). *The Desktop Guide to Complementary and Alternative Medicine: An Evidence-Based Approach* (2nd ed.). Mosby: London.

Concise, well-organized quick-reference resource, provides a more conservative approach based on very stringent evidence requirements that cannot yet be met by many beneficial herbs.

Harkness, R., & Bratman, S. (2003). *Mosby's Handbook of Drug–Herb and Drug–Supplement Interactions*. St. Louis, MO: Mosby.
Useful reference to check on interactions between herbs or between herbs and medications.

Lake, J., & Spiegel, D. (2007). *Complementary and Alternative Treatments in Mental Health Care*. Washington, DC: American Psychiatric Association.
Chapters are written by experts in different areas of CAM, for example, Chinese medicine, homeopathy, Ayurveda.

CHAPTER 4 OUTLINE

CHAPTER 4

Food, Glorious Food

Diet, Vitamins, and Nutrients

WAS IT SOMETHING I ATE?

Jimmy was rarely invited to birthday parties, but there was a new kid in his class whose mother had never seen him in action, so he got an invitation. At first, he just seemed a little excited, like the other kids, running around playing in the yard. At lunch he was a bit restless at the table, making funny faces and goofing around with the food. He helped himself to a third glass of soda while munching M&Ms and chips. By the time the cake and ice cream arrived, he was revved, his eyes glazed over as he babbled and jostled the kids sitting next to him. He kept ducking under the table and popping back up like a Jack-in-the-box, pausing only to stuff chunks of dessert into his mouth. His friend's mother was kind, even when he spilled his drink. The ducking and popping got rougher until he knocked the table so hard that all the soda cups came tumbling down. As he rolled laughing on the floor, he caught a glimpse of the mother dashing for the phone to call his parents.

What happened to Jimmy? What turned him into a party monster? Was it the soda, candy, chips, sugar, artificial colors and flavors, having to sit still, overstimulation from the other children—all of the above? There are many opinions on these questions.

When we read about a scientific study showing benefits from a dietary treatment, it is important to assess the quality of the evidence. There are many ways to do a scientific study, as we have noted, and some methods produce more solid, significant, and higher-quality evidence than others. In general, studies with larger numbers of participants and those that use a *randomized, double-blind, placebo-controlled method* are considered to be more convincing than smaller studies that do not use a control group. (See the discussion of research evidence in Chapter 2.) Here we sort through the evidence and suggest ways to evaluate the possible impact of food on symptoms of ADHD that you and your family may be experiencing.

DIETARY TREATMENTS: WORTH THE TROUBLE OR NOT?

Dietary treatments can involve eliminating certain foods, adding foods or supplements, or both. Changing the diet of children, especially by not letting them eat the foods their friends get to enjoy, is difficult at best and sometimes disastrous. Many parents wonder if it is worth the struggle. Will this make enough of a difference to be worth the effort, the fights, the tears, the tantrums? The answer is: sometimes yes and sometimes no. Although many individuals believe that food can profoundly affect their ADHD symptoms, findings from research on elimination diets have been consistently inconclusive. However, studies are making progress investigating why certain people with ADHD are affected by specific foods, artificial food additives, and particular supplements. Whether or not you will benefit by avoiding sugar, eliminating artificial food colorings, or taking supplements probably depends upon several factors:

- Your genetic composition and polymorphism profile (see Chapter 2 for discussion of polymorphisms or genetic variants)
- Whether you have deficiencies of essential vitamins or minerals due to diet or poor absorption.
- Whether you have allergies to specific foods or food additives.
- Whether you have been/are exposed to environmental effects such as toxins, pesticides, smoking.

Here are four simple rules that may help you make decisions about whether to add dietary treatment to the burden of tasks involved in managing ADHD:

Rule 1: Observe your own reactions to food.

Rule 2: What's good for your brain is good for your ADHD. Conversely, what's bad for your brain is bad for your ADHD.

Rule 3: Compare your subtype and characteristics with those that have been shown to be associated with positive responses to dietary interventions.

Rule 4: Use your common sense.

Here are some questions to consider when deciding whether to add dietary treatment to the many tasks involved in managing ADHD:

- Do I (or my child) have characteristics similar to those of people who are known to benefit from dietary changes?
- Which dietary changes are easiest to make with minimal disruption to normal eating patterns and food preferences?
- How strong is the evidence that dietary treatments really work?
- Which dietary changes or supplements would have additional health benefits to make them worth the effort and expense?
- Which supplements have been shown to help ADHD? What are the subtypes and characteristics of people most likely to benefit from these supplements?
- How do supplements work? Why are they important?

ELIMINATION DIETS

While some people swear by diets that eliminate all but a few foods, for most people, such an extreme approach is not necessary. There is some evidence that artificial food colorings, benzoate preservatives, sugars, and artificial sweeteners may cause problems in some cases. Studies suggest that approximately 50% of children may benefit from eliminating these culprits.

Characteristic: Allergic Tendencies

One characteristic of people who are most likely to benefit from dietary elimination are those who have specific food allergies or hypersensitivity to artificial food additives. This may seem obvious, but the identification of specific allergies is not. An allergy to strawberries that causes itchy hives is easy to spot, but an allergy that causes tiredness, mental fuzziness, or hyperactivity in an already hyperactive child is not. Fortunately, food allergies that exacerbate ADHD occur in only a minority of children. They are usually found in preschool children who have difficulty sleeping, irritability, atopy (allergic tendencies), asthma, allergic rhinitis, rash, behavioral problems, and sometimes high copper levels. If you suspect a food allergy, you can test it by process of elimination; that is, avoid that food for 2 weeks and see if that makes a noticeable difference, then try eating it again and see what happens. If the answer is not crystal clear, you can ask your doctor to do allergy testing.

Sugar—How Sweet It Is

Unfortunately, many of the studies on sugar elimination have used questionable methods. Even well-designed studies have failed to demonstrate that eating sugar worsens behavior in children with ADHD (Krummel, Seligson, & Guthrie, 1996). As a result, the issue of the role of sugar is still unresolved. It is important to understand why there is a lack of clear scientific evidence that sugar or artificial sweeteners can aggravate ADHD. It is extremely difficult to prove that one very common food component, such as sugar, causes ADHD for the following reasons:

1. It is difficult to isolate the effects of sugar because most sugary foods also contain other ingredients, such as artificial coloring and flavoring, which might contribute to the effects being observed.

2. It is impossible to totally eliminate sugar from the diet.

3. Families that allow their children to eat a lot of junk food may differ in other ways that could affect the outcome of scientific studies. For example, they could also be more lax about structuring the child's

behavior, less disciplined, less attentive to providing other forms of treatment or educational support, less able to provide a calming or predictable home environment, and so forth.

The bottom line: Since excess amounts of sugar are not particularly healthy anyway, if you find that indulging in sweets seems to aggravate ADHD symptoms, then it makes sense to curb your sweet tooth.

TOXIC FOOD—YOU DON'T HAVE TO TAKE IT ANYMORE!

Neither the food industry nor our government is moving quickly enough to reduce the amount of toxic substances entering the food chain and affecting our health and the health of our children. We focus on the most common additives and the worst contaminants while offering practical ways for you to find healthier foods.

Artificial Food Additives

Natural food colorings from plants such as beets and carrots are available. Yet most food manufacturers prefer to use artificial dyes because they are cheaper and more durable. Food dyes are complex chemicals derived from petroleum. Many contain more than 10% impurities, including carcinogenic, genotoxic (adverse effects on DNA), and neurotoxic (adverse effects on brain cells) contaminants. The Food and Drug Administration (FDA) deals with these problems by establishing limits on the maximum amounts of these carcinogens that can be present in foods. However, these limits do not take into account the fact that a person may consume carcinogens from multiple food sources, that the number of foods containing these chemicals increases every year, and that the total amount ingested by an individual could exceed the legal limits considered "safe" (Jacobson & Kobylewski, 2010).

The British government sponsored two studies of four dyes and a preservative (sodium benzoate) that found increases in hyperactive behavior in children with and without ADHD. Based on this and other information, the government ordered food companies to eliminate these ingredients in 2009. The European Parliament followed by requiring all foods containing these additives to be labeled as follows: "May have adverse effects on activity and attention in children." Consequently, major companies such as McDonald's, Mars, Kraft, and PepsiCo use no artificial dyes in certain food products sold in the United Kingdom, but continue to use them in the United States. The FDA has lagged behind in banning unhealthy food additives, leaving consumers with the burden of reading food labels containing long lists of ingredients in tiny fonts and then the frustration of not being able to control access to food additives when their children have food away from home.

Not So Mellow Yellow and Not So Rosy Red

Let's look at the most common offenders. Three of the dyes identified as causing allergic hypersensitivity reactions that could aggravate hyperactive behavior are Red 40 (Allura red AC), yellow 5 (tartrazine), and yellow 6 (sunset yellow). These three account for 90% of the food dyes certified by the FDA each year. In 2009, that would add up to about 13,500,000 pounds per year to brighten candies, cereals, gelatin desserts, bakery treats, and other child-oriented foods. These dyes are also used in sausages and cosmetics.

A double-blind, randomized, placebo-controlled study of 277 children found evidence that artificial food coloring and benzoate preservatives exacerbated hyperactive behavior in 3-year-old children. Although the parents noticed this effect, it was not detected by a simple clinic assessment (Bateman et al., 2004).

More recent studies suggest that people with the histamine gene polymorphism *HNMT* are more likely to experience increased hyperactivity in reaction to food additives, especially azo (yellow and red) dye food colorings and a preservative (sodium benzoate). We introduced this study in Chapter 2 (Stevenson et al., 2010). Stevenson's group compared the effects of two drinks containing a mixture of artificial additives with a placebo drink (no additives) on the behavior of children who were not diagnosed with ADHD. Mix 1 contained sunset yellow, carmosine, tartrazine, ponceau 4R, and sodium benzoate; Mix 2 had sunset yellow, carmosine, quinoline yellow, Allura red, and sodium benzoate. Children with the histamine gene polymorphism *HNMT* showed greater increases in hyperactive behaviors when given either Mix 1 or Mix 2 for 6 weeks. Although the exact incidence of this *HNMT* polymorphism in the general population is not known, in the Stevenson study, about 30% of the children had this polymorphism. That translates into a huge number of children (millions), with and without a diagnosis of ADHD, who could exhibit hyperactive behaviors when they ingest these food colorings. One limitation of this study was that it did not distinguish which of the components

Table 4.1 Food Additives Linked to Hyperactivity

Food additive	Name of dye	Uses in certain commercial products[a]	Hyper-sensitivity reactions	Carcinogen
Yellow 5	Tartrazine	Lemonade, desserts, flavored yogurt, cheddar-flavored snacks, pickles, candy	X	X
Yellow 6	Sunset Yellow	Bakery items, cereals, beverages, macaroni & cheese mixes, candy, gelatins, sausage, candy sprinkles	X	X
Red 40	Allura Red AC	Fruit punch, cake mixes, Bac-Os, candy, sodas, cotton candy, children's medicines	X	X
Red 3	Carmosine	Bacon bits, ice cream, gum, frozen pie, candy, dessert sprinkles, popsicles	X	X

[a] These additives are found in some commercial brands, but not in others. Consumers should read food labels and check other resources to identify specific products that may exacerbate attentional problems in some children.

of each drink was most responsible for the adverse effects. Ponceau 4R and quinoline yellow have been banned in the United States, but the food dyes called tartrazine (Yellow 5), sunset yellow (Yellow 6), carmosine (Red 3), and Allura red AC (Red 40) have not.

In Table 4.1 you will see examples of foods that may contain these dyes. For each food type, there are certain companies that use unhealthy dyes and others that do not. We have not identified the manufacturers whose products contain the dyes. However, you can find this type of information by reading food labels very carefully, searching websites, or by reading the Nutrition Action Health Letter (Jacobson & Kobylewski, 2010). The simplest way to avoid harmful food additives is to buy foods labeled "no artificial colorings or preservatives."

Because artificial food additives have no nutritional value and may have adverse effects on hyperactivity, not to mention cumulative or long-term carcinogenic or neurotoxic effects, you may want to eliminate these products as much as possible. This means taking the time to read package labels and reduce your use of products containing those artificial colorings, flavorings, and preservatives that have been associated with negative effects. (You may need a magnifying glass to decipher those cryptic food labels.)

Q&A

Q: What about children's vitamins?

A: Unfortunately, many of them do contain food additives. In fact, some of the most popular and widely advertised children's vitamins contain Red 40, Yellow 6, and Blue 2. Just read the labels carefully. What a cruel irony that we find these unhealthy additives in the supplements we give our children to stay healthy. It would be easy to eliminate these artificial colors and replace them with natural healthy vegetable dyes, such as beet juice.

Q: What can we do about the presence of artificial food additives in our food supply?

A: The first action to take is to *educate ourselves and others* about the widespread use of toxic additives. The second action to take is to *read the labels* on all the foods and supplements you buy. While writing this chapter, I remembered that the manufacturer of my calcium plus vitamin D tablets had recently changed the color from white to pink. Although I had noticed the color change, I had not given it much thought. Uh-oh! I dashed to the kitchen, flung open the cabinet, grabbed the bottle, and slowly read the label. There it was –Red 40 and Yellow 6—right there on my calcium supplements! Why did they change the tablets to pink? I guess some marketing genius decided that women prefer pink, but we *don't* when it means ingesting toxic substances every day. When you consider how much calcium women take, especially when they are pregnant, breast feeding, or postmenopausal, this is deeply disturbing. But, that wasn't all. I remembered that my multivitamins were orange. Sure enough, the label said Red 40 and Yellow 6—and I had been taking them for over 30 years—including when I was pregnant! What about those colorful antacid tablets my husband sometimes uses? Sure enough, a rainbow of carcinogens: Yellow 5, Yellow 6, and Red 40.

The third action to take is to *stop buying products containing these dyes* and switch to those that are free of these toxins when possible. From now on, I will use only calcium tablets that are white—the natural color of calcium—and multivitamins labeled "no artificial food colorings." When enough consumers (1) stop buying products containing unsafe artificial food colorings, (2) write to their public representatives, and (3) confront manufacturers and store managers about the unacceptability of these toxins, perhaps there will be changes in our FDA requirements and warning labels. Meanwhile, check all the cans, boxes, and bottles in your cabinets and arm yourself with a good magnifying glass that folds in and out of its case whenever you go shopping. For more information on food additives, check the websites in the Resources section at the end of this chapter.

Toxic Heavy Metals, Chemical Pollutants, Pesticides, and Free Radicals

Rule 2: What's bad for your brain is bad for your ADHD.

Toxic Heavy Metals

Although more research is needed on the effects of heavy metals (e.g., lead, cadmium, mercury, aluminum, or arsenic) on ADHD, there is evidence that in excess levels, they are toxic to neurons (brain cells), particularly when the brain is developing rapidly in utero and during childhood. Studies of children have shown that those with higher blood lead levels have increased risk of neurobehavioral deficits and ADHD. Studies conducted to date suggest that excess lead may reduce attention, response inhibition (control of impulsivity), and executive functions (the ability to get things done) (Roy et al., 2009). Even low-level lead exposure has been associated with increased risk of a clinical diagnosis of ADHD (Eubig, Aguiar, & Schantz, 2010). It is important to check your home for lead paint or corroding pipes, your water quality, and your neighborhood to be sure your family is not being exposed to environmental toxins.

In the United States, public health efforts have significantly reduced the incidence of lead poisoning, but people living in areas with higher industrial pollution may be at risk. If you suspect exposure to heavy metals, ask your doctor to do an evaluation. Through a careful history, physical examination, and blood tests, your doctor will be able to tell you if heavy metal levels are too high. Doctors can remove excess heavy metals from the body by prescribing oral (pills taken by mouth) chelating agents. These agents link metal ions together, forming complex structures called *chelates*, which are then readily eliminated from the body, primarily through urination. Beware of private clinics that do their own nonstandardized testing and offer expensive intravenous chelation regimens. If you are told that you have heavy metal poisoning and that you need chelation, get a second opinion and testing at an independent standard laboratory. Most people with ADHD do not need chelation (removal of heavy metals or pollutants from the blood) unless they have been exposed to an industrial area contaminated with heavy metals or lead paint. Chelation should be considered only when toxic levels of a heavy metal have been found in a blood sample analyzed by a standard, accredited laboratory. Chelation requires medical monitoring to minimize health risks. Adverse effects of chelation include elevated levels of liver enzymes and skin reactions (Bradberry, & Vale, 2009). Also, chelating agents can remove some of the heavy metals that your body needs such as copper and zinc, resulting in deficiencies unless supplements are provided.

Organic Chemical Pollutants: Pesticides, Dioxin, Polychlorinated Biphenols, and Hydrocarbons

Organochloride pesticides are contaminating our soil, water, and food supply. Although the FDA limits the amounts of allowable pesticides in foods, evidence is growing that certain pesticides, particularly polychlorinated biphenyl (PCB) and p,p'-dichlorodiphenyl dichloroethylene (p,p'-DDE) can cross the placenta and affect fetal neurodevelopment. A recent study by the Department of Environmental Health at Harvard School of Public Health found that increased levels of PCBs in umbilical cord blood samples were associated with a higher risk for ADHD-like behaviors in children (Sagiv et al., 2010). A study of 1,139 children, 8–15 years of age, identified 119 who met the criteria for ADHD. Those with ADHD had higher levels of organophosphate pesticides than those who did not have ADHD (Bouchard et al., 2010). Scientists are discovering more connections between pollutants such as pesticides and increased risk of developing ADHD, even if the exposure is simply from eating foods containing organic chemical pollutants (Kuehn, 2010).

While pesticides should be minimized in everyone's diet, this is especially important for women of childbearing age, for those who are pregnant, and for children. Children 2–5 years old who ate conventional foods were found to have urinary organophosphorous pesticide levels that were six times higher than those who ate organic fruits, vegetables, and juices. Pesticide levels on conventional diets exceeded the U.S. Environmental Protection Agency (EPA) guidelines that place the children in the category of "uncertain risk," whereas levels in children who ate organic produce were in the range of "negligible risk" (Curl, Fenske, & Elgetun, 2003).

It makes sense for everyone to reduce pesticide consumption as much as possible. This can be done by finding out which foods are most likely to contain toxins, shopping carefully, choosing organic products, and thoroughly washing or peeling all produce. Because PCBs are fat soluble, they tend to concentrate in animal fat and are found in fish, meat, and dairy products; PCB residues are also found on fruits and vegetables. Here are ways to minimize food exposure to PCBs:

1. Avoid commercial fish that are high in PCBs: Atlantic or farmed salmon, bluefish, wild striped bass, flounder, and blue crab. Prepare fish by removing the skin and trimming the fat. Broil, bake, or grill fish so that fat drips away.

2. Look for certified organic meats. Beef from grass-fed cattle is leaner.
   Buy lean meats and trim off the fat before cooking. You can reduce the amount of pesticides by broiling, grilling, roasting, or pressure cooking and discarding the fat. Do not fry in lard, bacon grease, or butter. Do not make gravies from meat fats or juices unless you use certified organic meat.

3. Use organic milk and dairy products for children. If you cannot find or cannot afford organic milk products, another way to reduce pesticides is to use low-fat milk products for children age 2 and older. Because organic pesticides are fat soluble, they tend to concentrate in the fat portion of milk rather than in the protein or water soluble components.

4. Whenever possible, choose organic produce. If you cannot buy organic fruits and vegetables, careful washing and scrubbing in cold water can eliminate 50% of pesticide residues.

5. Avoid certain fruits and vegetables that tend to have the higher pesticide residues (see Table 4.2).

If you cannot afford to buy all organic produce, then you could shop strategically by choosing organic produce from primarily the high-pesticide residue group. To learn more about foods that may contain PCBs and how to avoid them, visit the website of the Institute for Agriculture and Trade Policy Food and Health Program (see Resources)

Table 4.2 Pesticide Residue Levels in Fruits and Vegetables

High	Moderate	Low
Apples, grapes (imported), nectarines, peaches, pears, red raspberries, strawberries, bell peppers, carrots, celery, green beans, hot peppers, potatoes, spinach	Apricots, blueberries, cantaloupe, grapefruit, grapes (domestic), honeydew melons, oranges, collard greens, cucumbers, kale, lettuce, mushrooms, sweet potatoes, tomatoes, and winter squash	Apple juice, bananas, mangoes, orange juice, papaya, plums, tangerines, watermelon, asparagus, avocado, broccoli, cabbage, cauliflower, onion, sweet corn, and sweet peas

Note. Adapted from the Institute for Agriculture and Trade Policy Food and Health Program.

Free Radicals

Free radicals are molecules that can damage cells by breaking down essential components such as cell membranes. One of the most common sources of free radicals is the smoke inhaled from cigarettes and recreational drugs. Many people with ADHD become readily addicted to smoking cigarettes because nicotine can improve alertness and attention. So, not only are they prone to regular nicotine addiction, but they are also drawn into smoking because it improves their ability to function. Unfortunately, there are long-range consequences due to the increased risk of cancers of the mouth, throat, lungs, and stomach, ulcers, and cardiovascular disease. Moreover, the free radicals in cigarette smoke also attack brain cells causing damage to their membranes, internal structures, and DNA. Over time this accelerates brain aging. People with ADHD who smoke to obtain short-term benefits need to weigh these against the long-term health costs.

SUPPLEMENTS: VITAMINS, MINERALS, AND NUTRIENTS—SOMETHING FOR EVERYONE?

Now that we have talked about what to get rid of, let's look at nutrients that might be worth adding. As we discuss each supplement, we note the characteristics of people most likely to benefit. Moderate levels of vitamin and mineral supplementation (not megavitamins) have been beneficial in studies of children who are deficient or who have relatively low levels of these nutrients prior to treatment. Lack of diversity in the diet, especially inadequate amounts of fresh fruits and vegetables, can contribute to deficiencies. In addition, poor absorption of nutrients due to medical conditions, age, or improper food storage and preparation can reduce vitamin levels. In general, fresher food is higher in vitamins and nutrients than food that has been sitting on a shelf in the cabinet, refrigerator, or freezer. The growth of farmers' markets and the movement to "eat local" are making fresh foods more available. Raw food enthusiasts believe that cooking is unnecessary and only destroys nutritional value. This is not entirely true. For example, many people cannot fully digest certain raw foods and may need to cook them in order to absorb nutrients. Overcooking can also cause loss of nutrients. We recommend cooking foods until they are just done, but not overcooked. For example, green vegetables should retain their color and some firmness. Also, vitamins can be lost when vegetables are cooked in water; steaming preserves more of the nutrients. If you have a local health food store, rummage through their book section to find a guide to healthier cooking.

Tables 4.6 and 4.7 at the end of this chapter provide a summary of treatment guidelines for all of the supplements in this chapter and a list of quality products and where to find them.

Supplementation with Vitamins for the Brain: B, Folate, and C

Children and adults with below-normal levels of essential vitamins—B1, B6, B12, folate, C, and D—may benefit from supplementation. People with ADHD often have suboptimal diets because they either don't have the organizational ability to shop and cook properly, or they don't have the patience to sit and eat regular meals. Moreover, their appetite may be suppressed by stimulant medications. Very healthy eaters are more likely to have adequate vitamin levels unless they have a problem with absorption (which may not be obvious). As we get older (over age 40) our ability to digest foods and absorb nutrients may decline. If you are concerned about possible vitamin deficiencies, you may ask your doctor to run certain blood tests for the more important ones, including methylcobalamin (B12), folate, and vitamin D.

A randomized, double-blind, 3-month study of 245 children with low serum levels of vitamins B or C found that treatment with vitamin supplements reduced levels of aggression and antisocial behavior as well as improving cognitive performance compared to placebo. In 20% of the children given supplements, the mean IQ scores increased 16 points (Schoenthaler & Bier, 1999).

Folate and B vitamins, particularly B6 (pyridoxine) and B12 (methylcobalamin), are essential for normal brain development as well as for the ongoing production of neurotransmitters, including serotonin, norepinephrine, and dopamine. Many children (and adults) recoil from eating foods rich in these vitamins, particularly spinach and other dark-green leafy vegetables. When creative recipes such as spinach cookies or crunchy kale bars fail, daily vitamin supplementation may be the easiest solution.

One vitamin preparation we often use is Bio-Strath®. Derived from baker's yeast grown on alpine antioxidant herbs, Bio-Strath is high in natural antioxidants, minerals, vitamins (particularly B vitamins), essential amino acids, and immune boosters. It does not contain any whole yeast and therefore is not a problem even for people who are prone to yeast infections. Liquid Bio-Strath contains 3% alcohol and should not be used by anyone recovering from alcoholism, even though the amount in one teaspoon is negligible (see Table 4.6 and 4.7 at end of chapter). Bio-Strath also comes in tablet form. In an open study of 18 children whose assessment on a medical questionnaire suggested ADHD, the children were given one teaspoon of Bio-Strath three times a day for 6 weeks. Compared to starting scores, computerized tests of visual and auditory attention and response control improved significantly over the 6 weeks in 12 out of 18 participants. The greatest improvements were found in attention to auditory stimuli, processing of visual stimuli, and auditory impulsiveness (König & Joller, 2006). Further studies are needed to identify who would most likely benefit from Bio-Strath.

Mineral Deficiencies

In mineral deficiencies, supplements are also useful. Many children with ADHD have inadequate diets, so it may be worth checking with your pediatrician, who can easily test the levels of vitamins and essential minerals before starting supplements.

Zinc Deficiency

The micronutrient zinc is an essential cofactor in the production of dopamine and norepinephrine, two neurotransmitters that have been linked to ADHD. Low serum levels of zinc have been found to correlate with inattention, but not hyperactivity/impulsivity, in a study of American children (Arnold & DiSilvestro, 2005). In Turkey and Iran, where zinc deficiency is more prevalent, two studies showed zinc supplements to be helpful for ADHD. In a 6-week controlled study of 44 children with ADHD, 15 mg elemental zinc given daily improved the effects of methylphenidate (Ritalin) more than placebo (Akhondzadeh, Mohammadi, & Khademi, 2004). Another 12-week controlled study of 328 boys and 72 girls with ADHD found that zinc sulfate 40 mg/day significantly reduced ADHD symptoms compared with placebo (Bilici, Yildirim, Kandil, et al., 2004).

A Canadian study of 43 children with ADHD found that 66% were deficient in zinc and 23% in copper (Kiddie, Weiss, Kitts, Levy-Milne, & Wasdell, 2010). Curiously, in the Canadian study no relationship was found between children's serum zinc levels and the amount of zinc in their food or their use of standard multivitamin–mineral supplements. This study raises several questions. For example, how do we account for the observation that the daily consumption of zinc did not determine the serum zinc levels? Do children with ADHD have lower zinc and copper levels because of poor absorption of these elements from food, or is there some genetically based difference in how these minerals are metabolized? Although taking vitamin–mineral supplements containing small amounts of zinc did not appear to increase zinc serum levels, would higher doses of zinc make a difference? The use of supplements for zinc deficiencies warrants further study. Until there is more evidence, it may be helpful to check serum zinc levels. If the level is low, it may be worthwhile to use a daily zinc supplement (rather than a standard multivitamin–multimineral supplement) for several months and recheck the serum level as well as re-evaluate ADHD symptoms to see if there is improvement.

Copper Deficiency

Copper is an important micronutrient in the synthesis of dopamine and norepinephrine. The Canadian study mentioned above (Kiddie et al., 2010) found that about 23% of the children with ADHD were deficient in copper. Studies of the potential role of copper in ADHD are needed before it can be recommended as a treatment.

Iron Deficiency

Iron is necessary for dopamine synthesis. Enhanced dopamine transmission is a feature of most of the medicines that are effective in treating ADHD. In one study, ferritin (a measure of iron stores) was low in 84% of 53 children with ADHD compared with 18% of 27 children who did not have ADHD. Lower ferritin levels correlated with more severe cognitive deficits and ADHD ratings (Konofal, Lecendreux, Arnulf, & Mouren, 2004). In iron-deficient adolescents, iron supplements have improved learning and memory (Bruner, Joffe, Duggan, Casella, & Brandt, 1996). In a controlled study of 23 children (ages 5–8 years) with low serum ferritin levels, iron supplementation (80 mg/day) appeared to improve ADHD symptoms (Konofal et al., 2008). Iron therapy was well tolerated. Larger studies are needed to explore the role of iron supplements in the treatment of ADHD.

Iron and Folate Deficiency: Restless Leg Syndrome

Tina was a little wiggle worm. Her legs were always moving. It was cute when she was 3, but as she grew older, it became more of a problem. She was forever kicking her chair or the chair in front of her. Although she seemed to be moving constantly, she was also tired, no matter what time she was put to bed. Tina's parents began to worry that she might have ADHD. One night, determined to find out whether Tina was sleeping or not, her mother sat in her room to watch. What she saw was that Tina's legs kept moving, even when she appeared to be asleep. When she described this to her pediatrician, the doctor ordered a blood test. When it showed a low level of ferritin (iron), the doctor explained that restless leg syndrome (RLS) is a condition in which a person's legs seem to keep moving when they sit or lie down. It can cause poor sleep quality and daytime tiredness. Low levels of iron and folate are among the many possible causes of RLS. Because RLS can be mistaken for hyperactivity, children with symptoms of ADHD or restless legs should be tested for iron and folate deficiencies. In most cases, RLS can be treated with supplements. This condition could also be a wakeup call for a better diet. Frequent consumption of foods that are rich in iron and folate, which include dark-green leafy vegetables (e.g., spinach, kale, collard greens), beans, and red meat, may prevent the development of deficiencies.

Q&A

Q: Who should be tested for iron deficiency and possible supplementation?

A:
1. Children with RLS.
2. People with anemia (low red blood cell count).
3. People with ADHD and poor dietary habits.
4. Since ferritin levels are not checked in routine screenings, you may need to discuss getting this tested with your doctor.

PUFAS: POLYUNSATURATED FATTY ACIDS

The body, particularly the brain, needs polyunsaturated fatty acids (PUFAs). Our bodies are not able to produce certain PUFAs, including omega-3 and omega-6 fatty acids. In order to stay healthy, we must eat foods containing these essential fatty acids. Fish, plant oils, nuts, seeds,

Table 4.3 Food Sources for Essential Polyunsaturated
Fatty Acids (PUFAs)

Omega-3 Fatty Acids	Food Sources
Alpha-linolenic acid (ALA)	Seeds and nuts (pumpkin seeds, English black walnuts, flaxseeds, almonds); beans (navy, pinto, soy); vegetable oils (olive, soybean, rapeseed, walnut, flaxseed); leafy greens (kale, collard greens, spinach); fish (salmon, rainbow trout, catfish)
Eicosapentanoic acid (EPA)	Oily fish, fish oil (cod liver, herring, mackerel, salmon, sardine, albacore tuna, swordfish); microalgae; human breast milk
Docosahexanoic acid (DHA)	Cold-water ocean fish and fish oils, shellfish, eggs, microalgae
Omega-6 Fatty Acids	
Linolenic acid (LA)	Cooking oils (safflower, grape seed, poppy seed, sunflower, hemp, corn, wheat germ, cottonseed, soybean, walnut, sesame, rice bran, pistachio, peanut, canola, linseed); egg yolk, chicken fat, meats; fish (salmon, rainbow trout, catfish)
Arachidonic acid (AA)	Animal sources (meat, eggs)
Gamma-linolenic acid (GLA)	Vegetable oils (evening primrose, blackcurrant seed, borage, hemp seed); spirulina

soy, dark-green leafy vegetables, and eggs provide most of the PUFAs in our diets. The most essential omega-3 fatty acids are eicosapentanoic acid (EPA), docosahexanoic acid (DHA), and alpha-linolenic acid (ALA). Omega-6 fatty acids are also important for metabolic functioning. Fortunately, most people get enough of them—arachidonic acid (AA), and gamma-linolenic acid (GLA)—in their diets. For a list of some foods containing PUFAs, see Table 4.3 and additional nutritional information in the Resources section at the end of the chapter.

What Do PUFAs Do?

PUFAs are components of many important molecules used to build cellular structures, such as the membranes that form the outer wall

Table 4.4 The Contribution of Omega-3 Fatty Acids to Neural
Development and Brain Health

- Maintain membrane fluidity.
- Support membrane enzyme activities.
- Provide antioxidant defense against neuronal
  damage from free radicals.
- Produce anti-inflammatory molecules
  (e.g., prostaglandins).
- Affect gene expression in brain cells

of cells, nuclei, and mitochondria. Healthy, flexible cell membranes make it possible for neurons to transmit electrical impulses throughout the brain in milliseconds. PUFAs are key building blocks of these membranes. If the body lacks an adequate supply of essential fatty acids, it will substitute unhealthy fatty acids as components of the cell membranes, leading to less fluidity, less flexibility, and decreased transmission efficiency. The consequences can include problems with mood, cognitive functions, and memory. While both omega-3 and omega-6 fatty acids are important, we emphasize omega-3 fatty acids supplements because most people in the United States get plenty of omega-6 fatty acids in their diets, whereas few get enough omega-3s. Table 4.4 summarizes the contributions of omega-3 fatty acids to overall health.

Research has established the importance of omega-3 fatty acids, especially DHA, in neuronal development (Bourre, 2006). DHA is an essential component of cell membranes. For example, infants given omega-3-enriched formula have shown improved brain and eye development, better problem solving at 10 months, and higher scores on a mental development index (Willatts, Forsyth, DiModugno, Varma, & Colvin, 1998).

Deficiencies in Omega-3 Fatty Acids

Dietary studies find deficiencies in omega-3 fatty acids (30–90% below the recommended daily allowance) in many countries, including the United States, Canada, Europe, and Australia. Changes in eating habits and food sources make it harder to fulfill daily needs for omega-3 fatty acids. With low-quality feed, the EPA and DHA contents in farm-raised salmon and trout have dwindled compared with fish living in the wild. Conversely, feeding omega-3 fatty acids to chickens pumps up the omega EPA and DHA in egg yolks by 20-fold.

Omega-3 fatty acid deficiencies have been found in a subset of boys with ADHD (Antalis et al., 2006). Further studies of essential fatty acids, particularly in patients with low serum levels of specific EPAs, are needed in ADHD to determine what level of response to expect.

Mixing and Matching Omega-3 and Omega-6 Fatty Acids

Aside from the fact that omega-3 fatty acids are generally good for the brain, research is showing that different combinations of essential fatty acids, both omega-3 and omega-6 fatty acids, can have positive effects on ADHD symptoms. To add to the confusion, various combinations of essential fatty acids may produce different effects in subtypes of ADHD (inattentive, hyperactive, or mixed). So the current challenge in research is to find the best mixtures of essential fatty acids and the best match of each mix with ADHD subtypes.

Excess omega-6 fatty acids can interfere with the benefits of omega–3 fatty acids. A high proportion of omega-6 to omega-3 fatty acids in the diet shifts the body towards developing diseases: increased inflammation, cardiovascular disease, and cancer. Dietary sources of omega-6 fatty acids include poultry, eggs, avocado, nuts, cereals, whole-grain breads, most vegetable oils (palm, soybean, rapeseed or canola, sunflower, corn, safflower, and flax/linseed), evening primrose oil, pumpkin seeds, acai berry, and spirulina (Ayachi, El Abed, Dhifi, & Marzouk, 2007; Herrero, Vicente, Cifuentes, & Ibáñez, 2007). We do not recommend spirulina (a nutritional supplement made from microscopic organisms capable of photosynthesis that grow in both sea and fresh water) for children because products vary widely and may contain contaminants such as heavy metals. Products tested and shown to be free of heavy metals may be safer.

The average American diet contains more than enough omega-6

fatty acids, but tends to fall short on the omega-3 fatty acids. Therefore, it is more likely that people with ADHD will have a deficiency
of omega-3 fatty acids than omega-6 fatty acids. Early studies using
omega-6 fatty acids for ADHD showed minimal benefits. More recent
studies have used combinations of omega-3 and omega-6 fatty acids
or just omega-3 fatty acids. Using a combination of omega-3 PUFAs—
containing twice as much eicosapentanoic acid (EPA) compared with
docosahexanoic acid (DHA)—may be more beneficial (Parker et. al.,
2006). You will find this combination in supplements marked "EPA/
DHA 2:1." However, these tend to be more expensive; you can save
money by taking a larger dose of regular fish oil. Cod liver oil has been
a popular remedy for generations. However, it is not the best source
of omega-3 fatty acids as the following case illustrates. When it comes
to cod liver oil, it may be too much of a good thing.

> When Alana's children were tested and diagnosed as having ADHD,
> she realized that she probably had it, too. Always juggling too many
> things, she kept putting off an endless list of household chores.
> She felt fuzzy-headed and overwhelmed most of the time. When
> she started taking Adderall the mental fuzziness improved by
> about 75%. She began to notice how certain foods affected her. For
> example, refined sugar and carbohydrates (found in white bread,
> pasta, and desserts), made her feel sluggish and sleepy. After trying
> numerous supplements, she found that taking two tablespoons of
> cod liver oil twice a day and maintaining a healthy diet, her men-
> tal clarity rose from 75 to 95%. She tested herself on her favor-
> ite brain-boosting computer games. On Adderall alone, she could
> not get past the intermediate level of difficulty. However, when she
> added cod liver oil to the Adderall, she quickly reached and han-
> dled the expert level.
>
> Alana enjoyed the benefits of cold liver oil, but she did not read
> the label carefully. When I (Dr. Gerbarg) suggested that she read
> the label, she found that one teaspoon contained a total of 1260 mg
> omega-3 fatty acids plus 700 IU (international units) of vitamin A.
> We did the math: (700 IU/tsp) x (3 tsp per Tbsp) x (4Tbsp/day) =
> 8,400 IU/day. We added this to the amount of vitamin A in her mul-
> tivitamin: 5,000 IU. Then we added an estimate of the amount of
> vitamin A she consumed on an average day from her food: 7,000 IU.

The grand total was 20,400 IU of vitamin A per day! The problem is that although vitamin A is important for vision, bone growth, and immune defense, excessive amounts can increase the risk of birth defects, liver abnormalities, osteoporosis, and a variety of cancers.

The Food and Nutrition Board of the Institute of Medicine has established tolerable levels for the daily intake of vitamin A. Retinol is the form in which vitamin A is absorbed into the body. Table 4.5 shows the tolerable daily upper intake amounts for healthy individuals in IUs. *These levels are for healthy individuals only.* People with malnutrition or specific vitamin A deficiency may require higher daily intakes.

Alana was relieved when I proposed a compromise. She could continue taking one tablespoon a day of her favorite cod liver oil and make up the rest of her omega-3 fatty acids using a different fish oil supplement that was much lower in vitamin A.

Pregnant Women and Infants

A balanced diet is necessary for healthy brain development starting in utero. Women who are pregnant need to be conscious of eating healthy foods every day, taking supplements recommended by their

Table 4.5 Tolerable Daily Upper Intake Amounts for Vitamin A by Age

Age (years)	Vitamin A[a]
0–1	2,000 IU
1–3	2,000 IU
4–8	3,000 IU
9–13	5,610 IU
14–18	9,240 IU
19+	10,000 IU

Note. Adapted from the Office of Dietary Supplements, National Institutes of Health (2010).
[a]IU = International Units

doctor, and absolutely avoiding anything that may cause toxic effects on the rapidly developing brain of their baby (e.g., alcohol, cigarette smoke, illegal drugs). While vitamins, minerals, supplements, and omega-3 fatty acids should be taken by everyone during pregnancy, couples with a personal or family history of ADHD should be especially careful to supplement their diet with additional omega-3 fatty acids, which have been shown to enhance brain development. During pregnancy a large amount of omega-3 fatty acids is incorporated into the baby's growing brain. This can deplete the mother's store, particularly in the later stages. Supplementation is needed both to supply the needs of the fetus's neural development as well as to maintain the health of the mother. It is vital to assure adequate levels of dietary omega-3 fatty acids, especially DHA, for women during pregnancy and breastfeeding and in infant formulas, particularly for premature infants. Some, but not all, prenatal vitamins contain omega-3 fatty acids. The product label should tell you how many milligrams of omega-3 fatty acids, EPA and DHA, are contained in each tablet.

ADHD Subtypes Respond Differently to PUFA Supplements

Recall that there are three subtypes of ADHD:

1. Predominantly inattentive
2. Predominantly hyperactive/impulsive
3. Combined hyperactive/impulsive and inattentive

For simplicity, as noted previously, we use *ADHD* to include all three subtypes and *ADD* to denote only the inattentive subtype.

Subtype: Inattentive

A Swedish study of 75 boys with ADHD, ages 8–18, found that those with the inattentive subtype (ADD) responded faster to a combination of omega-3 and omega-6 fatty acids treatment. About one quarter of the children with ADD reported a 25% improvement in symptoms after 3 months, and about half of the entire group improved after taking the supplement for 6 months (Johnson, Ostlund, Fransson, Kadesjo, & Gillberg, 2009).

Oppositional Defiant Disorder versus Less Hyperactive/Impulsive

Oppositional defiant disorder describes children who show a pattern of negativistic, hostile, defiant behavior more frequently than is typical for children their age. These behaviors must be severe enough to cause significant impairment in social or academic functioning. Some children have both ADHD and oppositional defiant disorder. A mixture of DHA, EPA, AA, and ALA was used in a study of ADHD children. Significant improvements were found in teacher ratings of attention and parent ratings of oppositional defiant disorder, but not on measures of other symptoms (Stevens et al., 2003).

Another study—a 15-week randomized, double-blind, placebo-controlled study—compared children with different symptoms of ADHD. One group had oppositional behavior symptoms; the second group had less hyperactive/impulsive symptoms; and the third group had both oppositional behavior and less hyperactivity/impulsivity. The children were given either one capsule per day of PlusEPA (containing 500 mg EPA plus 2.7 mg DHA + 10 mg vitamin-E-mixed tocopherols) or a placebo (Gustafsson et al., 2010).

- Among those with *oppositional* behavior symptoms, 52% of the children given PlusEPA showed at least 25% improvement in oppositional behaviors and attention, but not in hyperactivity, on the Conners Teacher Rating Scales (CTRS), compared to 9% in the placebo group.

- 36% of children with *less hyperactivity/impulsivity* symptoms reported more than 25% improvement on the CTRS, but this was not statistically significant compared to the placebo group (18%).

- Children with both *oppositional behavior* and *less hyperactivity/impulsivity* had a 61% rate of response to PlusEPA, with more than 25% improvement on CTRS, compared to 11% with placebo.

Overall, children with both oppositional behavior and less hyperactive/impulsivity showed the highest rate of response to a combination of EPA, DHA, and vitamin E.

How to Use Omega-3 Fatty Acid Supplements

The use of purified fish oil supplements has become more appealing due to growing concerns about contaminants such as mercury and polychlorinated biphenyls (PCBs) in fish, and recommendations to limit consumption of fish to one serving per week. Nuts (particularly walnuts), flax, and dark green vegetables are also good sources of omega-3 fatty acids. However, flax contains ALA, not DHA. Although we have enzymes that convert a small amount of ALA into DHA, it is too little to meet the body's needs. Understandably, vegetarians prefer flax to fish, but unfortunately, the ALA from flax provides far fewer physical benefits than EPA and DHA from fish oil (Nettleton, 1991).

In sorting through all this information, or waiting for a clear answer, our recommendation is to apply Rule 4: *Use your common sense.* Because each research study selects different groups of children and uses different combinations of essential fatty acids and vitamins, collecting enough data to predict which supplements are most likely to be effective for any individual is likely to take years. In the meantime, since the essential fatty acids are both beneficial and benign (no serious adverse effects), you can try your own mixing and matching. Remember to allow time—at least 10 weeks—for each supplement to evaluate how well it is working before adding or changing to another. In addition to assessing yourself (or your child) for changes, it helps to get feedback from others who know you (or your child) well.

S-ADENOSYLMETHIONINE (SAME): THE SUPER METABOLITE

S-adenosylmethionine (SAMe) is a natural substance found in all the cells of our bodies. This generous metabolite donates clumps of itself (methyl and sulfate molecular groups) to help build many of the most important molecules in the body, including neurotransmitters and our home-grown antioxidants. Always busy, SAMe participates in over 200 chemical pathways in all body organs and tissues (Brown, Gerberg, & Bottiglieri, 2000). In short, SAMe is a super metabolite. Among the many neurotransmitters that are beholding to SAMe, dopamine is the one that needs boosting in ADHD. SAMe increases dopamine transmission and enhances the response to amphetamine stimulant medications. In other words, if you are experiencing only partial improvement from taking a stimulant such as Ritalin or Adderall, then you may get a better response by adding SAMe.

Brain waves of people with ADHD show abnormal increases in the slow frequencies: low alpha and theta. Shifting from slow alpha waves to faster alpha (alpha-2) and beta waves is associated with increased alertness, faster processing, and better behavior control (see Chapter 6 for a detailed discussion of brain-wave frequencies in ADHD). In an EEG (electroencephalographic) study of elderly subjects, SAMe increased the faster brain-wave frequencies—alpha-2 and beta. Although EEG studies of SAMe in ADHD have not yet been done, it is likely that SAMe would also improve the faster frequencies in people with ADHD. A 4-week open study of eight men with adult ADHD found that 2400 mg/day of SAMe improved ratings on measures of ADHD and mood in six out of the eight. The two who did not improve had not responded to previous trials of methylphenidate (Ritalin). Side effects were not significant (Shekim, Antun, Hanna, McCracken, & Hess, 1990). Larger and longer-term studies are needed to explore the use of SAMe in children and adults with ADHD.

SAMe is best known as an antidepressant. Many studies have shown that it is as effective as prescription antidepressants, works faster, and has fewer side effects. So, it is particularly useful in people suffering from both ADHD and depression. SAMe combines well with *Rhodiola rosea* to form a dynamic duo.

Many people are successfully treated for ADD in childhood or adolescence. For others, the right treatment may not come along until later, after many years of underperformance at school and failed relationships. This was the case with Jeremy, who sought help at age 27 when he was flunking out of graduate school. Jeremy had struggled with chronic low-level depression, severe dyslexia, and ADD since childhood. He told Dr. Brown that he was "never happy." In fact, Jeremy was intensely restless, easily distressed, and filled with self-blame. It was hardly surprising that he was failing in graduate school, particularly because he chose to study history, a field requiring immense amounts of reading. Dating was also a disaster. No woman wants to sit in a restaurant trying to hold a conversation with a man who is so distracted by other people's conversations that he can't even listen to what she says, or who interrupts her as soon as she tries to talk. Being late or forgetting every date is also not an endearing quality. Jeremy had tried nearly every medication available for his condition—all with unbearable side effects. Finally, a course of SAMe relieved his depression. When *Rhodiola rosea* was added to the mix, he felt even better. Within a short time, his mood and energy improved. He was able to focus, complete his work with fewer errors and, for the first time ever, stop procrastinating. Jeremy wisely left graduate school for a good job as a salesman that capitalized on (rather than penalized) his high-energy qualities. He was even able to sustain his first long-term relationship.

How to Use SAMe: Side Effects, Dosage, and Timing

Although SAMe is generally well tolerated, some people report experiencing nausea, loose stools, agitation, or transient sleepiness. SAMe is best absorbed when taken on an empty stomach about 30 minutes before breakfast and lunch. Doses range from 600 to 1200 mg twice a day. Because SAMe is rapidly oxidized when exposed to air, it should be purchased only in blister packs (each pill in a separate foil blister). Bargain brands tend to have low potency and may cause more side effects. The quality of the SAMe and the tablet manufacturing is of particular importance with this supplement. See Table 4.7 on quality supplements at the end of this chapter to find a list of high-quality brands. SAMe may be worth trying in cases with incomplete response to medications, habituation (loss of effectiveness over time) to stimulants, coexisting depression, or intolerance of prescription stimulants.

SAMe is well-tolerated by most people, but it can cause nausea, agitation, or anxiety in sensitive individuals. Although SAMe is usually taken on an empty stomach, if nausea occurs, it should be taken with a light snack to settle the stomach. People with bipolar disorder can be triggered into manic episodes by prescription antidepressants as well as by SAMe. Therefore, it should not be given to those with known bipolar disorder. If agitation, hostility, racing thoughts, or excessively elevated, inappropriate mood occur, SAMe should be discontinued because that individual may have undiagnosed bipolar disorder.

Q&A

Q: Who is likely to benefit from SAMe?

A: SAMe can be very helpful for the following indications:

- A history of improving on prescription stimulants such as Ritalin or Adderall, but inability to tolerate the side effects.
- ADHD plus depression.
- Incomplete response to medications
- Habituation (loss of effectiveness over time) with stimulants
- Combines well with *Rhodiola rosea* (see Chapter 3) for synergistic benefits
- May enhance and accelerate response to biofeedback (see Chapter 6).

PICAMILON

Picamilon is a combination of two natural compounds: the B vitamin niacin and a calming neurotransmitter called gamma-aminobutyric acid (GABA). One of its main effects is to increase blood flow within the brain by decreasing cerebral blood vessel tone. When blood flow increases, brain cells receive more oxygen and nutrients. This may be why picamilon can improve cognitive function as well as alertness and decrease anxiety and depression. Although Picamilon has mild stimulative properties, it reduces aggressive behavior in animal studies. In our clinical work we find that picamilon can be very helpful not only for ADHD, but also in patients with cerebral vascular disease, stroke, traumatic brain injuries, and those recovering from a stroke. People with ADHD may have difficulties remembering appointments and keeping track of time. Some are constantly late and as a result they may lose friends who interpret their lateness as a sign of unreliability or a lack of consideration. One of Dr. Brown's patients was always late even for very important appointments.

> Judy missed her first two appointments with me [Dr. Brown]. Although she was being treated for anxiety, depression, and an eating disorder, I began to think that she might also have ADHD. I called the night before to remind her of the next appointment and she managed to come, though 15 minutes late. She apologized profusely and told me tearfully that she had lost most of her friends because she always forgot to keep the dates she made with them. "People think I don't care about them when I forget or I'm an hour late. They accuse me of being inconsiderate, but I can't help it. I do everything I can think of to be on time, but it just slips away from me and then, when I realize, it's too late."
>
> By the age of 50, Judy had been through many different antidepressants, mood stabilizers, and major tranquilizers. In the past, Provigil, a stimulant, had been more helpful than the other drugs. She was being treated by a cognitive behavior therapist.
>
> Judy had heard about picamilon from other patients with ADHD, and she wanted to give it a try. From the first day, starting with just 100 mg, she noticed a change. At a full dose of 200 mg in the morning and 100 mg in the afternoon, she was less scattered, much more focused and organized. She was able to think more clearly. Depression, motivation, and energy all improved markedly. She cleaned her long neglected brushes, set up an easel, and took up painting again.

How to Use Picamilon: Side Effects, Dosage, and Timing

Picamilon is very low in side effects, even when given to elderly people. In rare instances it may lower blood pressure and cause lightheadedness, dizziness, or fainting. It is best to start with 50–100 mg daily and increase gradually to a maximum of 200 mg in the morning and 100 mg in the mid-afternoon to minimize the risk of side effects.

Q&A

Q: Who can benefit from picamilon?

A: Anyone with ADHD could possibly benefit from picamilon.

- Picamilon can be especially helpful for those who have ADHD with either anxiety or depression
- Picamilon can also help recovery from brain injury and stroke.

AMINO ACIDS: TRYPTOPHAN, PHENYLALANINE, LEVODOPA, AND L-TYROSINE

Amino acids are the building blocks of proteins. Studies of amino acid supplements, including tryptophan, phenylalanine, levodopa, and l-tyrosine, have shown only short-term benefits in ADHD with loss of effect after a few weeks. At this time we see no sufficient evidence of benefits for any significant period of time in ADHD. Vegetarians who are not getting adequate amounts of protein in their diet may need to use protein supplements with a full complement of the essential amino acids.

Q&A

Q: Who should use amino acid supplements?

A: In general, we do not recommend amino acid supplements for ADHD. It is better to invest in other supplements with more proven benefits.

L-CARNITINE AND ACETYL-L-CARNITINE

Acetyl-l-carnitine is a form of the natural substance, carnitine. Carnitine is made in muscle and liver tissues and is found in meat, poultry, fish, and some dairy products. Studies show that it improves cell membrane function, energy metabolism, synthesis of ATP (adenosine triphosphate, high-energy molecules) and neurotransmitters, essential fatty acid utilization, and possibly the attention component of the cholinergic system, the neuronal network that uses the neurotransmitter acetylcholine. (See Chapter 2 for a discussion of the role of acetylcholine in ADHD.)

L-Carnitine in ADHD, Inattentive Subtype

In a 16-week randomized pilot study involving 112 children with ADHD, ages 5–12, L-carnitine given in weight-based doses from 500 to 1500 mg twice a day was compared to placebo. Although the overall group scores showed no difference, there was significant improvement in attention in ADD (the inattentive type of ADHD), but not in the combined type (ADHD with both inattention and hyperactivity/impulsivity).

How to Use Carnitines: Side Effects, Dosage, and Timing

Side effects have been negligible in reported studies. L-carnitine deserves further study for possible benefit in the inattentive type (Arnold et al., 2007). Carnitines are safe and have shown promise in preliminary studies. Doses range from 500 to 1500 mg twice a day. We prefer to use acetyl-L-carnitine because it is better absorbed into brain cells and therefore likely to be more effective. While waiting for further research, it would be reasonable to try acetyl-L-carnitine as a complementary treatment in the people with the inattentive subtype of ADHD.

MECLOFENOXATE (CENTROPHENOXINE) AND DIMETHYL-AMINOETHANOL

The nootropic meclofenoxate is a combination of a dopamine booster DMAE (dimethyl-aminoethanol) and a synthetic form of a plant growth hormone called PCPA (p-chlorophenoxyacetic acid). As a cognitive enhancer meclofenoxate is well studied, inexpensive, and low in side effects. Meclofenoxate carries the DMAE rapidly into the brain where it becomes part of the nerve cell membranes. Once embedded in the membranes, DMAE scavenges free radicals to prevent them from causing damage (Zs-Nagy, 2002). DMAE increases dopamine activity and contributes to the synthesis of choline needed to produce the neurotransmitter acetylcholine.

In Chapter 2 we discussed the importance of acetylcholine for learning, short-term memory, attentional effort, and the allocation of visual attention (Klinkenberg et al., 2010). Choline and acetylcholine are essential for brain function, especially memory, but there are two problems. First of all, it is not easy to get choline into brain cells where it can be converted into acetylcholine for neurotransmission. Second, many people are now following diets that limit the amounts of foods that are richest in choline—fatty meats, organ tissues, and egg yolks. As a result, we may not be supplying enough choline for our brains to function at their best. One study found that when pregnant animals were fed a diet high in choline, they bore offspring with better cognitive function and a reduced incidence of dementia when they reached old age (Meck, Williams, Cermack, et al., 2007). Meclofenoxate improves the ability of choline to enter brain cells. Also, the herb ginkgo can enhance the cognitive effects of meclofenoxate.

How to Use Meclofenoxate: Side Effects, Dosage, and Timing

Meclofenoxate has minimal side effects, unless it is given in excess doses or combined with other cholinergic agents (medications such as donepezil [Aricept] that increase acetylcholine transmission). In doses that are too high for an individual, it can cause headache, irritability, muscle tension, small muscle tremors, insomnia, agitation, or facial tics. Therapeutic doses range from 250 mg per day in children over the age of 12 to 500–2,000 mg per day in adults. Some people are sensitive and may get some side effects even on 500 mg a day. In such cases, the dose can be reduced.

Q&A

Q: Who could benefit from Meclofenoxate?

A: Meclofenoxate is particularly helpful for improving memory problems associated with ADHD. Because meclofenoxate is not activating, it is more useful when the person does not need a highly stimulating agent.

USING NATURE'S BOUNTY WISELY— ONE STEP AT A TIME

We have introduced you to many wonderful natural supplements. Now what do you do with this information? Do you rush to your nearest health food store and buy one of everything? Of course not. Please take your time. If you are interested in a particular supplement, reread the section on it carefully so you are clear about how it works, what to expect, what side effects could occur, and how to use it correctly. Here are some general suggestions to help you use these treasures safely and effectively:

1. Discuss your use of supplements with your primary health care provider. It is especially important to involve your pediatrician or family practitioner before giving supplements to children.

2. Check the lists of precautions and warnings to be sure that you do not have any contraindications for using each product.

3. Be sure to get good-quality brands. This is especially important with herbs that may not be closely regulated for quality, purity, and effectiveness. Table 4.7 at the end of this chapter will guide you to some of the better brands. As we mentioned above, you can also visit websites that independently rate products.

4. Start slowly, take your time increasing the doses, and if you begin to experience mild side effects, back off to a lower dose and wait at least a week before trying to increase it again.

5. Be patient. It may take time for you to get up to a high-enough dose to see the benefits. Do not exceed the maximum doses listed in the supplement guidelines of Table 4.6. More is not always better and can cause side effects.

Natural medicines and nutrients are not magical cures, but they can often help reduce symptoms of ADHD, especially when combined carefully with other supplements and complementary treatments. Mother Nature has provided us with many natural medicines. It is up to us to use them wisely.

Table 4.6 Treatment Guidelines for Vitamins, Nutrients, and Nootropics

CAM	Clinical Uses	Dose (mg/d)	Side Effects and Interactions[b]
Acetyl-l-carnitine L-carnitine	Inattentive ADD	500–1500 mg/d	Minimal
B vitamins	ADHD		Minimal See cardiac stents[c]
B-complex		B50 or B100 1qd	
B6 (pyridoxine)		B6 25 mg/d	
B12 (methyl-cobalamin)		B12 1,000 mcg/d	
Bio-Strath B vitamins + antioxidants	ADHD	Adult 1½ tsp or 1 tab b.i.d. Child ½ tsp or 1 tab b.i.d.	None (keep the liquid refrigerated) See cardiac stents[c]
Folate	Folate deficiency	200–400 mg/d	Minimal See cardiac stents
Meclofenoxate	Mild ADHD, memory	500 mg/d or more	Minimal
Omega-3 Fatty Acids (PUFA) EPA/DHA 2:1	ADHD	1200–2400 mg b.i.d.	Minimal; GI distress, belching
Picamilon	ADHD	50 mg b.i.d., up to 100 mg t.i.d.	Minimal. High dose: hypotension.
Pycnogenol®	ADHD	50 mg b.i.d.	Minimal
Racetams	Learning disabilities, dyslexia, medicine-related cognitive impairment		Minimal, but rarely: anxiety, insomnia, agitation, irritability, headache
Aniracetam		Aniracetam 750 mg b.i.d.	
Piracetam		Piracetam 3600 mg/day	
Pramiracetam		Pramiracetam 600 mg b.i.d.	

CAM	Clinical Uses	Dose (mg/d)	Side Effects and Interactions[b]
SAMe (S-adenosyl-L-methionine)	ADHD	400–4,000 mg/d	Occasional: nausea, loose bowels, agitation, anxiety, insomnia. Rare: palpitations. Avoid in bipolar disorder—can cause mania.

Note. ADHD = attention-deficit/hyperactivity disorder (includes all three subtypes); BP = blood pressure; CAM = complementary and alternative medicine; DHA = docosahexanoic acid; EPA = eicosapentanoic acid; GI = gastrointestinal; PUFA = polyunsaturated fatty acid.; mcg = micrograms; ↓ = decreases; mg/d = milligrams per day; tab = tablet; qd = per day; b.i.d. = twice a day; t.i.d. = three times a day; mg = milligrams, mcg = micrograms.

[a]The doses in this table are meant only as guidelines. People who are more sensitive may need to use lower doses. Readers should discuss the choice of supplements and the adjustment of doses with their personal physician.

[b]Common side effects are listed. There are additional rare side effects. Individuals with high blood pressure, diabetes, pregnancy (or during breastfeeding), or any chronic or serious medical condition should check with their physician before taking supplements. Patients taking anticoagulants should consult their physician before using supplements. Parents are advised to consult a qualified physician to prescribe and monitor supplements given to children.

[c]One study suggests that folate with B_{12} and B_6 may increase the risk of restenosis in cardiac stents in men only whose serum homocysteine level is greater than 15μm/L (Lang et al, 2004)

Table 4.7 Guide to Quality Vitamins, Nutrients, and Nootropics

CAM	Company	Brand Name	Source	Cost/day[a]
L-carnitine, Acetyl-l-carnitine	Life Extension Foundation (LEF), Smart Nutrition	L-Carnitine ALCAR	800-544-4440 www .lef.org www.smart-nutrition.net	$0.50– 1.50
B vitamins, B-complex, Bio-Strath, B6 (pyridoxine), B12 (methylcobalamin)	International Antiaging Systems (IAS), Smart Nutrition		www.antiaging-systems.com www .smart-nutrition.net	
Bio-Strath, B vitamins, antioxidants	Bio-Strath	Bio-Strath Strath Food Supplement	www.bio-strath. naturesanswer. com/default.asp	$0.50–1.00
Folate	major brands		Health food stores	
Meclofenoxate (Centrophenoxine)	IAS	Lucidril	www.antiaging-systems.com Fax: 011-44-208-181-6106	$0.50– 2.50

CAM	Company	Brand Name	Source	Cost/day[a]
Omega-3 fatty acids: EPA/DHA 2:1	Vital Nutrients, IAS, Nordic Naturals, Twin Labs, Solgar	Pure fish oil	1-888-328-992 www.vitalnutrients .net www.antiaging-systems.com Health food stores	$1.60– 2.60
Phosphatidyl serine (not bovine)	Phosphatidyl serine (PtS)	Jarrow and others	Health food stores	$0.50
Picamilon	IAS, Smart Nutrition	picamilon	www.antiaging-systems.com www.smart-nutri-tion.net	$0.40– 1.20
Pycnogenol®	Horphag Research	Pycnogenol	www.pycnogenol. com	$0.25
Racetams Aniracetam Piracetam	IAS, Smart Nutrition	aniracetam piracetam	www.antiaging-systems.com www.smart-nutrition.net	$1.80
SAMe (S-adenosyl-L-methionine)	IAS, Nature Made, LEF, GNC, Now Foods, Jarrow, Geroformula	Donamet®, Samyr® SAM-e, SAMe	www.antiaging-systems.com www.naturemade. com www.lef.com Local health food stores	$1.00– 4.00

Note. DHA = docosahexanoic acid; EPA = eicosapentanoic acid; GNC = General Nutrition Centers.

[a]Costs of products may vary. This table lists approximate costs at the time of publication.

RESOURCES

Here is a list of websites, books, and journals where you may find additional information about foods, vitamins, and nutrients to help reduce symptoms of ADHD.Websites for Organizations

Agriculture and Trade Policy Food and Health Program: http://iatp.org/foodand health/.
Grassroots organization started in the 1980's to save the family farm. Advocates for healthy sustainable food supply, fair trade, and human rights. Supports family farmers and rural communities.

Center for Science in the Public interest: www.csinet.org.
> See the report, "Food Dyes: A Rainbow of Risks" by Kobylewski and Jacobson (2010).

ConsumerLab.com: www.consumerlab.com.
> Rates many brands of herbs and supplements on some measures of quality and labeling accuracy. Does not assess for shelf life, that is, the possible loss of potency over time prior to purchase. Provides useful free information. For in-depth reports on specific supplements an annual fee is required.

Drugs.com: www.drugs.com.
> Concise updated presentation of CAM, including risks and interactions.

National Center for Complementary and Alternative Medicine, National Institute of Health, National Library of Health Complementary and Alternative Medicine Specialist Library (NeLCAM): www.library.nhs.uk/cam.

Natural Medicines Comprehensive Database: www.naturaldatabase.com.
> Good source for comprehensive information on herbs, but tends to overemphasize side effects.

The Research Council for Complementary Medicine: www.rccm.org.uk/default .aspx?m=o.
> Aims to develop and extend the evidence base for complementary medicine in order to inform practitioners and their patients about the effectiveness of CAM treatments of specific conditions. New database: CAMEOL.

Supplement Watch: www.supplementwatch.com.
> Corporation of scientist, physiologists, nutritionists, and other health professionals offers free access to a database on supplements. To obtain detailed reports on particular supplements requires a $25 annual fee.

U.S. Food and Drug Administration: www.fda.gov/medwatch.
> Provides safety information, reports serious problems, and issues warnings.

Other Websites

Dr. Richard P. Brown and Dr. Patricia L. Gerbarg: www.haveahealthymind.com.
> Provides updates and a free newsletter on Complementary and Alternative Medicine.

Vaughns' Summaries: www.vaughns-1-pagers.com/food/artificial-food-colors.htm
> Information on artificial colorings in candy.

Books

Brown, R.P., Gerbarg, P.L., & Muskin, P.R. (2009). *How to Use Herbs, Nutrients, and Yoga in Mental Health Care*. New York: Norton. —Balanced, well-documented information on how to use herbs, nutrients, nootropics, other supplements, and mind-body practices. Includes risks, benefits, and clinical guidelines. Covers anxiety, depression, PTSD, cognitive function, life stage issues, hormonal changes, sexual enhancement, substance abuse, schizophrenia, and medical issues.

Ernst, E., Pittler, M.H., & Wider, B. (Ed.). (2006). *The Desktop Guide to Complementary and Alternative Medicine: An Evidence-Based Approach* (2nd ed.). London: Mosby.
Concise, well-organized as a quick reference resource. The viewpoint is quite conservative and at times unnecessarily cautious.

Lake, J., & Spiegel, D. (2007). *Complementary and Alternative Treatments in Mental Health Care*. Washington, DC: American Psychiatric Association.
Chapters are written by experts in different areas of CAM; for example, Chinese medicine, homeopathy, Ayurvedic treatments.

Journals

BMC Complementary and Alternative Medicine: www.biomedcentral.com.
Peer-reviewed journal publishes articles on CAM.

Evidence-Based Complementary and Alternative Medicine: www.hindawi.com.
Peer-reviewed journal publishes articles on CAM.

Herbalgram: Journal of the American Botanical Council: www. Herbalgram.org.
In depth, authoritative articles on herbs from around the world.

Journal of Complementary and Alternative Medicine: www.liebertpub.com.
Peer-reviewed journal publishes articles on CAM.

CHAPTER 5 OUTLINE

CHAPTER 5

When the Body Talks, the Brain Listens

Mind–Body Practices for ADHD[1]

Some people tend to think of the mind and the body as being separate, but they are not. The brain and the body are in constant, dynamic communication. Mind–body practices include a wide variety of techniques that combine physical and mental activities. Although many different schools have evolved, in this chapter we use the general term *yoga* to include them all. The following example shows how a very simple practice called *coherent breathing* solved the problems of inattention, school failure, anxiety, and inability to sleep in a child with ADD (inattentive type).

Like his father, Alex had the inattentive type of ADD. Like his mother, he had generalized anxiety disorder. He would get extremely anxious under pressure, such as when taking tests or having to give a talk in front of the class. His parents were determined not to put him on medication because they were concerned about side effects, and he seemed to be doing well enough. Since Alex was not hyperactive, he was generally well behaved, cooperative, and sociable. In the lower grades he was able to pick up enough information in class and dash off small amounts of homework well enough to get by. However, the more demanding curriculum in fourth grade was overwhelming. He could not focus or

[1] The authors wish to thank Joy Bennet, Kim Sutherland, Amy Weintraub, Master Robert Peng, Stephen Elliot, and Sat Bir Khalsa for their support in the preparation of this chapter.

sustain his attention long enough to complete reading or writing assignments. Although math had been his best subject, having to read word problems now became an insurmountable obstacle. Being unprepared for classes and tests set off anxiety to the point where his stomach ached. He could not sleep at night because he was worrying about school the next day. A trial of biofeedback (see Chapter 6) was of no help.

Alex's mother turned to Dr. Brown for advice. He taught her a calming breath practice, coherent breathing, and she then taught Alex so that they could practice together at home. They listened to a CD with chime tones that timed their breathing to five breaths per minute. The first time he tried it, Alex felt calmer. He began by practicing with his mother, but soon learned to use the CD himself every night at bedtime. One month later, Alex's mother checked with Dr. Brown to see if it was all right that he was breathing with the CD for an hour at bedtime. His anxiety was much better during the day, and he was sleeping well at night. Since Alex really liked doing coherent breathing and it seemed to be helping, Dr. Brown suggested that she just let him continue and see what would happen. With no other interventions, over the next 3 months Alex felt better and better. With improved focus, he could study, finish assignments, and do well on tests. Free from anxiety, he was able to sleep at night. Alex felt a lot better about going to school and about coming home with the A's and B's he deserved.

HOW MIND–BODY PRACTICES HELP ADHD

In Chapters 1 and 2, we discussed the symptoms of ADHD, inattention, hyperactivity, and impulsivity, as well as hypoarousal, reward deficiency, and emotional self-regulation problems. Mind–body practices can be extremely helpful for all of these symptoms of ADHD. Yoga practices that improve alertness, attention, mental clarity, calmness, emotional self-regulation, physical self-control, and awareness of oneself and others are beneficial for children and adults with ADHD.

When people think of yoga, they tend to visualize people holding odd poses or postures, but yoga began as a complete system for physical, mental, and spiritual development. Many of the more popular schools of yoga, such as Kripalu, Shambhala, Iyengar, Kundalini, Ashtanga, Anusara, Shanti, and Sudarshan Kriya, stem from the "eight limbs of yoga" described by Patanjali (200 c.e.). The eight limbs (Feuerstein, 1998) included:

1. Ethical and moral standards
2. Study of scriptures
3. Physical yoga postures with meditation on the body to experience the self
4. Yoga breathing techniques
5. Turning attention away from the senses toward the inner world of self-experience
6. Concentration to focus attention
7. Meditation with mental clarity and total calmness
8. The happiness that occurs when one is reunited with the true self, universal energy, or the divine.

Modern yoga studios often focus on the physical aspects, mainly yoga postures, which can be beneficial, but there is much more to be gained if we mine the wisdom of thousands of years of yogic evolution.

Yoga was and is a science of the mind. Picture the ancient yogis sitting hour after hour, day after day, year after year. What were they doing? They were experimenting, trying different ways to alter the functioning of their minds through body movements, breathing, and meditation. In the process, over thousands of years, they discovered myriad ways to change how their minds and bodies worked. For example, they could change their heart rate or their ability to tolerate pain (think of those beds of nails and the hot coals). They could change their mental focus, how thoughts flowed, their emotional reactions, and their state of consciousness. Modern scientists have discovered that adept yogis and Buddhist meditators can change the pattern of their brain waves at will, activate and deactivate parts of their brains, and even influence the development of certain brain structures (Lazar et al., 2005). Many of these ancient practices can be used therapeutically to help the ADHD mind by improving alertness, attention, processing, coherence, integration, impulsivity, overreactivity, mood, and calmness.

Most mind–body programs include some form of movement, breathing, and meditation. There are differences in specific techniques and in the emphasis placed on each of these essential components. Rather than trying to review hundreds of mind–body practices, we focus on a select set that is supported by evidence and that we have found to be particularly beneficial in working with people who have ADHD, with or without other concurrent diagnoses.

YOGA MOVEMENTS AND POSTURES

Starting with movements helps to release the physical tension, frustration, and excess energy that tend to build up in people with ADHD. Maintaining yoga postures and redirecting attention to physical sensations experienced during these postures improves attention, self-awareness, and physical self-control. Performing the postures slowly helps the individual learn to slow down, gain control over physical actions, and improve balance and motor skills. Synchronizing movements with breathing enhances the effects. In general, we breathe in with rising movements and breathe out with descending movements.

Although intense physical yoga can provide many health benefits, yoga programs that entail slow, gentle movements are more beneficial for calming the system and focusing the mind. It is best to learn yoga postures from an instructor. If you cannot get access to yoga classes, there are many DVD programs. The Namaste Yoga television program is a good example of calming practices.

In the section below on yoga programs in schools we describe and illustrate a set of basic movements and postures suitable for children and adults. We recommend starting yoga with movement practices, especially for people with ADHD who need to reduce their level of restlessness in order to relax. See the Resources section at the end of the chapter for more information.

Breathing Practices

Specific breathing practices can be used to increase alertness, calm the mind, quiet distracting thoughts, focus attention, reduce anxiety, improve emotion regulation, and improve memory and other brain functions. There are hundreds of different breathing practices. We have selected a few that we find to be easy to learn, rapidly effective, and safe: coherent breathing, resistance breathing, breath moving, and "*ha*" breath.

Coherent Breathing

The ideal breath rate for balancing the stress response system can vary with age, height, and physical condition. On average, for most adults, it ranges between five and six breaths per minute. Coherent Breathing is simply slow, gentle, relaxed breathing at five to six breaths per minute using equal time for inhalation and exhalation. This special rate also optimizes cardiovascular function and oxygenation (Bernardi, Porta, Gabutti, Spicuzza, & Sleight, 2001). Coherent Breathing is a modern adaptation of ancient practices known to Qigong masters and Zen Buddhist monks. Qigong can be thought of as Chinese yoga. Studies show that for each person there is an optimal breath rate using equal lengths of inspiration and expiration for balancing the stress response system and calming the mind. This breath rate has been used by Paul Lehrer's research group in a technique called resonant breathing (Song, & Lehrer, 2003; Vaschillo, Vaschillo, & Lehrer, 2006).

The resonant breath rate for most adults and adolescents is between four and a half and six breaths per minute. For people over 6 feet tall, it is about three or three and a half breaths per minute. Coherent Breathing, using a rate of five breaths per minute, falls in the middle of the resonant breath range, and works well for most people over the age of 10. Younger children have higher resonant breath rates depending on their age and size. Formal studies on the optimal breath rates for children have not been published. However, we find that children under the age of 10 can comfortably breathe between 6 and 10 breaths per minute.

How to Learn Coherent Breathing Coherent Breathing is a safe way to reduce anxiety, insomnia, depression, fatigue, anger, aggression, impulsivity, inattention, and symptoms of posttraumatic stress disorder (PTSD). It is easy to learn how to breathe at five breaths per minute by listening to sound tracks on *The New Science of Breath Respire* 1 CD (see Resources). On one track a voice tells the listener when to breathe in and breathe out. On another sound track the breathing is paced by bell tones. On one bell tone you breathe in and on the next bell tone you breathe out. You can relax, close your eyes, breathe in through the nose and out through either the nose or the mouth, and let the bells pace your breathing. It is important to relax completely and breathe gently and slowly without forcing or straining to get the best results. Eventually, you can learn to breathe at five breaths per minute even without the bell tones. Those who are able to learn resistance breathing (described below) can use the *Respire 1* CD for even greater effects.

How to Use Slow Breath Practices Safely Coherent breathing is safe for children, adults of all ages, people with medical illnesses, and during pregnancy. However, some people with severe or acute asthma may find that when they first try to do coherent breathing, their breathing becomes more difficult. If they are taught to add a special modification, called *Breath Moving*, their airways will remain open and they will breathe more easily. You can learn breath moving by taking one of our Breath~Body~Mind workshops. Alternatively, you can learn a basic form of Breath Moving from our book, *The Healing Power of Breath* (Brown & Gerbarg, 2012).

Resistance Breathing

Also called *Ujjayi, victorious breath*, or *ocean breath*, resistance breathing uses a slight contraction of the upper throat muscles to produce a sound like the ocean while breathing through the nose. This increases stimulation of the vagus nerve and helps to control the rate of airflow more precisely. Another form of resistance breathing is lip pursing. The pursed lips partly obstruct airflow during exhalation only. In Qigong and in Resonant Breathing, resistance is created by exhaling through pursed lips. It is best to learn resistance breathing from a teacher who can check to be sure you are doing it correctly to avoid straining.

Breath Moving

Using the imagination to move the breath in circuits to different parts of the body can be found in Qigong, Hawaiian breathing, yoga, and martial arts. Developed to the highest degree by Russian Orthodox Christian monks, it was used to prepare for "The Jesus Prayer" and to attain deep states of prayer and meditation. The monks also taught breath moving to Christian knights to enhance strength, endurance, and skill while defending the realm from invaders. Traces of these practices are still part of Russian Special Forces training (Vasiliev, 2006).

How to Use Breath Moving Breath moving can be combined with coherent breathing and resistance breathing. It reduces distracting thoughts, improves mental focus, and relieves stress. It is also especially helpful in people who have asthma. When people with asthma first do slow breathing, their initial reaction can be difficulty breathing due to narrowing of the airways. However, when they use the technique of breath moving, this does not occur and they are usually able to perform coherent breathing without difficulty. In the long run, daily practice of these breath techniques improves respiratory function and awareness.

"Ha" Breathing

Many traditions use some form of *"ha"* breathing, that is, forceful exhalations while saying *"ha"* loudly and sharply. There are many ways to do *"ha"* breathing. Here is one that is simple and effective.

Stand up straight, bending the elbows, palms pointed upward, curve the fingers into a loose fist (see Figures 5.1 and 5.2). Inhale breath deeply through the nose while retracting the elbows behind

Figures 5.1 and 5.2

the back, palms facing upward, hands in fists. As you exhale sharply, say the sound "*ha!*" loudly, extend the arms and throw the hands forward, letting the palms turn downward as though you are flinging water off the tips of your fingers. Inhale deeply, bending the elbows, palms upward, hands in fists. Exhale sharply with the "*ha*" sound, repeating the same movements. This should be done briskly at approximately one breath per second. It can be done for 15 repetitions (about 15 seconds) or for up to a maximum of 3 minutes continuously, depending on your physical capacity and on how much is needed to activate your system. For example, it is useful when you need to study or do intellectual work for a prolonged time and find that your mind is getting "fuzzy" or unfocused. This type of breathing will tend to increase mental alertness. For most people we recommend using only short bursts of "*ha*" breaths, as brief as 30 seconds and no longer than 2 minutes.

How to Use Forceful Breathing Practices Safely Rapid breathing with forceful exhalation can immediately improve attention and alertness by stimulating the sympathetic nervous system. This should be done only for very short periods of time, just a few minutes. We described a forceful breathing practice call "*ha*" breathing above.

Another fast, forceful breathing practice, *Kapalabhati*, is a widely used stimulating practice that can be done at different rates. A study using Kapalabhati for 5 minutes at a rate of 120 breaths per minute in healthy adults showed improvements in attention, concentration, and accuracy on standard testing (Telles, Raghuraj, Arankalle, & Naveen, 2008).

Rapid or forceful breathing practices should not be done by people who have uncontrolled hypertension, seizure disorder, asthma, obstructive lung disease, recent surgery, or who are pregnant. Also, rapid breathing can trigger panic attacks in patients with panic disorder, flashbacks in people with PTSD, or manic episodes in those with bipolar disorder. Healthy adults can benefit from Kapalabhati or "*ha*" breath. However, it is important to learn correct techniques from a qualified instructor and to limit the amount of time doing this practice.

Where to Learn Breathing Practices

Some of these breath practices are taught in a wide range of yoga and other mind–body courses. All of these practices are included in our Breath~Body~Mind programs for reducing stress, anxiety, depression, insomnia, and PTSD. They can also be learned from our book, *The Healing Power of the Breath* (Brown & Gerberg, in press).

Combining Breath Practices with Standard Treatments

Breathing techniques can be used in conjunction with other treatments such as stimulant medications. Here is an example of a patient who used coherent breathing and "*ha*" breath along with medication to successfully overcome the problems caused by her ADHD.

Jenna was in a panic because she was on the brink of failing her first year at a prestigious college. She could not concentrate enough to write her final papers or complete her art projects. She was terribly upset and crying as she told me that her professors thought she wasn't trying. They didn't know that she had to lock herself in her room for 10 hours just to write one page of an assignment. Jenna wanted desperately to please her professors and felt deeply hurt that they thought she didn't care about her work. She had not told them about her ADHD. The constant worry and anxiety made her even more distracted and disorganized.

I (Dr. Gerbarg) asked how she had managed to do well enough in high school to get admitted to such a competitive college. She explained, "My mother always sat at the table while I did my homework. She would explain anything I didn't understand, keep me focused, and help organize my essays. I had good ideas but I couldn't express them in writing without her help. They were really my ideas, I'm not stupid. I just needed help to write them down clearly. When I got to college, I just couldn't do it all myself."

When I asked whether her family knew she had ADHD, she nodded, "Oh, yes. It's just that they don't believe in using medication. Even though I wanted it, they wouldn't let me. But now, I need it or else I will lose my scholarship and everything." I agreed to write her a prescription for Adderall because it would work quickly, hopefully in time to salvage her semester, but I also suggested she learn some breath practices. Jenna's face showed relief and gratitude. I also counseled her to tell her teachers that she was just starting treatment for her ADHD.

Over the next few weeks, Jenna's concentration got much better. By spending long hours in the studio, she was able to catch up and complete her projects in time to get credit and even praise. Three of her four teachers were very understanding and supportive when they discovered that it was the ADHD and not a lack of motivation that had caused her poor performance. The fourth teacher was unsympathetic, viewing the ADHD as just another excuse. Unlike the other three, he made no accommodations for her problems. They were willing to give her extra time to complete her tests and projects if needed.

Jenna learned to do "*ha*" breathing before sitting down to study and every few hours whenever she became tired or distracted. "*Ha*" breathing is energizing; it wakes up the brain and sharpens mental focus. She practiced coherent breathing to the point where she could do it with her eyes open while listening to the chime track on her CD. She used coherent breathing while working on her computer, reading, writing, or even painting. It kept her calm and focused. During vacations, Jenna took a break from Adderall and just used the breath practices as needed. As soon as she had to study or produce work, she resumed her integrative regimen of Adderall combined with coherent and "*ha*" breathing.

Jenna's case illustrates the benefits of integrative treatments. If she were living in a different situation, say on a farm in the 1800s, Jenna would not have needed to take Adderall to succeed in planting, harvesting, feeding chickens, milking cows, cooking, etc. But in the 21st-century, heading for a college degree and a competitive career, she needed the medication to fulfill her ambitions. The breathing practices further enhanced her response to the medication by reducing anxiety and distraction to the point where she was able to do challenging intellectual work.

RELAXATION, CONCENTRATION, MINDFULNESS, AND MEDITATION

Relaxation techniques and meditation help to calm, balance, and strengthen the nervous system. Meditation and guided imagery can be used to reduce negative thinking and increase self-esteem as well as positive emotions. Many people with ADHD find it difficult to meditate because they cannot focus their mind enough to attain a meditative state. For people interested in meditation, breathing practices and yoga movements may help to settle the mind and bring the person to the threshold of meditation, making it possible for him or her to meditate more easily. ADHD often impairs the ability to relax and to concentrate. By first using movement and breathing to release physical tension and focus the mind, it becomes easier to relax, concentrate, and meditate.

Meditation may involve emptying the mind of all thoughts, focusing the mind on one word or one image, or moving through a series of visualizations. It can be challenging for anyone to empty the mind of all thoughts or to maintain focus on one word or one point—for people with ADHD it can be extremely difficult. We do not recommend these forms of meditation for beginners unless the person is intensely motivated and willing to devote a great deal of time. For the majority of people with ADHD, it is easier to meditate by listening to a teacher or a CD providing a sequence of images, or by shifting the focus to different parts of the body—for example, by tensing and relaxing different muscle groups, by walking while meditating, or by doing a simple body scan (see Brown & Gerbarg, in press). This kind of approach is more dynamic and holds the attention better. Another deeper form of attention practice, called *Open Focus Meditation*, uses a sequence of mental exercises to develop the ability to shift between a narrow and a wide focus of attention (Fehmi and Robbins, 2007). Maureen Murdock's (1987) book *Spinning Inward* contains guided imagery exercises that can be fun for adults as well as children.

Mindfulness uses focused attention to develop awareness of thoughts, feeling, and sensations. Increasing awareness is a first step towards developing the capacity to observe one's internal reactions without self-criticism rather than being flooded and caught up in those reactions—and to become better able to choose how to respond (Siegel, 2011). Mindfulness is a challenging practice, particularly for people with ADHD in that it requires long periods of maintaining mental focus. By shortening the length of time focusing on each object, it may be easier for people with ADHD to learn these practices. Furthermore, when mindfulness is directed toward enhancing awareness of the body during yoga postures and awareness of the breath during breathing practices, then it serves to increase their effectiveness and prepare the mind for deeper meditation. We think that cultivating the conscious awareness or mindful focus on breath and postures complements the input from sensors that register changes in the internal states of the body (*interoceptions*) to the brain (see the discussion of interoception below), leading to more powerful and long-lasting effects from the yoga practices. For more information on meditation and mindfulness, see the Resources section.

Q&A

Q: Do I have to meditate many years to change my brain?

A: No, in fact, brain scans of people who had never meditated before showed that after participating in a mindfulness-based stress reduction program for 8 weeks, there were changes in the concentration of gray matter (reflecting increased density of neurons) in areas of the brain involved in learning, memory, emotion regulation, and perspective taking. These areas included the hippocampus, posterior cingulate cortex, temporoparietal junction, and cerebellum (Hölzel et al., 2011).

INTEROCEPTION: HOW THE MIND LISTENS TO THE BODY

While studying the use of yoga for anxiety, depression, and PTSD, we became fascinated with the way breathing can affect the mind. People in extreme states of distress often don't respond to words— their own or those of other people who are trying to help. When your mind is worrying at warp speed, words such as *calm down*, *relax*, *don't worry*, or *it will be fine* won't make it so. We have to find a different way, a nonverbal way, to communicate with the emotional mind because words do not compute when we are in a state of panic. This is where an alternate network comes into play, the body's own communication Internet.

Most people know about the five senses: sight, smell, hearing, taste, and touch. But there is another set of internal sensors that contribute to *interoception*—the perceptions of subtle feelings that come from inside the body, including the sense of heat, cold, vibration, hunger, fullness, pain, cramps, stretching sensations, air hunger (the sense of not getting enough air), and more. Interoception includes everything that occurs within our bodies from moment to moment. There are literally millions of sensors throughout the body that register every little change and send micro-messages through the interoceptive system to tell the brain what's happening. Most of this information travels

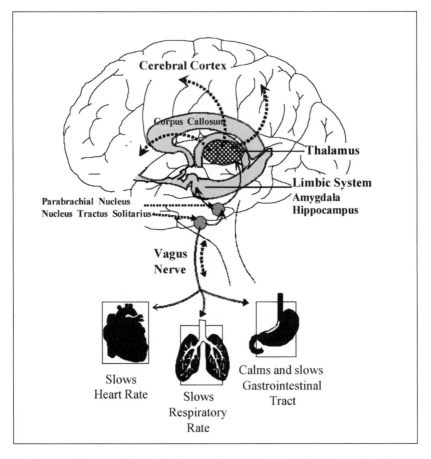

Figure 5.3 *Vagus Nerve Pathways between the Body and the Brain*

Information travels up and down through two nerves, the right and left vagus nerves. Their branches innervate all organs and tissues of the body where they pick up messages to carry directly into the brainstem. These messages go through relay stations and are delivered to the major areas of the brain where they influence our emotions, feelings, perceptions, thoughts, decision-making, and behavior.

through two nerves, the right and left vagus nerves (parasympathetic system). Their branches innervate all organs and tissues of the body, where they pick up messages and carry them directly into the brainstem. These messages pass through relay stations that send them on to the major areas of the brain where they influence our emotions, feelings, perceptions, thoughts, decision-making, and behavior (see

Figure 5.3). We could say that interoception provides input from the body that the brain needs to make up its mind about how to feel, how to react, and what to do (Craig, 2003; Critchley, 2005; Porges, 2001).

Suppose the stomach is telling the brain that it's hungry, and the throat is telling the brain that it's thirsty, and the lungs are telling the brain that they need air—all at the same time. What will the brain pay attention to first? If your brain chose to listen to your stomach when your lungs needed air, you would be dead within a few minutes. The brain has to listen to what is most critical for survival first—breathing. If we are choking or drowning or suffocating, our brain has to pay immediate attention and devote all of its efforts to getting enough oxygen to survive. Fortunately, the design of our interoceptive system makes sure that the connections between the respiratory system and the brain are very fast and strong. This may be one of the reasons why input from the respiratory system can have profound, rapid effects on how the brain is working.

Breathing: Our Portal to the Body's Internal Communication System

Breathing is the only autonomic function that most people can control at will. Breathing is usually automatic, but we can easily change the rate, pattern, and depth of our breathing. Breathing is our portal, our way of accessing the interoceptive messaging system and sending the messages we want to send to our brains—messages that reach all parts of the cognitive and emotion regulation centers of the brain—messages that the brain cannot ignore. We can "log onto" the body's internal Internet and send messages in the form of respiratory information in a nonverbal, body-based language that the brain understands.

When words fail, when logic fails, we can use coherent breathing and other slow breath practices to convince the mind that we are safe, that it is time to stop worrying and just relax. Specifically, slow breathing stimulates the vagus nerves, the main pathways of the soothing, healing, recharging (parasympathetic) part of the nervous system. We can send nonverbal messages through the portal of breath into the parasympathetic and other regulatory systems of the body up to the brain centers that determine how we feel, how we think, and how we react. Because these messages are in the language of the body, the whole brain—even the nonverbal, emotional, unconscious, and automatic parts of the brain—will understand and respond to these messages. This is particularly important for modulating reactions of the autonomic and stress response systems.

The autonomic nervous system, which is responsible for all of the automatic functions of the body, has two main counterbalancing branches involved in stress response and recovery: the *sympathetic* and the *parasympathetic*. The sympathetic system drives the stress response. Once the threat is gone, the parasympathetic system soothes the mind and recharges the body. A simple way to think of the sympathetic system is that it gets you ready to fight or run away (fight–flight) when you feel threatened. The sympathetic system developed during a time in the distant past when most of the day was taken up with slow, tedious activities such as gathering nuts and berries. Long periods of sameness were broken up by sudden life-threatening dangers, such as the appearance of a tiger. As soon as we saw that tiger, the sympathetic system turned on and sent messages to increase the heart rate, speed up respirations, and divert blood flow to the muscles of the arms and legs—all preparations for fight or flight. When the danger was over, the sympathetic system turned off and the parasympathetic system turned on, sending messages to slow the heart and respirations, relax the gut, redistribute the blood flow, calm the mind, restore energy reserves, repair any damage to the body, and reduce inflammation. The problem today, particularly for people with ADHD and concurrent diagnoses, is that the autonomic system is often out of balance. One or both branches may be underactive, overactive, slow to react, or erratic.

Q&A

Q: What are the consequences of imbalance in the stress response system?

A: The short-term consequences involve feeling tense, worried, fearful, overly sensitive, overly reactive, under-reactive, irritable, and fatigued. These imbalances can worsen problems of inattention, cognitive processing, emotion regulation, anger, and sudden aggression. The long-term consequences are acceleration of diseases such as cardiovascular disease and other stress-related conditions (Thayer & Brosschot, 2005).

Q: What kinds of imbalances occur in the stress response system in ADHD and how can we address these problems?

A: The relationship between specific imbalances in the stress response system and ADHD are only beginning to be studied. So far, it appears that different kinds of imbalances in the stress response systems may be associated with different symptoms in people with ADHD.

People with ADHD who experience agitation, aggression, and problems with impulse control tend to benefit from practices that are calming. For example, the activity of the parasympathetic system was studied in children ages 12–17 years, including 17 with ADHD, 20 with aggressive conduct disorder (CD), and 22 who had neither ADHD nor CD. Those with ADHD or CD showed underactivity of their vagal parasympathetic system (Beauchaine, Katkin, Strassberg, & Snarr, 2001). They also had lower thresholds for fight–flight reactions and were at increased risk for aggressive behavior. In other words, it didn't take much to trigger them to either become combative (fight) or run away (flight). This is an example of a parasympathetic system being too weak to counteract the influence of a sympathetic system in overdrive.

Along these lines, an open pilot study using autonomic nervous system biofeedback (see Chapter 6) found that improvements in symptoms of ADHD correlated with increases in parasympathetic nervous system activity (Eisenberg, Ben-Daniel, Mei-Tal, & Wertman, 2004). In ADHD, the parasympathetic system is underactive, while the sympathetic system can be overactive or erratic (usually underactive, but at times overactive). We usually use calming practices that increase parasympathetic function. However, when a person with ADHD is having difficulty focusing attention on a task, we find that a more stimulating breath practice such as "*ha*" breath can be helpful. In our treatments we combine coherent breathing, resistance breathing, and breath moving to balance and strengthen the stress response system and to improve symptoms of ADHD.

RESEARCH ON MIND–BODY PRACTICES

Numerous studies have found that mind–body practices such as yoga, breathing, and meditation increase activity of the parasympathetic system and decrease activity of the sympathetic system, thus balancing the stress response system (Bernardi et al., 2001; Brown & Gerberg, 2005a; Raghuraj, Ramakrishnan, Nagendra, & Telles, 1998; Telles, Gaur, Balkrishna, 2009).

Since 1995, a group of researchers in China and the U.S. have been studying integrative mind-body training (IMBT), a program combining body-mind techniques derived from ancient Chinese practices with aspects of meditation and mindfulness. The techniques include body relaxation, breathing adjustment, mental imagery, and mindfulness training with comfortable background music. It is designed to reduce the need the struggle to control thoughts while learning to improve attention and the ability to control stress. Programs are designed for children and adults. In a randomized controlled study of 80 Chinese college students, those who were given a twenty-minute session of integrative mind-body training (IMBT) for 5 days showed greater improvements in attention, self-regulation, and conflict compared to those who were given relaxation training only. The IMBT group also had lower scores on anxiety, depression, anger, and fatigue as well as significant decreases in stress-related cortisol levels (Tang, Yinghua, Junhong, et als., 2007).

A second randomized study of 86 Chinese college students used heart rate variability (a measure of the activity of the parasympathetic and sympathetic systems), electroencephalogram (recordings of brain wave activity) and brain scan (single photon emission computed tomography—SPECT) to evaluate the effects of the 5-day IMBT. Students who were given IMBT showed better regulation of the autonomic nervous system (sympathetic and parasympathetic systems) compared to those given relaxation training only. (Tang, Yinghua, Fan, et al, 2009)

Two small controlled meditation studies on children with ADHD found improvements in attention, particularly in the classroom (Arnold, 2001). These studies were presented as dissertations, but not published in a peer-reviewed journal. While they provide encouraging data, larger studies that have gone through the rigorous scrutiny of the peer review process are needed to provide stronger evidence of efficacy. A review of meditation therapies for ADHD was inconclusive because there were too few studies and most were not of adequate quality (Krisanaprakornkit, et al. 2010). More studies of higher quality would have to be published for the scientific evidence supporting the use of meditation for ADHD to reach a level that would be considered conclusive.

More and more studies are showing that mind–body practice such as yoga, Qigong, and Tai Chi can improve stress, anxiety, mood, and attention (Brown & Gerbarg, 2005b, 2009; Brown et al., 2009; Descilo, et. al. 2010). Evidence indicates that some of the ways that mind–body practices improve attention, cognition, emotion regulation, and behavior are through balancing the autonomic system—activating the parasympathetic system and increasing or stabilizing the activity of the sympathetic system (Brown et al., 2009).

Mind–body practices such as yoga breathing combined with yoga postures calm the mind, improve mental focus, and reduce aggressive behavior. Cyclical meditation is one such practice that alternates yoga postures with guided relaxation. Shirley Telles and colleagues found that cyclical meditation improved attention, concentration, memory, and anxiety in normal adults (Sarang, & Telles, 2006, 2007; Subramanya, & Telles, 2009)

In a small open study of 19 boys with hyperactive/impulsive ADHD, ages 8–13, a program of yoga postures, yoga breathing, and relaxation led to significant improvements on standardized ADHD tests. The degree of improvement correlated with the number of yoga sessions attended and with the amount of home practice each student performed (Jensen & Kenny, 2004).

In a randomized controlled study, 19 children with ADHD were assigned to either a yoga program or a conventional program of motor exercises. The yoga training was superior for all outcome measures, including attention scores and parent ratings of ADHD symptoms (Haffner, Roos, Goldstein, Parzer, & Resch, 2006).

Inattentive behaviors range from mild to severe even in children without a diagnosis of ADHD, and research has shown that children without ADHD who are easily distracted can benefit from mind–body practices. A small study of 10 elementary school children (ages 6–10) with documented attention problems but without ADHD (i.e., these children did not fulfill all of the required diagnostic criteria) were selected for this study, based on observations that they spent less than 80% of their classroom time on task (Peck, Kehle, & Bray, 2005). Time on task meant time when the students made eye contact with the teacher or the task and performed class assignments. Twice a week for 3 weeks the students watched yoga videotapes, *Yoga Fitness for Kids Ages 3–6* (Gaiam, 2002) and *Yoga Fitness for Kids Ages 7–12* (Gaiam, 2001), that led them through deep breathing, physical postures, and relaxation with guided imagery. Time-on-task measures improved significantly during the 3-week intervention but dropped off gradually after the program ended. This study demonstrated the feasibility of using a brief yoga intervention to improve attention as well as the need to have an ongoing program to maintain the benefits. Although the children in this study did not have symptoms severe enough to warrant a formal diagnosis of ADHD, their inattention was interfering with their ability to finish assignments, listen to directions, concentrate, and organize their work. While they clearly benefited from the videotape intervention, more symptomatic children with ADHD would probably need a live instructor and a longer program.

WHAT MAKES YOGA THERAPY?

Everyone can benefit physically and emotionally from participating in yoga classes. However, for yoga to be the most therapeutic for individuals with ADHD, only instructors who have a deep understanding of, and sensitivity to, the emotional and psychological needs of their students should teach it. The qualities of the most effective yoga teachers are compassion, love of people, commitment, and awareness of their own emotional issues as well as those of their students. Setting the tone, creating a "safe container" of caring, gentle, noncritical support is essential, especially when working with children or adults who may have ADHD as well as other emotional challenges. The work must be done slowly and without pressure, ideally with a trained yoga therapist (Williams, 2010; see also the Resource section at the end of this chapter). It requires great patience.

Yoga therapy is developing at the crossroads of yoga and mental health as well as yoga and medical treatments. Yoga therapists include psychotherapists who want to incorporate yoga into their work with patients as well as yoga teachers who want use psychotherapeutic knowledge in their work with students and clients. Joy Bennet, a registered yoga teacher (ITY 500), exemplifies the sensitive and skillful use of therapeutic yoga. Trained as a Kripalu instructor, she studied Integrative Yoga Therapy with Joseph LePage and LifeForce Yoga® with Amy Weintraub. Founder of Joyful Breath Yoga in Providence, Rhode Island, Joy uses yoga therapeutically for individuals with emotional challenges. She also developed a program for teaching yoga to boys with ADHD and other disorders who were sent to a special school because they could not be managed in the public school system. I (Dr. Gerbarg) had an opportunity to interview Joy, who embodies the essential qualities of a yoga therapist.

The Joy of Teaching Yoga to Boys with ADHD

Joy Bennett's work shows that yoga practices can be adapted even for children with extreme behavioral problems due to ADHD. As we describe some of Joy's teachings, you may look at Figures 5.4 through 5.9 for illustrations of the poses.

I sat facing Joy in her quiet office. She made sure I was comfortable by placing a folded blanket under my feet, then she sat in her simple cotton dress waiting for my first question. "Would you tell me exactly how you teach yoga to a class of boys with attention-deficit disorder?"

She closed her eyes a moment to collect her thoughts. "Twice a week I teach two groups, grades 1–3 and grades 4 and 5 with 11 in each group. You understand that they come from very difficult situations—broken homes, foster families and some from the local orphanage. Besides ADD, they have learning disabilities, emotional problems, and one has Asperger syndrome. Five adults assist in the room."

"I must be mentally ready, very centered and calm, before they are brought into the room and taken to their mats. To provide a stable presence, I stand still, allowing the other teachers to help settle the children on their mats. I make silent eye contact with them as they come in and nod slightly to greet them. I create a holding container by using a steady, compassionate voice."

"I start with, 'Coming to a seated position, inhale while you...'" "Wait," I interrupted, "Is that what you actually say? How can they understand what you mean by *inhale*?" "You see," she smiled, "we teach them the words they need for a yoga class using a diagram of Dan-the-Man. They like Dan. I ask them, 'Can anyone show me your hip?' Some

Figures 5.5 and 5.6. Mountain Pose

point to their knee or their ankle. One boy points to his hip. 'Good, Charlie, can you come up and show us where Dan-the-Man's hip is?' They love that, being able to come to the board and show what they know."

"If they come in all charged up, sprawled all over the mats, I have to get them moving. I begin with Mountain Pose: 'Coming to a seated position, fingertips to the earth, inhale as you bring your arms up, up over your head. As you exhale, arms float back down to earth.'" As she spoke, Joy's graceful arms moved up and down with her breath (see Figures 5.5 and 5.6).

Spinal Movements

Joy teaches a sequence of movements for the spine. She prepared the boys for this by first teaching them about the spine. Using a Halloween skeleton and Dan-the-Man, the boys discovered where the spine is located and how it moves.

Spinal movements are part of core yoga and Qigong practices for adults. They are illustrated in many yoga books, such as *Yoga for Depression* by Amy Weintraub (2006), and can be learned in yoga classes or from DVDs. Joy adapted these yoga movements for children by incorporating images to which they could relate and by keeping the atmosphere playful but calm.

Spinal movements begin in a seated position: "Bringing awareness to your left hand and allowing that hand to glide along the floor to the left side, on the next exhale, your right arm comes up, trying to touch the ceiling . . . moving your hand (*she makes a rotating motion at the wrist*). Take a big breath in and exhale as you come back to the middle." These movements are then repeated on the other side (see Figures 5.7 and 5.8).

Next come spinal twists, forward bends, shoulder rolls forward and backward, and the cow and cat tilt (see Figures 5.9 and 5.10). Since children enjoy imitating animals, they easily come into a "table position" with hands and knees on the floor. Joy reminds them to keep their hands directly under their shoulders and both knees under their hips: "As we inhale, bring that tail bone up toward sky and let the belly hang down toward the earth. Looking forward, we exhale, com-

Figures 5.7 and 5.8. Spinal Movements

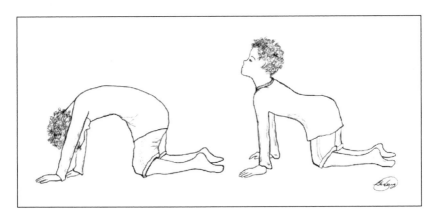

Figures 5.9 and 5.10. Cat and Cow Tilt

ing into cat tilt, bringing chin to chest, and arching the back towards the ceiling. Again, bring your tail up, coming into your cow, face forward. Let me see your shining faces. Let's bring sounds into the cow this morning. What does your cow say?" Many moos are heard. "What does your cat sound like? Let's hear those cat sounds." Making sounds is a good release for excess energy.

Good Vibrations

Within yoga traditions, different sounds are believed to stimulate specific energy centers called *chakras*. From a modern scientific viewpoint, making these sounds creates vibrations in different parts of the body. Sensors throughout the body register these vibrations and transmit this information through the interoceptive system we described earlier. As these messages reach the brain, they help to induce calmness and mental clarity. It is also possible that the vibrations produce healing effects in the body organs and tissues, but this has not yet been explored through modern science.

From the cat pose, it is easy to lower down in the child pose. Joy continued: "'Move your body back, bringing your hips all the way back to your heels, stretching arms forward and bringing your forehead down to the mat. Let's use that sound of the letter *m*. Big breath in . . . and . . . *m-m-m-m-m-m-m-m-m-m-m-m-m-m-m-m-m-m-m-m*'" (see Figure 5.11).

"'Bringing your body back up to table position, your head coming up to your shoulders, let's curl our toes under our feet. Whenever you're ready, lift your hips toward the sky, grounding your hands, getting your arms long, stretching. Your knees can be soft as you lower one heel down, then the other. One heel, and then the other, three times (see Figure 5.12). What kind of dog do you want to walk today?'

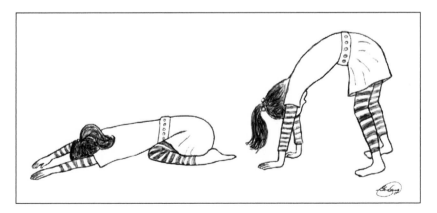

Figures 5.11 and 5.12. Child Pose and Downward Dog

They shout out, 'Beagle!—St. Bernard!—I'm walking my puppy!'" Joy continues: "'Now let's bring that dog into stillness. Let's be as still as a statue dog. Who can be the most still with their statue dog? Beautiful. Look between your hands. Walk your hands to your feet, your feet to your hands. Hanging like a rag doll, rotate slightly to your left, your right, and back to center. Let your head be heavy, your arms limp and loose, like noodles in your soup.'"

"They love to make sounds. All day long people tell them to be quiet. So I have them extend their arms up, up, and hold the breath, hold it then exhale with a whistle. Boys love to whistle." Joy demonstrated another pose used to blow off excess energy and focus attention. From a sitting pose, she leaned forward letting out the sound, "ha!" She explained, "Many of the boys don't talk about what has happened to them. They suppress it and as a result, they may have tightness in the throat. This helps."

Grounding

In yoga, grounding—feeling connected to the ground—promotes a sense of being anchored, secure, steady. For people with ADHD, whose thoughts and bodies tend to fly all over the place, grounding techniques help them feel more centered within their own body and more connected to the place where they are here and now. Joy continued: "Grounding through your feet, knees soft, begin to rise up, rise up, coming to stand, rolling shoulders back, opening the heart space. Grounding through your feet, lift up all the toes and allow them to spread. Slowly bring toes back down to earth."

When the Force Is with You

In Eastern traditions, the energy of the life force has many names. In yogic traditions it is *prana*, in Qigong it is *chi*, in Aikido it is *ki*. Whatever the name, this energy is intangible. Yet we are able to sense when we are more energetic and when we have lost our get-up-and-go. Our bodies generate and run on microvolts. In a sense, we are all living batteries of energy. However you conceptualize the energy in your body, awareness of that energy can be used in mind–body work for ADHD. Children with ADHD tend to be unaware of their own bodies, and this lack of awareness contributes to incoordination and lack of control over their physical actions. When children can think of the energy in the body as "The Force," they become interested in learning about it, feeling it, and using it—just like a Jedi knight.

Joy increases her students' awareness of energy by saying this: "Close your eyes in standing position. Feel *The Force* moving in your body. Maybe your fingers feel sparkly or your face feels warm or maybe another feeling. Just notice that."

Breathing Buddies

Joy described how she concludes her class: "We finish with each boy lying down with his breathing buddy—a Beanie Baby placed on the navel. On the inhale, they give the Beanie Baby a ride up, on the exhale, a ride down (see Figure 5.13). At first I only used Beanie Babies with the lower grades, but when the older boys saw, they wanted Beanie Babies, too, even the 12-year-olds. I have them imagine they are someplace special: 'Imagine you are lying in a park or on a cloud, just you and your Beanie Baby.' As I count slowly backward from 15 to 1 we make the image more real, watching the birds or the blue sky. Then I let them rest. Sometimes they roll to one side and just lie there holding onto their Beanie Baby" (see Figure 5.14).

Children are willing to do things that make them feel good. For the

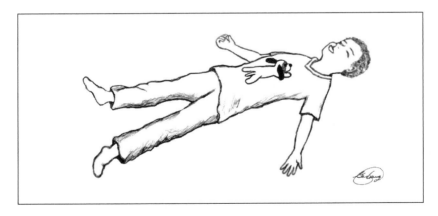

Figure 5.13. Breathing Buddies

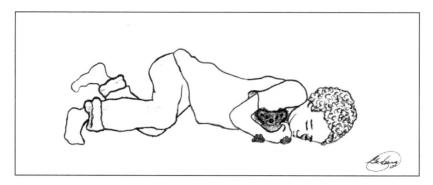

Figure 5.14. Rest

child with ADHD, feeling good could mean having a calm, quiet mind free from constant inner chatter; being able to keep track of what is going on instead of becoming confused or overwhelmed; having a small success that is recognized by praise; or feeling soothed, comforted, loved, happy, or safe. The key to yoga therapy is much more than instruction in techniques. It involves forming a bond of trust and closely observing each child's needs and responses to discover what makes him or her feel good enough that he or she wants to try more and more. Over time, starting with very simple brief activities, until the child's attention and physical skills improve, a complete program can be built to guide the child to better levels of mental, emotional, and physical functioning.

Yoga in the Classroom

Over the past 20 years, more and more schools have been adopting yoga programs. For children who respond to yoga classes with improved attention, calmness, and self-control, these benefits tend to carry over into their regular classrooms. Teachers note increased abilities to focus on schoolwork, complete assignments, behave appropriately in class, and relate to their classmates (Slovacek, Tucker, & Pantoja, 2003). Classroom teachers who participate in the children's yoga classes can learn how to use the same methods to help students calm down, maintain self-control, reduce impulsive behaviors, and sustain the focus they need to complete tasks. Yoga interventions in the classroom may take just a few minutes and can prevent having to deal with disruptive behaviors.

A Classroom Teacher's Point of View

Kim Sutherland, MEd, has been a special education teacher for 16 years. She worked with Joy Bennet for 2 years in a school for children with special needs. The boys in her fourth- and fifth-grade classes have ADHD, and most also have PTSD from emotional or physical abuse and neglect. Their behaviors are extreme. They have very little or no ability to regulate their emotional states or control their sudden impulses. These children often lose control, becoming violent, scream, throw chairs, assault others, and require physical restraint. They require so much attention that each class has six students and three teachers. Fortunately, most children with ADHD are able to attend regular schools. Although they may engage in disruptive behavior, it is usually to a lesser degree. Kim's description of the effects of yoga on severely affected children highlights the potential benefits for children who have milder forms of ADHD.

Kim explained: "Joy's yoga program helped the kids in many more ways than we imagined. We teachers took the classes with them. By watching the teachers do yoga in class, kids saw the teachers in a more collaborative way. We try to engage the kids to create a sense of community where we are all working together, students and teachers, towards educational and social developmental goals. Unfortunately, there are times when a child loses control, and we have to pin him or her down with physical restraint. As a result, kids tend to see teachers more as wardens than as educators, even though we are careful to process those experiences. In the yoga class students felt more comfortable and less intimidated by teachers. They wanted to sit near the teachers. It helped them to see us trying, getting frustrated with our own efforts to do the yoga, and having to find strategies to deal with our stress."

She continued: "Yoga was an *equalizer*. Everyone can do yoga—it doesn't matter what shape you're in, or how smart you are or aren't, or your level of learning and development. The yoga class was noncompetitive and fostered acceptance of each person regardless of his or her level of performance. Kids thrive on *consistency*. Yoga was so consistent and calming. They have no control over the rest of their lives, which are often noisy, scary, and chaotic. Children with abuse histories do not feel safe in their bodies. One way they may develop to protect themselves during abuse is to disconnect or dissociate from their bodies in an attempt to escape painful physical sensations. This disconnection can become habitual, creating unawareness, mistrust, and loss of control of the body. Yoga enables kids to feel safe in their bodies with gentle physical activities in a safe environment. At the same time, yoga helps develop directed *focus*. A simple example would be, 'Wiggle your toes. Now wiggle your hands.' This simple exercise requires mental focus and enhances body awareness. Within the structure, they have freedom to move. Your mat is your space. You stay in your space. You can move in your space. With yoga they became more aware of their bodies. They become better able to control their bodies and impulses, rather express their feelings by acting out physically, for example, by running, hitting, or kicking. Many kids required less frequent physical restraint, and when it was needed, they regained control more quickly.

"In regular class, these children are usually distracted, restless, tapping their pencil or kicking the wall. Physical postures release and channel excess energy while encouraging mental focus. By the end of the relaxation practices, they are calm and still. When their minds wander, they may think of something distressing from the past. Trauma memories can overtake their minds, triggering fear, trembling, rage, or physical violence. In Joy's class, whenever we noticed a child starting to become agitated, we could often prevent a meltdown by having him or her do yoga breathing for a few minutes. If a child started to get frustrated with schoolwork, we would offer him or her a chance to practice yoga in a separate place, either alone or with a teacher. The children usually calmed down quickly with yoga breathing or sometimes by doing whatever yoga postures they liked. Processing and praise would follow: 'You did a really good job calming yourself down. How do you feel?'

"The kids really enjoyed and looked forward to the yoga sessions. They asked for a way to practice at home. Joy created a booklet for them with pictures of the different poses to guide them. Some families bought their children yoga mats. Others were given a mat by the school. The teachers also looked forward to yoga as a time to relax and decompress during their very wearing work day. They also learned from the yoga teacher new ways to observe, understand, and help the children. Joy's ability to create a compassionate atmosphere supported the school community."

As the parent of a child with ADHD, you may not have easy access to skilled yoga teachers or special schools. We wanted to give you an example of what can be achieved by a gifted yoga therapist working in a school with dedicated teachers willing to fully participate in her work in order to help extremely dysfunctional children. For children with milder forms of ADHD and for children with attentional problems in general, school yoga programs can be very beneficial. Let's look at current and future directions in research on yoga and the teaching of mental health hygiene in schools.

When to Choose Individual Yoga Therapy versus Group Yoga Classes

Most adults and children with mild ADHD can participate in yoga classes. However, a period of individual instruction may be necessary for those who have more severe inattention, hyperactivity, overreactivity, or concurrent diagnoses such as anxiety disorders, PTSD, obsessive–compulsive disorder, learning disabilties, neurodevelopmental problems, or Asperger syndrome (an autism spectrum disorder). These individuals first need private sessions to attain better levels of attention, physical control, and mastery of basic techniques before taking on the challenges, distractions, and stimulation of being in a group class.

TEACHING MENTAL HEALTH HYGIENE AND STRESS RESILIENCE IN SCHOOLS

Parents, teachers, and administrators are looking for new and practical methods to improve the abilities of children to cope with stress, regulate their emotions, reduce anger, focus attention, gain more self-esteem, develop better relationships, and achieve greater academic success. Rather than waiting until a child is far behind or in deep trouble, it makes more sense to take a preventive approach to foster positive emotional development and robust stress resilience.

Based on studies of the relaxation response (Benson, 1976; Benson and Klipper, 1982, 2000), mindfulness (developing the skills to concentrate on the activity one is performing and bring the attention back to that activity when distractions occur), and yoga, a program called Yoga Ed was developed and evaluated in elementary and middle schools (Slovacek et al., 2003). Classes included movement and awareness of breath, thought, emotion, behavior, and the environment. Students who participated in yoga class 1 or 2 hours per week over the course of 1 year showed improvements in self-esteem, behavior, physical health, academic performance, and attitudes toward school. Although there were limitations in this study, it gave support for further program development. Yoga Ed programs are now offered in many schools.

Sat Bir Khalsa, PhD, assistant professor of medicine at Harvard Medical School, and Jessica Noggle, PhD, Harvard Medical School Research Fellow, are studying methods to introduce effective yoga programs into school systems. Their long-range vision is to make education in stress resilience and *emotional hygiene* part of every child's education. Emotional hygiene includes methods to maintain mental health throughout life and to prevent the detrimental effects of stress and adversity. Funded by the Institute for Extraordinary Living at Kripalu Center for Yoga and Health (see Resources), Drs. Khalsa and Noggle completed a preliminary study of yoga in a suburban high school (Noggle & Khalsa, 2010). In this controlled study, 120 students in grades 9–12 were randomly assigned to either a Kripalu yoga class or regular physical education (PE) two to three times a week for about 45 minutes each session for one semester. The Kripalu program included a standard set of yoga postures, breathing practices, and relaxation/meditative techniques.

By the end of one semester, significant differences were found between the two groups. Students in the regular PE group showed increases in scores for negative mood, fatigue, inertia, tensions, anxiety, and confusion. At the same time, they showed a drop in scores for stress resilience and anger control. In contrast, students in the yoga group maintained or slightly improved their scores in these areas. In other words, the yoga intervention protected the students from whatever adverse experiences and stressors were wearing down the comparison group. This study suggests that a regular yoga program could prevent the decline in mental health and stress resilience seen in many high school students. In other words, yoga could serve as a method for mental hygiene.

Dr. Khalsa's group and others are conducting larger studies in schools with more diverse populations as part of their efforts to adapt programs to the needs of a wide range of students and to scientifically demonstrate the short- and long-term benefits of yoga. Funding is needed to study the effects these programs may have on the children's lives not only while they are in school, but also as they enter adult life. It is possible that by teaching stress resilience and emotion regulation from elementary through high school, children might have a significantly better chance to maintain their mental health, control their anger, improve their relationships, and attain greater success at school and at work. If this is so, as preliminary studies suggest, then we need to support the research efforts that are necessary to determine if yoga programs should be implemented in our schools.

HOW TO USE MIND–BODY PRACTICES TO REDUCE SYMPTOMS OF ADHD

Mind–body practices provide multiple benefits for all of the symptoms of ADHD we described in Chapters 1 and 2:

- The core symptoms of ADHD: inattention, hyperactivity, and impulsivity
- The three faces of ADHD: hypoarousal and impulse control problems, reward deficiency, and disorders of emotional regulation

Children learn to focus attention and awareness on their bodies in order to perform yoga postures. Learning to stay on a yoga mat and hold each position for a period of time helps reduce hyperactivity and impulsivity. The effect of yoga on the mind is to create a state of calm alertness that is a healthier, more balanced state of arousal. The effects of yoga practice are positive, pleasurable feelings, including a sense of peacefulness, relief from anxiety, and a sense of mastery. These good feelings, combined with positive feedback and praise from the yoga teacher, provide the rewards that motivate continued practice. By quieting and balancing the stress response system, yoga and breathing practices improve emotional regulation. For these reasons, we recommend that everyone with ADHD get involved in yoga and breathing practices, and we advise practitioners to consider adding mind–body practices to their ADHD treatment plans. Combining these practices with the complementary treatments described in the other chapters is even more effective.

Physical yoga should be slow-paced, calming, and at a level appropriate for each person's physical abilities. A combination of regular daily calming breath practices and intermittent stimulating practices (as needed for work and study) is effective for many people.

To move forward toward improvement through mind–body practices, we recommend the following steps:

1. Learn more about the different types of yoga programs available in your area.
2. Discuss your ideas about starting yoga with your doctor or your child's pediatrician or therapist. Make sure that you have no physical limitations that might be contraindications. Find out what your health care providers knows about your local mind–body teachers. Check the yellow pages and the Internet for programs.
3. Finding a teacher or program that's right for you or your child may require some time.

4. Interview the yoga teacher and observe a class. This will help you assess not only the level of the class, but also the personal style and character of the teacher. Look for a trainer who is patient, calm, kind, supportive, and available to talk.

5. If you or your child has special needs, discuss these with the yoga teacher and create a plan to address these needs.

4. Once you find a good teacher, it may take time—perhaps weeks or month—to see results. Be patient and stay with it.

5. Making time to practice yoga every day is also challenging, especially if you have children or are busy with schoolwork and activities. You may be able to manage it only three times a week. That would be a strong start. Make 7 days a week your goal, but give yourself flexibility on those inevitable impossible days.

6. Talk with your family about why you want to practice yoga and how you hope it will help. You may need your family's cooperation to help you carve out time for regular yoga practice.

7. If you find it difficult to stay with your practices, as many people do in the beginning, participate in a class at least once a week to give yourself support and reinforcement. You can also talk with your yoga teacher or therapist about ways to increase your motivation and remove obstacles to your practice.

FINDING OR CREATING YOGA PROGRAMS FOR ADHD

If your school does not offer yoga, bring it up at PTA meetings and with the school counselors and administrators. You are likely to find others who will agree that such a program would enrich the school. Form a committee to develop a program. There may be a teacher in your school who is already trained in yoga practices.

If your school has a yoga program, you could discuss your child's special needs with the yoga teacher to find ways for your child to participate in the available classes or to develop a special class for those who are not ready to join an established group. With increased interest and support from parents and educators, more yoga teachers will be trained to work with children, including those with ADHD.

Many organizations all over the world have developed yoga programs for children and adults. You will find a list of some of these in the following Resources section. Finding yoga therapists experienced in ADHD and programs specifically designed for children with ADHD is more challenging.

RESOURCES

The following resources provide information on mind-body practices through websites, organizations, journals, and books.

Websites for Organizations

Atlantic Canada's Yoga Teachers Association: www.yogaatlantic.ca.
   Central resource for yoga within Atlantic Canada, fosters professional yoga training through a network of yoga teachers representing all traditions and styles of yoga.
Art EXCEL Course: All Round Training in Excellence: www.artofliving.org.
   Self-development programs for children ages 8–13.
British Yoga Teachers' Association: www.britishyogateachersassociation.org.uk.
   Place to find yoga teachers and yoga teacher training in the UK.
The Center for Mind–Body Medicine: www.cmbm.org
   Global Trauma Relief Program trains mind-body teachers and community leaders to deal with stress and trauma of war and natural disasters. Offers training in mind-body medicine, nutrition, and integrative oncology (cancer treatment).
International Association for Human Values: www.iahv.org.
   International humanitarian, educational, non-governmental organization (NGO) partners with governments, educational institutions, other NGOs, corporations, and individuals, to develop programs for personal development and to encourage the practice of human values. Offers disaster relief programs worldwide.
International Association of Yoga Therapists: www.iayt.org.
   supports research and education in Yoga, a professional organization for Yoga teachers and Yoga therapists worldwide.
The International Yoga Federation and The World Yoga Council: www.worldyoga council.net/members.html.
   Provides information on leading yoga teachers and organizations.
Kripalu Yoga Center for Health and the Institute for Extraordinary Living: www.kripalu.org.
   Provides courses, workshops, teacher training, and research.

Mind & Life Institute: www.mindandlife.org.

Non-profit organization that seeks to understand the human mind and the benefits of contemplative practices through integrating knowledge from the world's contemplative traditions with findings from contemporary scientific study to relieve human suffering and advance well-being. This approach includes publication of dialogues with the Dalai Lama, research and training institutes.

Yoga Teachers' Association of Australia: http://www.yogateachers.asn.au/join-ytaa /benefits.html.

Professional yoga teacher association promotes high standards of teaching.

Yoga Alliance: www.yogaalliance.org.

Online community for registered yoga teachers to connect and communicate.

Youth Empowerment Seminar: www.youthempowermentseminar.org.

Yoga self-development programs for youth ages 14–18.

Other Websites, CDs, DVDs, and Newsletters

www.coherence.com.

Coherent breathing site by Stephen Elliot offers *Respire-1* CD with tracks for pacing respirations at five breaths per minute. Offers additional aids to enhance effects on the autonomic system.

www.gaiam.com

Website for Gaiam Yoga: yoga videos and DVDs for adults and children).

www.haveahealthymind.com.

Website of Dr. Richard P. Brown and Dr. Patricia Gerbarg provides information on Breath~Body~Mind training, courses, mind-body programs for disaster relief, Integrative psychiatry, updates, and a free newsletter.

www.joyfulbreath.com.

Joy Bennett offers individual and group yoga therapy and yoga programs for children and adults.

www.LetEveryBreath.com.

Systema training in Russian martial arts with Vladimir Vasiliev.

www.openfocus.com.

Les Fehmi provides courses and CDs for training in open focus meditation and biofeedback.

www.robertpeng.com.

Elixer Light Gigong Master Robert Peng provides Qigong teachings, courses, DVDs.

www.yogaed.com/about.html.

Yoga Ed. produces health/wellness programs, trainings and products for teachers, schools, parents, children and health professionals that improve academic achievement, physical fitness, emotional intelligence and stress management.

www.yogafordepression.com.
    Amy Weintraub's Yoga for Depression and LifeForce Yoga® site offers DVD programs at all levels, courses, newsletter.

www.yogaforthemind.info.
    Heather Mason's Yoga for the Mind offers classes, private consultations, a CD set of breathing practices, and a YouTube video on how to do ocean breath (*Ujjayi*): http://www.youtube.com/watch?v=PqR_HSDXuEk.

Books

Brown, R.P., & Gerbarg, P.L. (in press). *The Healing Power of the Breath*. Boston: Shambhala.
    Book and CD teach basic breath practices from our Breath~Body~Mind program. Readers learn how to use breathing practices for emotional self-healing, stress reduction, relationships, and enhanced performance at work and at play.

Feuerstein, G. (1998). *The Yoga Tradition: Its History, Literature, Philosophy, and Practice*. Prescott, AZ, Hohm Press.
    Classic comprehensive volume on yoga.

Murdock, M. (1987). *Spinning Inward. Using guided Imagery with Children for Learning, Creativity, & Relaxation*. Boston: Shambhala.
    Contains many appealing visualizations that add a creative dimension to practices for children.

Sumar, S. (1998). *Yoga for the Special Child*. Evanston, Il: Special Yoga Publications.
    A therapeutic approach for infants and children with Down Syndrome, cerebral palsy and learning disabilities.

Weintraub, A. (2004). *Yoga for Depression*. New York: Broadway Books.
    Inspirational description of Amy Weintraub's development of yoga practices for depression. Clear and scholarly presentation of yoga practices.

Williams, N. (2010). *Yoga Therapy for Every Special Child*. Philadelphia: Singing Dragon.
    Excellent descriptions of teaching yoga to children of all ages.

Journals and Magazines

ADDitude: www.additudemag.com.
    Excellent newsletter that covers many topics relevant to home, school, work, parenting, and relationships.

Australian Yoga Life: www.ayl.com.au.
    Magazine and website offers stories and articles about yoga. Information about yoga retreats, schools, teachers, and teacher training in Australia.

International Journal of Yoga Therapy: www.iayt.org/
    Peer-reviewed Journal of the International Association of Yoga Therapists
    includes scientific research and articles by yoga teachers and researchers.

The Yoga Journal: www.yogajournal.com.
    A yoga magazine with articles on yoga practices, music, and celebrities.

CHAPTER 6 OUTLINE

CHAPTER 6

Neurofeedback Therapy and Brain Stimulation[1]

Brain waves recorded on Electroencephalograms (EEGs) reflect the moment-to-moment brain functioning in ADHD, and they can be used to improve how the brain is working. With emerging technologies, people can learn how to improve their own brain waves to overcome many symptoms of ADHD. In this chapter we provide the information you will need to take advantage of these new treatments and to keep up with the many advances that will occur in the next few years.

In order to do mental work such as thinking, analyzing, understanding, attending, planning, organizing, and generating appropriate responses, the brain has to speed up its activity. One of the problems with the ADHD brain is that when it is time to concentrate and do mental work, the system *slows down* instead of speeding up. In other words, when it's time to go, it gets stuck. The cell assemblies shift to the wrong "gears" and generate slow waves (called *alpha*) instead of the faster waves (called *beta*) that are associated with active, concentrated thinking.

Using a variety of biofeedback methods, most people can learn how to change some of their brain waves. The results can be improve-

[1] We wish to thank Dr. Stephen Larsen, Dr. Rollin McCraty, Dr. Laurence Hirshberg, and Dr. Leslie Sherlin for their assistance in the preparation of this chapter.

ments in learning and behavior. Many of the mind–body practices we described in Chapter 5, particularly breathing practices, can also improve brain-wave activity. In this chapter we discuss other methods for correcting imbalances in brain wave patterns, including neurofeedback therapy, cranial electrotherapy stimulation, interactive metronome, heart rate variability feedback, coherence training, HeartMath®, and Early HeartSmarts®. Before learning more about these treatments, we first take a quick dip into the pool of scientific terms needed to follow the discussion.

WHAT YOU NEED TO KNOW ABOUT BRAIN WAVES

Knowing some basic information about brain waves is a key to understanding how and why brain stimulation techniques can improve brain function in ADHD. You will need this information to help you decide how these treatments could fit into an integrated approach and whether you want to pursue them.

Brain cells work by generating electrical activity. Electroencephalography uses electrodes attached to the scalp at specific locations to record the brain's electrical activity over a period of time, usually 20–40 minutes in clinical work. The electrical activity of a single neuron is too small to be picked up by one of these scalp electrodes. Instead, the EEG reflects the sum of synchronous activity of millions of neurons.

Figure 6.1. depicts the three frequencies being used the most in working with ADHD: theta, alpha, and beta. In people with ADHD, a common brain-wave imbalance involves too little fast activity (beta) and too much slow activity (alpha and theta). This reflects the tendency of the brain to run at a low speed when a higher speed is needed for alert, active, concentrated thinking.

Brain waves are divided into different types based on their frequency. The hertz (Hz) is the unit of frequency, that is, the number of cycles per second. One cycle includes one peak and one valley. So, for example, if you look at the graph of the theta waves (Figure 6.1.), you see about six peaks (indicating a frequency of 6 Hz) in the 1 second

Figure 6.1 *Brain-Wave Patterns*[a]

Theta Waves

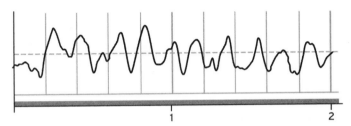

Theta is the frequency range from 4 to 7 Hz. Theta is seen normally in young children. It can appear during drowsiness or arousal in older children and adults. Theta also occurs with relaxed, meditative, and creative states. In ADHD there is too much theta when mental work has to be done.

Alpha Waves

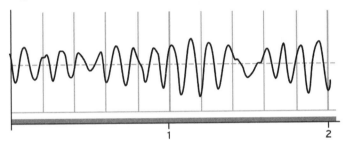

Alpha is the frequency range from 8 to 12 Hz seen mainly over the posterior areas of the brain on both sides. It emerges when the eyes are closed and the individual is alert but idle. Alpha diminishes when the eyes are open or during mental exertion. In ADHD there is too much alpha when the brain needs to do active mental work.

of the recording (the total on each EEG strip here is 2 seconds). This is within the defined range of 4–7 Hz for theta.

The peaks represent amplitude, that is, the sum of the current being generated by a large group of brain cells and recorded from an electrode placed at a particular spot on the head. As more and more brain cells shift into the same frequency, the amplitude increases to form a peak. If we think of a bandwagon carrying just one lonely saxophone player, no one will hear his or her music. But, as the other musicians jump onto that bandwagon and start to blow their horns,

Beta Waves

Beta frequency range is 12–28 Hz. It is distributed symmetrically on both sides, mainly in the frontal area. Low-amplitude beta with multiple varying frequencies often occurs with active, busy, or anxious thinking and with active concentration. It becomes the dominant rhythm when people are alert, or anxious, or have their eyes open. In ADHD there is not enough mid-beta when active concentration and mental work is needed. Specifically:

- 12–15 Hz, the slow beta range along the motor strip, is called the *sensorimotor rhythm* (SMR).
- 15–18 Hz is mid-beta and is associated with concentration or thinking.
- 18–28 Hz is hi-beta and usually indicates anxiety, trauma, hypervigilance, or insomnia.

Note. Different systems may use slightly different frequency ranges to delineate the types of brain waves.

[a] Printed with permission of Leslie H. Sherlin, PhD

the volume (amplitude) will rise higher and higher. The amplitude peaks each time they all blow as hard as they can, and it subsides (into a valley) each time they ease off. Similarly, as more and more cells jump on the bandwagon by generating the same frequency, the amplitude of that frequency rises. A band playing "When the Saints Go Marchin' In" will produce more frequent sound peaks than a band softly playing back-up for a soulful love song.

BRAIN WAVES AND ELECTRICAL POTENTIALS IN ADHD: JUST A PINPRICK

Historically, research and treatment have focused on abnormal activity in the alpha, beta, and theta frequencies associated with ADHD.

Table 6.1 Guide to Brain Waves: Comparison of EEG Frequencies

Type	Frequency	Location	Associated Activity *Imbalances Seen in ADHD*
Delta	up to 4 Hz	frontally in adults, posteriorly in children	• normal in adults during slow wave sleep • normal in babies • during some continuous attention tasks
Theta	4–7 Hz	Found in locations not related to task at hand	• *In ADHD there is too much Theta when mental work has to be done* • normal in young children • seen during drowsiness in older children and adults • seen during relaxed, meditative or creative states or when the brain is just idling • associated with inhibition such as when a person is actively trying to repress a response or action
Alpha	8–12 Hz	posterior regions of head; central sites at rest	• *In ADHD there is too much alpha when mental work has to be done* • Relaxed, reflecting, closing the eyes • associated with inhibition control
Beta	12–28 Hz 12-15 Hz 15-18 Hz 18-28 Hz	both sides frontal, symmetrical	• *In ADHD there is not enough fast Beta when mental work is needed* • alert, working, active, busy thinking • Slow Beta called Sensorimotor rhythm (SMR) • Mid-Beta with active concentration or thinking • Hi-Beta usually indicates anxiety, trauma, hypervigilance, or insomnia.
Gamma	28–100 +	Somatosensory cortex	• Neuron network activity during cognitive or motor functions • sensory processing that combines two different senses, such as sound and sight • short term memory matching and recognition of objects, sounds, or tactile sensations

More recently, scientists have become interested in *evoked potentials* (EPs). Evoked potentials are like your response to being pricked with a pin—"Ouch!" The pinprick is an event or stimulus. Whenever an event occurs, the brain responds within a certain time frame (time-locked), usually measured in milliseconds. We could measure how long it takes you to say *ouch* after you are pricked with a pin. You probably don't wait 15 minutes. You let loose with the *ouch* about 1 second after the pin penetrates your skin. We could measure the time it takes you to respond by repeating the pinprick at regular intervals, measuring how long it took for each *ouch*, adding up the times, and taking the average. We would discover that your *ouch* is time-locked, that it occurs within a specific time frame following the event of the pinprick. EPs occur in a certain time frame in response to the "prick" of a stimulus. The stimulus could be a painful sensation (e.g., the pinprick) or a flashing light or a repeating sound.

Rather than just recording the EEG as the brain tools along on its own, the brain is stimulated to respond to a repeating signal, such as a light flashing, at a certain rate. The EP is the electrical response of the brain to the sensory stimulus, in this case, a flashing light. *Slow cortical potentials* (SCPs) are event-related potentials that reflect preparation for the activation of large groups of cells. As the brain prepares to respond to a stimulus, we can think of an SCP as being the "Get ready, get set," before the "Go!" Table 6.2 summarizes some commonly used neurofeedback training protocols.

Neurofeedback Therapy (Neurotherapy)

Neurofeedback therapy, also called neurotherapy, trains patients to become aware of and influence their state of alertness based on real time EEG brain wave recordings. Sensors on the scalp are connected to computer software that records the brain's electrical activity in the form of an EEG. While the brain activity is being monitored on the EEG, different kinds of feedback are given. As the person responds to the feedback, for example, information or images on a computer screen, changes occur in the EEG which are fed into the training program. The training program feeds the information back to the person

Table 6.2 Commonly Used Neurofeedback Training Protocols

---

1. Theta/Beta training:
   a. decrease theta slow waves (4–8 Hz)
   b. increase faster beta waves (13–25 Hz)
2. Sensorimotor rhythm training
   a. increase slow beta (12–15 Hz)
3. Slow Cortical Potentials (SCP)
   a. Improve self-regulation of slow cortical
      potentials

---

using objects or games on a computer screen or, as in more recent developments, radio carrier waves.

Theta–Beta Training

As an example, theta–beta training uses a screen on which something changes in response to a change in the user's brain waves, as recorded from a sensor, usually on the vertex (top of the head) in this protocol. It can be as simple as two bars on a computer screen. The challenge is to make the bar on one side of the screen shorter by reducing theta activity, while at the same time making the bar on the other side of the screen taller by increasing beta activity. The person is also instructed to reach a relaxed yet attentive state of mind. The feedback is seeing the changes in the height of the bars. Over time, the person learns to decrease theta and increase beta without having to use the computer screen. Elaborate, colorful computer games have been developed to be fun and engaging for children. In another example of neurofeedback therapy, the person may sit in a chair and simply look briefly at a small beam of light that provides the feedback (Robbins, 2000; Fehmi & McKnight, 2001).

The original neurofeedback studies used a flashing light signal until it was discovered that the therapeutic effect was due to radio frequencies, not the light. More recently, neurofeedback therapy has been using radio frequencies as carrier waves such that modifications of the patient's own EEG can be used as the feedback signals. Just as vocal vibrations are superimposed on a radio carrier wave to produce the sounds we hear on a radio, so too, the EEG signal is superimposed on a radio frequency carrier wave. Len Ochs developed the low energy neurofeedback system (LENS; previously called *Flexyx*), using the slightly modified electrical signals from the patients' EEGs to provide feedback to the brain using low-energy radio carrier waves at a level of intensity far below those of a cell phone (Glieck, 1988; Ochs, 2006). This quick, painless procedure requires minimal cooperation and is easily tolerated even by young children. However, it does require multiple treatments over a period of time. LENS has been reported to reduce symptoms of ADHD, PTSD, affective disorders, pain syndromes, chronic fatigue, and fibromyalgia in many cases (Larsen, 2006; Larsen, Harrington, & Hicks, 2006). Randomized controlled studies are needed to validate these positive clinical reports.

Slow Cortical Potential Training

Slow cortical potentials (SCPs) are the result of the electrical change that occurs when a large group of nerve cells (*assemblies*) are activated. When the SCP is shifted in the negative direction, cell assemblies have a lower threshold of excitation; in other words, they are more easily activated, more responsive to events or stimuli. When the SCP is shifted in the positive direction, cell assemblies have a higher threshold and are more difficult to activate (Leins et al., 2007).

Picture a horse having to jump over a hurdle in training for a race. If the hurdle (threshold) is too high, the horse can't gallop forward. If the horse is not strong enough to clear the hurdle, the top bar has to be lowered so that the horse can continue training. Children with attention problems have reduced shifts, in the negative direction, in cell assemblies in anticipation of a task. This means that when the ADHD brain gets ready to respond to a task, the threshold of excitation may not be low enough for the cell assemblies to be activated and do whatever mental work is needed. This can result in poor performance in reading, writing, math, comprehension, or any other mental task. Studies of children have shown that they can learn to regulate their SCPs through neurofeedback therapy (NFT). For example, after SCP training, 23 children with ADHD (ages 8–13) showed improvements in attention, IQ tests, and behavior. These improvements were sustained when they were retested 6 months later (Strehl et al., 2006).

CASE EXAMPLES

Dr. Stephen Larsen, director of the Stone Mountain Center for Counseling and Biofeedback near New Paltz, New York, has helped thousands of clients with ADHD, learning disabilities, developmental disorders, seizures, and brain injury (see Resources at the end of the chapter). Dr. Larsen described the treatment of 100 of his cases using the LENS technique in his book *The Healing Power of Neurofeedback* (2006). We are fortunate to be able to collaborate with him for the benefit of our patients. Dr. Larsen is a skilled psychologist as well as a biofeedback specialist who treats both children and adults. The following are two cases in which Dr. Larsen's neurotherapy contributed to the success of our integrative approach.

The Bull in a China Shop

Nigel was adopted from a hospital nursery. His adoptive father, a business executive, suffered from lifelong drinking problems and mood instability. He described his adoptive mother as a career-obsessed media personality. Nigel felt "driven like a motor" and was very distractible. His ADHD had been diagnosed when he was 8 years old. As a child, he was constantly banging into things or dropping, bumping, and breaking whatever wasn't glued down. Even as an adult he was physically uncoordinated. Despite many years of medication trials and psychotherapy, fundamentally, he didn't think he was much better than he had been during childhood.

Nigel grew to be a tall, handsome young journalist. His previous psychiatrist had put him on Adderall for ADHD, but he continued to be distractible and to have terrible rages. Lisa, his fiancée, dreaded those rages.

When I (Dr. Brown) began to work with Nigel, I put him on a low dose of a stimulant, Ritalin, combined with the herb, *Rhodiola rosea.* As his rages came under control, Nigel began to like himself much better. He still complained that he had to smoke marijuana to calm down and sleep because the stimulant medications revved him up too much. He was also working with a psychotherapist who specialized in treating ADHD.

Thinking that Nigel might benefit from a course of neurotherapy, I referred him to a biofeedback specialist, Dr. Stephen Larsen. During the evaluation, Dr. Larsen gave Nigel a subjective symptom rating scale in which he rated the severity of his problems on a scale from 1 (no problems) to 10 (worst problems). He had high scores: 9 for explosiveness, 8 for hyperkinesis (feeling like a motor running constantly), 7 for distractibility, 6 for insomnia, and 6 for mood instability. He also mentioned a lifelong problem with being "clumsy." Nigel was delighted when Dr. Larsen told him the medical term for clumsiness, *dyspraxia,* meaning difficulty in carrying out intended movements or motor tasks, even after one has tried repeatedly to learn them. Nigel's eyes lit up. "That's right on! I have to tell you that as a journalist I always prefer a Latinate term to a word as crude and ugly as *clumsy*! From now on I will tell people I suffer from *dyspraxia*!"

Dr. Larsen described Nigel's treatment: "While Dr. Brown continued to manage the meds, we began our brain mapping and treatment. We were used to seeing quick results with LENS, but we were also familiar with how difficult adult ADHD can be to treat. Frankly, we were surprised at Nigel's rapid response. After the first session he reported sleeping very well, even in an unfamiliar place (the B&B near our office). He told us the following morning, 'There was less chatter in my head.' Lisa, his fiancée, said that 'Nigel just woke up and was more present and aware.' Over the next several weeks there were ups and downs. At first the dyspraxia worsened, but then it got better. He noticed that his executive functions (his abilities to plan, organize, follow through, and get things done) improved. Nigel also began to make better progress in psychotherapy—for example, realizing how self-centered he'd been and vowing to be more attentive to Lisa's feelings and needs.

"At Dr. Brown's request I gave Nigel HeartMath training [see below]. To further balance Nigel's stress response systems, Dr. Brown taught him coherent breathing. HeartMath and the breathing practice increased Nigel's calmness and composure in the stressful environment where he worked. Dr. Brown started Nigel on SAMe (see Chapter 4) and continued a tiny dose of Ritalin (10 mg/day). Nigel really liked how he felt on this combination—alert, focused, calm, energetic, but not revved up. Dr. Brown continued fine-tuning his regimen by adding to the Ritalin another herb, *Eleutherococcus senticosus*, and a nootropic, aniracetam (see Chapter 3). He felt best using *R. rosea*, SAMe, *Eleutherococcus senticosus*, and aniracetam on most days and only taking the Ritalin occasionally when needed.

"Throughout this time Nigel continued neurofeedback therapy once every 1 or 2 weeks. He described feeling better without the amphetamine medications: 'I can deal with the stress at work. I stayed calm, even when we were moving to a new office and a new apartment at the same time. When I feel myself becoming irritated, I just bark once and then it's over. Lisa and I are getting along better than ever. Everything is soaring now, everything I want is happening.'

"Eight months after starting neurofeedback treatments, Nigel's self-assessment scale confirmed his progress: 1 for explosiveness; 0 or 1 for hyperkinesis; 0 for distractibility; 2 for insomnia; 0 for mood instability. By the 10th month of treatment all of the self-assessment scores were 0. I noticed that Nigel was moving quite gracefully and comfortably in the office. 'You know, you don't look very clumsy to me at all,' I quipped. 'Please,' he parried, 'don't you mean my *dyspraxia* has dwindled away?' Touché!

"Nigel continued to see Dr. Brown every couple of months. Eleven months and 28 LENS treatments from the start, we were very happy to see him finish and say 'Goodbye.' Nigel was as surprised and pleased by the outcome as we were. He hadn't asked to have ADHD in the first place, but he had taken the bull by the horns, and brought it to its knees! Eventually Nigel and Lisa got married. Now he is enthralled with their 18-month-old son."

When You're Hot, You're Hot

Gary was a very serious, polite, soft-spoken young man who looked at the floor when talking about his problems. About to graduate from parochial high school with mediocre grades, he was terrified of going to college because, "Words don't get off the page into my mind." Stimulant medications such as Adderall, Ritalin, Provigil, and Focalin had helped his attentional problems, but they also escalated his anxiety, prevented him from sleeping, and made his mind race around like a mechanical toy on a track.

Dr. Brown's approach, using a small dose of Provigil combined with omega-3 fatty acids, vitamins, minerals, and tyrosine (an amino acid), had helped Gary feel better, but he was still struggling with school-work. Dr. Brown decided to refer Gary to Dr. Larsen for an evaluation regarding the possible use of neurotherapy. The initial brain map showed slow brain waves in the frontal area of the cortex and a "hot spot" at the back of the brain where the brain-wave amplitudes were twice as high as normal. Hot spots usually appear on the brain map in areas where there has been a focal injury to the brain. When asked about any brain injuries, Gary recalled being hit by a car and thrown into the air when he was 10 years old. He was knocked unconscious and hospitalized for 4 days. This brain injury probably explained why Gary had not responded well to medications or other treatments.

Gary's initial subjective assessment revealed high scores: 10 for concentration problems, 10 for learning difficulties, 10 for procrastination, 10 for irritability (especially to noise), 7 for anxiety, 7 for lack of stamina, and 5 for sleep disturbance. After 20 weekly neurotherapy sessions, his scores improved: 5.5 for concentration; 5.5 for learning difficulties; 4 for procrastination; 2.5 for anxiety; 4 for lack of stamina; 8.5 for irritability (noise); and 0 for sleep disturbance. With better sleep, Gary had more energy. He became less anxious, more self-confident, and more optimistic in looking forward to college.

This case shows how a head injury can complicate the treatment of ADHD. If a person is not responding well after a series of appropriate treatment attempts, then it is time to look deeper into the situation. Head injuries are extremely common, particularly in children. They are often forgotten and not mentioned until a clinician jogs the person's memory years later. Even relatively mild concussions can bruise the brain and cause some permanent damage when the soft brain tissue bumps up against the inside of the hard boney skull. Fortunately, neurotherapy can help improve recovery from brain injury as well as ADHD.

STUDIES OF EEG BIOFEEDBACK

Excess theta (slow rhythms) low quality alpha, and reduced beta (faster rhythms) have been noted on EEGs of people with ADHD. This cortical slowing may reflect sluggish activity, for example, in the attention and inhibitory circuits we discussed in Chapter 2. Promising results have been reported using neurotherapy to increase alpha and/or beta rhythms, but further studies are needed (Lubar, Swartwood, Swartwood, & O'Donnell, 1995; Nash, 2000; Ramirez, Desantis, & Opler, 2001).

In a 12-week nonrandomized study of children with ADHD between the ages of 8 and 12 years, 22 children were given neurotherapy and 12 were treated with a stimulant medication, methylphenidate (Ritalin). Children whose parents preferred an alternative to medication were assigned to neurotherapy treatment. Both treatments significantly improved scores on ADHD assessments and attention and behavior in school (Fuchs, Birbaumer, Lutzenberger, Gruzelier, & Kaiser, 2003).

One hundred children with ADD/ADHD, 6–19 years old, were treated for 1 year in an outpatient program where they all received methylphenidate (Ritalin), and academic support at school, and the parents received counseling. EEG biofeedback therapy was also given to 51 of the participants. Post-treatment testing while using Ritalin showed significant improvement in the symptoms of ADHD. However, at 1-year follow-up, only those children whose parents employed consistent reinforcement strategies at home and who had received EEG biofeedback sustained these gains when tested without Ritalin. There was also significant reduction in cortical brain-wave slowing only in patients who had received EEG biofeedback (Monastra, Monastra, & George, 2002). These findings would be strengthened by a fully randomized study.

In a controlled study of 18 children with ADD/ADHD, 6 of whom also had learning disabilities, the children were randomly assigned to two groups. One group was given EEG biofeedback once a week for 40 weeks, and the other group was put on a waiting list. Children who received EEG biofeedback had a 28% decrease in inattention compared to a 4% increase in the wait-list group (Linden, Habib, & Radojevic, 1996). Although this was a small study, it provides additional evidence for the benefits of EEG biofeedback for children with ADD, ADHD, and learning disabilities.

The effects of neurofeedback training, including both theta–beta and slow cortical potential training, were compared to a computerized attention skill training program in a large, multicenter, randomized, controlled study of 103 children with ADHD. The children treated with neurofeedback showed significantly greater improvements on measures of ADHD, behavior at home, and performance of homework (Gevensleben et al., 2009). Six months later, 61 of these children were available for follow-up retesting to determine if their improvements were long-lasting. On average, the benefits were sustained. Of the children who had received neurofeedback training, 50% showed a reduction of 25% or more on a standardized ADHD test, compared with 30.4% of the children in the attention skill training group (Gevensleben et al., 2010). This study provides strong support for the use of neurofeedback training as a complementary treatment for many people with ADHD. We anticipate further improvements in the effectiveness of neurofeedback protocols as the techniques are studied and adapted to the needs of individuals.

In people with ADHD, stimulant medications are believed to improve attention by increasing activity in dopaminergic neurons in the prefrontal cortex. Naturally, the question arose: Does neurotherapy have a similar effect? This question was addressed by a group at the University of Montreal where they documented changes in the functional magnetic resonance imaging (fMRI) of 15 children given 40 one-hour neurofeedback sessions during a 15-week study. The brain images showed an increase in activity within the anterior cingulate gyrus, an area of the prefrontal cortex that is associated with attention, concentration, and impulse control. The study also found significant correlations between the increased brain activity on fMRI and improvements in scores on tests of attention and concentration, as well as parent ratings of attention and hyperactivity (Lévesque, Beauregard, & Mensour, 2006).

WHAT NEW TECHNOLOGIES CAN DO FOR ADHD AND LANGUAGE DIFFICULTIES

Language difficulties can occur in any population, but they are more frequent in people with ADHD. The following is an example of a man who had symptoms of ADHD, but who sought treatment for a more distressing condition: stuttering. It is possible that in this case quieting the right prefrontal cortex stopped the stutter. His story also shows how rapidly new treatments are being developed as scientists and clinicians figure out how to use the flood of new information about how the brain works with the new technologies that are available.

Running was the one place where Jim felt he excelled. Having ADHD and a stutter, Jim often felt embarrassed and ashamed. Running set him free. As part of a national championship running team, he had the honor of carrying an Olympic torch through three states. That torch became his prized possession.

After retiring from his job as an engineer, Jim wanted to fulfill his lifetime dream of coaching sports teams, but he was terrified that he would stutter while making a call on a play. It was difficult enough to stammer, to have people treat him as stupid, to be disrespected because of stuttering, but the dread of looking foolish in an arena filled with fans overwhelmed him with anxiety. For 6 months he tried stimulant medications, but they caused nausea and dry mouth while doing nothing for his symptoms. Finally, he consulted a neurotherapist, Dr. Laurence Hirshberg, director of the Neurodevelopment Center at the Alpert Medical School of Brown University. He was given treatments for ADHD, memory, and stuttering. The treatments directed at improving his brain-wave balance reduced his forgetfulness.

For the stuttering, Dr. Hirshberg's strategy was based on research findings of increased activation in the right prefrontal cortex compared to the left during speech in stutterers. Since the left prefrontal area, called Broca's area, is considered to be predominant in speech, Dr. Hirshberg thought that the excess activity of the corresponding area on the right side could be creating interference, resulting in stuttering. He therefore applied neurotherapy to increase alpha (slow resting frequency) activity in the right prefrontal area to deactivate it (i.e., put it to rest). The response was unexpectedly rapid. After the first 15-minute session, Jim experienced no stuttering for 24 hours. After the second (30-minute) session, he was fluent (stutter free) for 2 days. After the third (1-hour) session, he was even more fluent for 4 days. With neurotherapy the effects usually last longer with increased training. When I (Dr. Gerbarg) interviewed Jim, he talked for 40 minutes with no actual stuttering. There were some brief periods of hesitancy in his speech, but overall he spoke quite well. For the first time, Jim is feeling hopeful and gaining self-confidence as he waits to see what further progress he will make with neurotherapy. If you are interested in following Jim's progress, Dr. Hirshberg posts updates on his blog (see Resources at the end of the chapter).

WHO IS MORE LIKELY TO BENEFIT FROM NEUROTHERAPY?

You are probably wondering if neurotherapy works for everyone or if there are some criteria to use in deciding whether or not to try this approach. Based on our combined experience and the available research, we have identified some general benchmarks you and your doctor can apply in deciding whether to pursue neurotherapy treatment.

- Based on EEG patterns. At this time, studies are showing that people who have increased theta or theta–beta ratios are more likely to benefit from treatment with stimulant medication, neurotherapy, or both (Sherlin, Arns, Lubar, & Sokhadze, 2010).
- Based on clinical symptoms. Current research suggests that neurofeedback is most effective for inattention and impulsivity. When

the main problem is hyperactivity, medication is a better option (Sherlin et al., 2010).

- Based on the presence of other disorders. Individuals with ADHD and a learning disability, brain injury, seizure disorder, or pervasive developmental disorder may benefit from the addition of neurotherapy to their treatment programs.

- Based on medication response. Neurotherapy should be considered for people who show:

1. Less than complete response to stimulant medication
2. Unwillingness to take stimulant medication
3. Intolerable side effects in reaction to stimulant medication

Despite many positive reports on the benefits of neurofeedback therapy for ADHD in both adults and children, many health care professionals are not familiar with it or do not yet accept its validity. In part this is because much of the early literature was based on case reports or nonrandomized studies. However, the quality of research is improving, increasing the solid evidence base to support these treatments (Monastra, 2008; Sherlin et al., 2010). Through research and greater clinical experience, more specific, targeted, effective treatments are evolving.

The main advantages of neurofeedback treatments are that they are painless, very low in side effects, beneficial in about 75% of cases when provided by a well-trained clinician, and the effects have been shown to last 6 months or more following a course of treatment. Some individuals are highly sensitive to neurofeedback. In such cases, the treatments may need to be briefer in order to minimize adverse reactions. Side effects may include headache, nausea, dizziness, sleepiness, or agitation. In contrast, medications have a higher rate of side effects and the benefits are lost when the medications are discontinued. The main disadvantages of neurofeedback are the need for frequent (one to three times per week), prolonged (2–12 months) treatments. This is costly, especially because neurofeedback is not yet covered by many insurance companies.

The International Society for Neurofeedback Research maintains a website with excellent information, articles on new developments, references, conferences, training workshops, and help in locating certified neurofeedback practitioners: www.isnr.org.

CRANIAL ELECTROTHERAPY STIMULATION

Cranial electrotherapy stimulation (CES) uses microcurrents, very low voltage electrical signals, applied to the head to improve brain function. CES has been used for over 40 years in Europe, the United States, and other countries to treat depression, anxiety, sleep disorders, headaches, pain, and to relieve spasticity in children with cerebral palsy. Two studies found that CES increased attention and concentration in normal adults (Hutchinson, Frith, Shaw, Judson, & Cant, 1991; Southworth, 1999). Clinical reports of benefits in treating ADHD are appearing, but controlled studies are needed to validate these promising findings.

Many cases do better when CES is combined with other treatments as was reported in the case of a nine-year-old boy with anxiety, dyslexia, and ADD (Overcash, 2005). The child was described as nervous, disorganized, and having frequent stomach aches and headaches due to anxiety about going to school. In the third grade, despite tutoring and working with a speech and language pathologist, he could not recognize all the letters of the alphabet and was reading at a Kindergarten level. Changing his Ritalin to Concerta and using Project Read reading program five days a week for three months produced no improvement. At that point the parents agreed to Dr. Overcash's recommendations to discontinue medication and begin Alpha-Stim CES for one hour every morning and evening to reduce anxiety and ADD symptoms. In addition he prescribed neurotherapy using the ROSHI/BrainLink one hour twice a week during his sessions with the reading specialist to improve his concentration and ability to learn. The parents and teachers began to report that the boy was more "settled' and easier to work with after CES treatments. He was also better able to concentrate and learn. By the end of 6 months treatment, his overall IQ increased from 97 to 112 with substantial improvements in concentration and memory. Reading improved to a third grade level, spelling to a fourth grade level, and math to a fourth grade level. The stomachaches and headaches stopped as he became less anxious. Follow-up two years after discontinuing neurotherapy showed that the benefits were maintained.

In clinical practice, we find that CES is often helpful for people with ADHD because it can improve attention, reduce anxiety, and relieve insomnia. Sometimes we get unexpected benefits, even in extremely difficult situations such as this—The Grinch that Stole Childhood.

For most children, each day is a new adventure. Children look forward to playing with their friends, learning new things, experiencing loving relationships, and enjoying feelings of pride as they master new skills. Severe ADHD can rob a youngster of the normal joys of childhood.

Daniel had had enormous problems all his life. In addition to ADHD, he suffered from depression, anxiety, insomnia, and multiple learning disabilities. Being impulsive, hyperactive, and inattentive, he repeatedly broke school rules, defied his father and school authorities, and cursed like a sailor. When his parents argued, he became agitated and had panic attacks. By the age of 11, he had developed an Internet pornography addiction. Other children could not stand to be around him, leaving him with no friends. He often thought, "Life is not worth living. I wish I wasn't alive."

Daniel was one of those children with ADHD who do not respond to stimulant medications. Trials of Ritalin, Adderall, Strattera, Atomoxetine, Trileptal (oxcarbazepine), serotonin reuptake inhibitors, and other antidepressants all failed. Treatment with two mood stabilizers (anticonvulsants), Depakote (divalproex) and Gabapentin (neurontin), yielded only slight improvement. Clonazepam and melatonin helped a little with sleep. Nothing worked well. His EEG during sleep revealed a severe parasomnia (an abnormal pattern of arousal) for which there is no known treatment.

Daniel started using marijuana and Ecstasy at age 13 and was hospitalized for a year in substance abuse treatment programs. He continued to abuse marijuana and was rehospitalized for 6 months. By this time he was being treated with multiple medications: Adderall, Seroquel (quetiapine), Zoloft (sertraline), Gabapentin, Remeron (mirtazapine), trazadone, and Zyprexa (olanzapine) with minimal improvements.

The family brought him to see me (Dr. Brown) for a consultation. I advised them to try a CES device (Fisher Wallace). The father's first reaction was, "How could that possibly help my son? You're supposed to be a doctor!" I finally convinced the boy and his parents to give this approach a try.

The CES began to work within the first month. Using level 2 (this device has four levels of intensity) for 20 minutes twice a day, Daniel was sleeping better, felt less anxiety, and noticed improvements in mental focus and energy. He admitted, "It's a real relief." Teachers began to compliment his work. The craving to abuse substances faded and he stopped using marijuana and quarts of caffeinated drinks. The dose of Adderall was reduced from 80 to 20 mg a day. He stopped seeking out Internet porn sites and became interested in more age-appropriate activities. For the first time in his life, he had friends who enjoyed hiking, canoeing, and camping with him.

Daniel told me, "I used to feel horrible waking up every morning. Now I wake up and look forward to the day. The CES helps with my organization, and I'm more independent. I don't think about death anymore. I'm thinking of getting a job."

Many people who feel better using a CES device begin to slack off, and Daniel was no exception. He came in 9 months later, sounding like he was getting worse again. He admitted that he was using the CES only once a day a few days during the week. I asked him, "Do you remember how awful it used to be? Do you want to go back to that?" Of course, he didn't. By increasing his use of the CES to once a day, *every day*, Daniel was able to remain well. When Daniel is inconsistent with CES treatment, his symptoms tend to worsen, but he has never slipped back to the state of severe dysfunction he suffered before treatment.

How Does Cranial Electrotherapy Stimulation (CES) Work?

Unlike electroconvulsive therapy (ECT), which uses high-amplitude currents, CES uses very small currents (less than in a cell phone) that do not cause seizures or convulsions. The currents are so low that usually the patient does not even feel them.

Studies show that 20 minutes of CES treatment increases the levels of neurotransmitters: serotonin, norepinephrine, beta-endorphins, GABA, and dehydroepiandrosterone (DHEA; Liss, & Liss, 1996). Norepinephrine is known to improve mental alertness, and serotonin is involved in the modulation of dopamine, learning, mood, and memory. In Daniel's case, there were clear improvements in alertness, learning, and mood. Although beta-endorphins are best known for their role in pleasure pathways, they are also involved in learning, memory formation, and the sense of reward (Routtenberg, 1978). In Chapters 1 and 2 we discussed reward deficiency syndrome, the inability to enjoy the usual sources of pleasure in life. Although it cannot be proven, it is certainly possible that the endorphin effects of CES contributed to changes in Daniel's ability to enjoy normal activities with his peers rather than having to seek excessively stimulating experiences. He acquired the ability to feel rewarded through recreational activities as well as from school achievements. The ability to experience pleasure and reward enabled him to wake up and look forward to each day. Increases in GABA are important because it is the primary inhibitory neurotransmitter in the brain. As such, it is essential for moderating and controlling over-reactivity. Such improvements in self-regulation may have helped Daniel to reduce his anger and control his destructive behaviors.

An additional mechanism that may contribute to the beneficial effects of CES is the stimulation of sensory nerves that could activate the parasympathetic system (calming). In Chapter 5 we discussed the importance of activating the parasympathetic system to balance the stress response system in ADHD. When these systems are well balanced, the result is calmness better problem solving, and improved emotion regulation, impulse control, and behavior. Furthermore, the CES also turns on the reticular activating formation, the network responsible for maintaining arousal, alertness, and attention.

We know that CES treatments can increase levels of neurotransmitters that are crucial for arousal, attention, learning, and memory. What we still don't know is exactly how the microcurrents bring about these changes in the neurotransmitters. Theories have been advanced, but so far, none has been proven (Klawansky et al., 1995). We do know that CES research is gearing up in major medical centers. This research should provide evidence that will confirm previous reports and our own positive clinical experience.

Are There Different Kinds of CES Devices?

There are eight FDA approved CES devices currently on the market. The most extensively studied are ALPHA-STIM® and the LISS Cranial Stimulator device (now marketed by Fisher Wallace). Most CES machines consist of a small handheld unit containing AA or 9-volt batteries. Current from the batteries travels through two wires to two electrodes that are attached to the head or earlobes. Treatments usually last 20 to 40 minutes. Depending on the severity of the condition, the CES can be used once or twice a day at a prescribed level of intensity. Results may be seen in 1 week, but may take as long as 2 months of daily use.

ALPHA-STIM® and the Fisher Wallace Stimulator have FDA approval for the treatment of anxiety, depression, and sleep disorders, and acute and chronic pain. Studies also suggest benefits for ADHD, headache, and obsessive–compulsive disorder. Further research evidence is needed to obtain approval for the specific FDA indication for use in ADHD.

A prescription from a physician is needed to order the CES. The advantages of this device are that it is very safe, even for young children, when used in the correct doses. It can be used to improve response to medications, to reduce the dose of medications, and sometimes to eliminate medications. The CES targets a wide range of symptoms associated with ADHD, including attention, hyperactivity, impulsivity, learning disorders, behavior problems, anxiety, depression, reward deficiency, and sleep. Although it is covered by only a limited number of insurance companies, it may still be worth the investment when one considers the ongoing cost of medications and doctor visits, as well as the toll that ADHD can take on the lives and happiness of the patient and family. Most companies have a money-back policy (minus processing charges) if the device is not effective within 1 to 2 months.

Who Could Benefit from Trying CES?

- Anyone with ADHD could benefit from a trial of Cranial Electrotherapy Stimulation (CES), particularly if there are symptoms of anxiety, panic attacks, phobias, agitation, insomnia, depression, processing problems, or procrastination.

- For those few people who may become overstimulated or agitated in reaction to CES, the duration of each treatment can be shortened, starting with 3 minutes and increasing very gradually, as tolerated.

- We recommend consultation and monitoring by a health care professional who is knowledgeable in the use of CES for adults and children.

CES can be combined with other treatments such as medication, neurotherapy, breathing practices, and remediation of learning disabilities for optimal results.

INTERACTIVE METRONOME: NEW TWIST ON AN OLD IDEA

For over 300 years metronomes have been used to drill timing into the hearts, hands, and minds of music students all over the world. Who could forget that relentless clicking of the metal lever swinging back and forth on its pyramidal throne? New computer technologies are harnessing the power of the metronome to help people with ADHD develop better motor planning, sequencing, and timing—all essential for attention, learning, and behavior control. For example, learning involves putting things in sequential order in the mind. Neural networks in the prefrontal and striatal areas are involved in timing and motor planning. These same areas were found to be hypoactive (below normal activation) on fMRI in children and adults with ADHD (Cubillo et al., 2010).

Preliminary studies are showing that computer-assisted technologies such as the Interactive Metronome® (IM) have the potential to improve attention and learning in ADHD and learning disabilities.

The IM system uses a computer, headphones, and two contact sensors. One sensor in the palm of a glove is triggered by clapping. The other sensor, a flat plastic back set on the floor, is triggered by pack foot tapping. When a subject hears a tone through the headphones, he or she claps or taps a response. The sensor transmits a signal to the computer, which notes how long the person took to respond. The IM analyzes the time delay and adjusts the guidance sounds—pitch of the tone and location (left-to-right) in the headphones—based on the accuracy of the tapping signals. Through thousands of repetitions, the person is trained to respond more rapidly and accurately to sequences of tones.

In a randomized study of 56 boys with ADHD, ages 6–12 years, those who were given 15 hours of IM training showed significantly greater improvements in attention, language processing, reading, and control of aggressive behavior (Shaffer et al., 2001). As with all treatments, the IM may not be as effective in all cases. For example, children with severe learning, cognitive, neurological, and emotional problems were excluded from the Shaffer study.

Multimodal Treatments

It is important to recognize that many ADHD children with learning problems can improve reading skills if given early intensive remediation. For example, combining IM with other interventions that are individually tailored for specific deficits, such as sensory stimulation, motor training, aerobics, and academic training, can be even more effective. A multimodal approach was given three times a week for 12 weeks to 122 children, ages 6–12, with ADHD. At the end of the 12-week training, tests found that 81% of the students showed significant improvements in parent symptom ratings, eye–hand coordination, overall academic performance, spelling, written expression, and listening comprehension (crucial for learning in class lectures). On a word-reading subtest, 84% gained 2 or more years of improvement in grade level. The main limitation of this study was that there was no long-term follow-up to see if these improvements were sustained (Leisman et al., 2010).

Bill struggled in college with ADHD, processing problems, procrastination, and depression. He was also not happy with his tennis backhand. Processing problems made it hard for Bill to absorb information during lectures. Due to procrastination, he fell behind in his coursework. When I (Dr. Brown) treated Bill with Adderall, it helped to some degree, but caused insomnia. Picamilon partly relieved the depression, and he seemed to benefit at first from neurofeedback therapy, but the effect plateaued. He tried R. rosea (Rosavin), SAMe, and numerous herbs. Although there was progress, he was still plagued with processing problems and procrastination.

I referred Bill for a course of IM and found that his processing improved. As a result, he showed increased reading comprehension, greater ability to absorb information from lectures, and better academic performance. Bill was also teaching part time. The IM treatment enhanced his ability to express and communicate ideas to his students. As for timing, he was thrilled to report a major improvement in his tennis skills, especially his backhand.

Fortunately, Bill was willing to try new things. When I suggested the CES LISS device (Fisher Wallace), he was game. As he increased the CES to level 2 for 20 minutes twice a day, his sleep got much better. After 6 weeks, his depression vanished, never to return. Since I didn't hear from him for 6 months, I called to see how he was doing. Bill was sailing through graduate school. He was still using the CES and taking Rosavin 100 mg twice a day, but he had stopped all other medications. As for procrastination—it was completely gone. Bill had never been so productive before. He was full of creative ideas and able to translate them into his work. He was "in the flow" and on his way to a rewarding career.

We don't always know at the outset which treatments are going to work best for a particular individual. Usually we have to work with each person over time to try a variety of approaches and combinations of treatments. Though this can be tedious or frustrating at times, it is well worth the effort to bring someone to his or her highest possible level of recovery and performance.

Additional large-scale controlled studies are needed to explore the potential benefits of IM as a complementary treatment for ADHD and learning disabilities. Nevertheless, given that IM is a noninvasive, time-limited treatment without adverse effects, there is enough research evidence and clinical experience to consider a trial of this emerging technology as an additional component in a multimodal treatment plan.

Who Could Benefit from treatment with the Interactive Metronome?

- People with ADHD and reading comprehension problems may benefit from IM combined with reading remediation.
- People with cognitive processing problems such as difficulty processing visual or auditory information or ideas.
- People with procrastination problems.

THE HEART–BRAIN CONNECTION: HEART-CENTERED BIOFEEDBACK

A variety of feedback methods can be used to improve brain function. In Chapter 5 on mind–body practices, we saw that breathing patterns can provide powerful feedback to the brain. Changing the patterns of breathing can affect brain function in numerous ways. You may wish to refresh your memory by revisiting Figure 5.3 (p. 148). Breathing affects interoceptive pathways from the body to brain areas involved in emotion regulation (limbic system) and cognitive functioning (thalamus and cerebral cortex). In addition, breathing can improve the balance between the sympathetic and parasympathetic nervous systems, shifting the brain into a relaxed, calm, attentive state. In this chapter, we reviewed the use of brain waves to provide feedback to retrain the brain. For example, theta–beta training involves shifting the balance of frequencies by reducing slow-wave theta and increasing fast-wave beta to correct deficiencies in ADHD.

The heart also provides feedback through the vagus nerves (interoceptive system) to brain areas involved in emotion and cognitive function. Figure 6.2 shows pathways carrying information from the

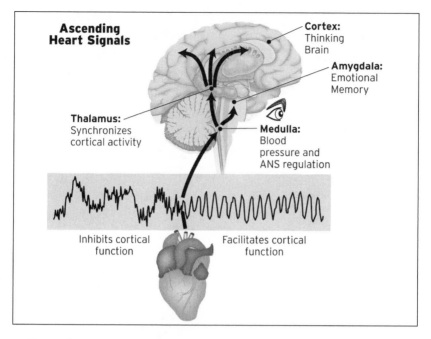

Figure 6.2. *Heart Activity Affects Brain Function*

This diagram illustrates afferent (ascending) pathways by which neurological signals generated by the heart are transmitted to key centers in the brain. These heart signals not only impact autonomic regulatory centers in the brain (e.g., the medulla), but also cascade up to higher brain centers involved in emotional and cognitive processing, including the thalamus, amygdala and cortex. Through these pathways, heart activity exerts a continuous impact on numerous aspects of brain function. As shown, when patterns of heart activity are erratic and disordered, such as during emotional stress, the corresponding patterns of neurological signals traveling from the heart to the brain produce an *inhibition* of higher cognitive and emotional functions. In contrast, the more ordered and stable pattern of the heart's input to the brain during positive emotions has the opposite effect—serving to *facilitate* cognitive function and reinforcing positive feelings and emotional stability. (From McCraty et al., 2006. © Institute of HeartMath) Reproduced with permission of R. McCraty and the Institute of HeartMath.

heart to the brainstem nuclei and from there to the amygdala (emotion processing and memory center) and the cerebral cortex (thinking area of the brain). These are the same brain areas we saw affected by voluntary changes in breathing patterns in Chapter 5.

New treatments are focusing on the heart itself to provide feedback to improve autonomic balance and brain function. *Heart rate variability* (HRV) is a measure of the change in the heart rate when we breathe in compared to when we breathe out. HRV is useful because it gives us a way to indirectly measure changes in the activity of the parasympathetic and sympathetic nervous systems. Many researchers utilize HRV as an indicator of the balance between the sympathetic (fight–flight) and the parasympathetic (safety, soothing) systems. Moreover, HRV can be used as feedback to enhance self-regulation. The electrical pattern on the left side of Figure 6.3 shows erratic changes in HRV compared with the smooth (coherent) pattern on the right side. Treatments that induce a shift toward a smoother, more coherent pattern are associated with improved cognitive function, emotion regulation, and positive emotions.

It is easy to monitor HRV using a simple sensor to register the pulse either from one finger or from an earlobe clip. Subtle changes in the variation in the pulse are computed to calculate moment-to-moment changes in HRV. Facing a computer screen, the subject places one finger inside the sensor, which is connected to a computer by a cable. As the computer registers changes in HRV, it creates different effects on the computer screen. When HRV increases, a rewarding response appears on the screen. By seeing the changes in images on the screen, the subject learns to shift how his or her brain is functioning to produce the desired result. In effect, the person learns how to create the state of mind associated with increased HRV, a state that is calm, alert, and more cognitively efficient.

We review two heart-centered treatments being used to treat ADHD and learning disabilities. One method uses HRV feedback. The other uses a combination of HRV, breath regulation, and mental focus on the heart and positive emotions.

Something Old, Something New

Mind–body practices have been used for thousands of years for emotion regulation, and computer-assisted technologies are now being rapidly developed for emotion self-regulation training. We are now seeing the convergence of ancient yogic and meditative

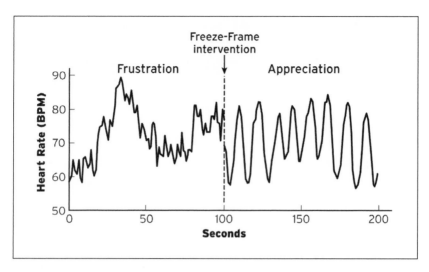

Figure 6.3. *Shift to Coherence*
The real-time heart rate variability (heart rhythm) pattern is shown for
an individual making an intentional shift from a self-induced state of frustration to a genuine feeling of appreciation by using a HeartMath positive
emotion refocusing technique ("Freeze-Frame intervention," at the dotted
line). Note the immediate shift from an erratic, disordered (incoherent)
heart rhythm pattern associated with frustration and emotional stress to
a smooth, harmonious, sine wave-like (coherent) pattern as the individual
uses the positive emotion refocusing technique to self-generate a feeling of appreciation. (From Bradley et al., Chapter III, 2007, © Institute of
HeartMath). Printed with permission of R. McCraty and the Institute of
HeartMath.

practices with modern neuroscience and computer technology. An
example of the synergy between ancient and modern techniques is
the Early HeartSmarts (EHS) program, a multimodal approach using
HeartMath with other heart- and breath-centered techniques. Before
describing this program, we need to understand a few concepts, starting with *psychophysiological coherence, intentional generation
of psychophysiological coherence*, and the HeartMath program. In
Chapter 5 on mind–body practices, we discussed coherent breathing,
one aspect of psychophysiological coherence. Recall that coherent
breathing uses a breathing rate of five or six breaths per minute and
is associated with increased HRV and an ideal balance between the
sympathetic and parasympathetic systems.

A simple way to think of *psychophysiological coherence* is as a state of mind–body synchrony. A more "scientific" definition would say that psychophysiological coherence reflects a state of increased synchronization, efficiency, and flexibility with and among physiological, cognitive, and emotional systems. Positive emotions, such as love, compassion, and gratitude, shift neurological systems toward greater psychophysiological coherence (Lloyd, Brett, & Wesnes, 2010).

Intentional generation of psychophysiological coherence occurs when a person intentionally shifts his or her attention to the physical area of the heart and deliberately brings to mind a positive emotion. Figure 6.3 shows the change from an erratic HRV during a negative emotional state of frustration to a smooth, coherent HRV when the person intentionally shifts to a positive emotion—in this case, appreciation (Bradley, McCraty, Atkinson, Arguelles, & Rees, 2007).

This is a "scientific" description of a method similar to the compassion meditation used for thousands of years by Buddhist meditators who focus the mind on compassionate thoughts to engender positive emotions and desirable physiological states. Brain-imaging studies are showing that such meditations and other mind–body practices can affect neurotransmitter systems, how the brain functions and, over many years, the architecture of brain structures involved in emotion processing and regulation (Lazar et al., 2005; Streeter et al., 2010).

The EHS program was designed to facilitate emotional self-regulation and social, emotional, and cognitive development in young children. It accomplishes these goals by teaching children how to recognize, understand, and regulate emotions; how to express positive feelings to family and friends; how to improve peer relations; and how to engage problem-solving skills. The program was tested in a controlled study of 309 preschoolers (3–5 years old). Children given the EHS intervention showed significantly greater improvements in social, emotional, physical, cognitive, and language development. The program was effective regardless of gender, ethnicity, or socioeconomic status (Bradley, Atkinson, Tomasino, Rees, & Galvin, 2007).

In a randomized controlled study, 38 children with ADHD (ages 9–13 years) were taught three HeartMath emotional self-regulation techniques. During each practice session the students shifted their focus of attention to the area around the heart while breathing easily and slowly, as if breathing through the chest area. HRV coherence feedback was used to help teach the "Heart Lock-In" technique to generate and maintain a positive emotional state. As described above, the HeartMath system used an earlobe clip pulse sensor to track HRV coherence and provide visual feedback through a computer game called the "Rainbow Game." At the same time, students listened to a music CD designed to promote physiological coherence and emotional balance. After 6 weeks of practice, the students given the HeartMath interventions showed significant improvements in cognitive functions and significant reductions in difficult behaviors. They learned to use the Heart Lock-In technique at home and at school to self-regulate their emotional states (Lloyd et al., 2010).

Programs that combine emotion regulation techniques, including HRV coherence feedback and the teaching of emotional awareness, intentional generation of positive emotions, and methods to increase psychophysiological coherence are being tested in school systems. As experience is gained, the programs will become even more effective with adaptations for specific needs of students. Similar techniques are already in use within a variety of therapeutic mind–body programs for adults (see Chapter 5). Such programs can be beneficial at any age, but they may be most effective during childhood when the neural connectivity has a higher degree of plasticity (capacity for change). Early intervention could correct neurophysiological imbalances, jumpstart healthier patterns, and enable children to enjoy the benefits of learning and social relatedness for the rest of their lives.

Q&A

Q: Is it possible to increase the activity of specific brain areas through stimulation?

A: Yes, it is. Ongoing research is needed to identify which specific areas are underactive in each individual, what kinds of stimulation are likely to be most beneficial and long-lasting, and how to best provide programs that are practical and affordable for the people who need them. We already have the technology to identify the level of activity in brain areas critical to learning, attention, emotion regulation, behavior control, and reward processing. In the foreseeable future, using both brain scan and EEG data to monitor brain activity, it should be possible to develop programs using neurofeedback, cranial electrotherapy stimulation, interactive metronome, heart-centered biofeedback, and other modalities to address many of the challenges that confront people with ADHD.

TAKING ONE STEP AT A TIME

We have introduced you to treatments using emerging technologies. In deciding whether to pursue these approaches, consider the following steps:

1. Learn more about treatments that interest you by exploring the websites and resources below.
2. Discuss these treatment options with your health care providers. They may be able to recommend local practitioners for you to interview.
3. Before you decide on a particular treatment, make an appointment to discuss it with the provider. Find out how much experience and knowledge the provider has regarding working with ADHD. If the provider does not have much experience, he or she may be able to recommend someone in the field who does.
4. It can be helpful to set up an initial evaluation. For example, a neurofeedback specialist who performs an initial QEEG (qualitative EEG) would be able to show you your brain-wave patterns and discuss how to go about improving them. Be sure to ask for an estimate of the number of sessions that would be required and the cost per visit.
5. Neurofeedback and brain stimulation techniques take time. Some people respond to their first treatment. But, it is best to allow at least 6 weeks for noticeable changes.
6. Do not expect a provider to be able to precisely predict how or when you will respond. Each person is unique. Depending on your response, the treatments may need to be adjusted and tweaked numerous times. Keep talking with your provider and asking questions so that you feel comfortable with how the treatment is progressing.

RESOURCES

The following websites, organizations, books, and journals will provide you with information to understand and access the treatments discussed in this chapter.

Websites for Treatments and Organizations

Alpha-Stim: www.alphastim.com.
Cranial electrotherapy stimulator that enhances alpha waves.

Fisher Wallace: www.fisherwallace.com.
Cranial electrotherapy stimulator based on LISS device.

HeartMath: www.heartmath.com.
Products and programs that reduce stress. Institute for HeartMath: Early HeartSmarts for ages 3–6; HeartSmarts for grades 3–5.

International Society for Neurofeedback and Research: www.isnr.org.
Information, conferences, training, research, referrals.

Neurodevelopoment Center, Alpert Medical School, Brown University, Providence, RI: http://www.neurofeedbackexperts.blogspot.com.
information on Dr. Laurence Hirshberg's work.

Stone Mountain Center for Counseling and Biofeedback: www.stonemountain center. com.
Dr. Stephen Larsen provides evaluation and neurofeedback.

Books

Larsen, S. (2006). *The Healing Power of Neurofeedback: The Revolutionary LENS Technique for Restoring Optimal Brain Functioning.* Rochester, VT: Healing Arts Press.
Comprehensive information about neurofeedback with 100 case examples.

Journals

Journal of Neurotherapy —research articles on the latest developments in neurotherapy.

CHAPTER 7 OUTLINE

Just Desserts

Congratulations for making it to our final chapter. After the previous six chapters, you may be feeling rather full of ideas, so we will keep this seventh course light. We hope you have learned a lot about ADHD and that you will benefit from some of the new approaches we have described. Hopefully, some of you will be taking this knowledge to your health care providers before ordering new supplements, while others will be rummaging through your cabinets, armed with magnifying glasses, reading all the food labels. You may be inspired to talk to your local grocer about offering more organic food options or writing to the head of some major food chain that needs to clean up its ingredients. You might join a yoga class or simply order a CD and slow your breathing down to five breaths per minute. Before you take this knowledge and run, we'd like to highlight some of the main points and tie up a few loose ends.

BEING A SEEKER

If you only remember one lesson from this book, we hope it will be this: *Be a seeker*. By that we mean continue to seek new information and more effective treatments for yourself and for those who are dear to you. You may need to try many different treatments, one after another. You may have to consult with different specialists. To be a successful seeker requires a lot of patience and determination. As a person with ADHD, you may tend to get easily frustrated and make snap decisions rather than wise decisions. Be sure to fully evaluate the effects of whatever treatment you are trying before moving on to the next. Sometimes a slightly higher dose or an additional few weeks can make all the difference. The same is true for doctors and consultants. If you decide to work with professionals, give them time to do their job. The following case illustrates how an impatient parent can disrupt a child's care.

> Allison phoned to make an appointment for her 17-year-old son Daren, who was suffering from ADHD and severe sleeplessness. He tossed and turned every night, never sleeping soundly. During the day he was drowsy, but he couldn't sleep. Allison, who also had ADHD, loved her son, advocated for his needs, and kept up with the latest treatments, but she tended to jump from one thing to another too quickly. For example, she wanted me (Dr. Gerbarg) to evaluate Daren to prescribe medication to help him sleep. Allison came into the office with Daren and began telling me about the many treatments they had tried. Meanwhile Daren sat on the sofa looking exhausted and agitated at the same time. One leg kept jiggling up and down while his hands fidgeted. Allison said she wanted me to prescribe medication to put Daren to sleep at night. During the discussion, I explained that a simple breathing practice might work better than medication to help Daren relax and put himself to sleep. Since he had not responded well to other medications, it would be better to let him try something new rather than just giving him heavier sedation. They both agreed to give it a try. I noticed that Allison was tense, tended to interrupt the conversation, and unintentionally agitated her son. I asked her to sit in the waiting room so that I could teach Daren how to use coherent breathing to get himself to sleep.
>
> As soon as she left the room, Daren asked to lie down on the sofa while I taught him coherent breathing with resistance breathing. As he shifted into breathing at five breaths per minute with his eyes closed, his entire body relaxed and became absolutely still. Within a few minutes, he fell asleep. When Allison returned to the room, I explained to her how well he had done and gave them both instructions for continuing the practice. At the end of the session, Alli-

son asked, "What about the medication?" I replied that we needed to use the time that day for coherent breathing and that we could discuss medication and other treatments during the next visit. We made an appointment and said good-bye. One week later, Allison left a message on my voicemail saying she was disappointed that I had not given Daren any medication, and she cancelled his appointment. They never returned, but I still remember Daren sleeping so peacefully on the sofa. Perhaps, he remembers, too. Maybe someday he will return to the breathing practice.

YOUR BRAIN IS ONE OF A KIND

You are unique and your brain is one of a kind. What works well for someone else may not work for you. Conversely, you may discover a special benefit that others will not get from a particular combination of treatments. So, it makes sense to combine the treatments that work best for you. Each successful treatment should bring you to a higher level of functioning, so just keep building on those successes.

In Chapter 1 we introduced you to Andy, the boy who kept visiting the ER with broken bones. Now, after reading this book, you have learned enough about complementary treatments to understand the steps Andy took over many years to solve his problems and create the life he always wanted. The curious child, always looking for new things, new adventures, grew into an explorer of new treatments.

We saved the details of Andy's story for the last chapter because they illustrate how one person found solutions to some of the more subtle symptoms of ADHD. There is no single complete description of all the things that people with ADHD experience. Andy is particularly talented at describing some of the less obvious aspects of his mental world. You may be experiencing thoughts or problems that have not been included in the ever-expanding diagnostic lists of ADHD symptoms. Listed or unlisted, some of these problems might respond to treatment.

Recall that Andy started using stimulant medications to help him focus and study in medical school. He wanted to find another way to manage his ADHD because he didn't like feeling speeded up by the medication. Andy was struggling with the following lifelong problems:

1. Poor attention, difficulty reading, slow processing, and difficulty absorbing information.

2. Memory problems. For example, Andy would dial a phone number—but by the time the person on the other end of the line picked up the phone and said hello, Andy would have forgotten whom he was calling.

3. Difficulty paying attention to the world around him and consequently failing to notice things.

4. Low energy, low mood, feeling worst in the evening.

5. Feeling insecure, worrying about imagined slights. For example, if someone didn't say hello or return a phone call, it really got under his skin, leading to ruminations (going over and over the same worries in his mind) and inability to stop the negative thoughts ("Why doesn't he like me anymore? What did I do to drive him away? What's wrong with me?")

About 10 years ago, I (Dr. Brown) started treating Andy with the herb, *Rhodiola rosea*, increasing his dose to 450 mg per day. Andy reported improvements in energy, alertness, attention, his sense of being in the present and engaged in the world, and a new feeling of well-being. Adding 2000 mg a day of omega-3 fatty acids (EPA + DHA) did not seem to affect his ADHD, but he continued to take them to improve his cardiovascular health and cholesterol levels. Using three capsules each morning of Clear Mind (Ameriden International)—an herbal blend containing *Rhodiola rosea, Rhododendron caucasicum* (Georgian snow rose; another energy-enhancing herb); Brown, Gerbarg, & Muskin, 2009), and *Ribes nigrum* (blackcurrant; believed to increase absorption of the other herbs)—further boosted his energy, mental clarity, and alertness. Instead of losing track of whatever he was trying to do, Andy was able to maintain his attention until he finished. Insecurities and negative thoughts did not vanish completely, but they faded into the background and didn't bother him as much. When he forgets to take Clear Mind for even a few days, his mood is off and he becomes less happy and more irritable.

Seven years ago, Andy found that using the LISS cranial electrotherapy stimulator consistently helped him sleep (see Chapter 6). Now he recommends it to many of *his* patients.

Five years ago, Andy learned a set of breathing techniques, called *Sudarshan Kriya*, that included resistance breathing (*Ujjayi*), rapid forceful breathing (*Bhastrika*), cyclical breathing (*Kriya*), yoga postures, and some meditation. At that time, Sudarshan Kriya opened his emotional awareness, leading to greater happiness. Although he no longer practices Sudarshan Kriya, he still uses resistance breathing to rapidly relieve anxiety and calm down. He sometimes uses rapid breathing practices to improve mood and mental focus.

Two years ago Andy added 100 mg a day phosphatidyl serine to his regimen. Phosphatidyl serine is a naturally occurring phosphorous-containing lipid in cell membranes and fat. Studies of phosphatidyl serine supplementation for memory and cognitive function have shown modest positive results in people over the age of 40 (Brown, Gerbarg, & Muskin, 2009). Nevertheless, the effect of the additional supplement was quite noticeable—improvements in attention, processing speed, memory, and absorption of information. Andy was able to dial a phone number and remember whom he was calling when the person answered the phone. He felt less "spacey" and more present. His wife especially appreciated his increased ability to pay attention to what other people were saying.

We have to admire Andy's determination. Even with all of these improvements, he continued seeking. Although his mood was considerably better, Andy was aware that his sense of well-being depended on vigorous physical exercise every day. On some days, for example, when he had to go early to the operating room and missed his morning workout, his mood dropped. About 6 months ago, he started taking Vivix (Shaklee Corporation), a concentrated form of resveratrol (a plant-derived compound that may have anti-oxidant, anti-cancer, anti-inflammatory, and blood sugar lowering properties) containing antioxidants. Resveratrol stabilized Andy's sense of well-being, even on days when he couldn't work out.

Before starting complementary treatments, Andy managed to do good work and to be a good husband, father, and friend, but it often required a tremendous effort to overcome his ADHD problems. By gradually building up layers of complementary treatments, it became easier and easier for Andy to improve his relationships and enhance his work productivity. By helping his brain to work better, complementary treatments enhanced his abilities to listen, notice, think, absorb, remember, plan, respond, and feel good about himself and his life.

At first glance, the complexity of Andy's treatments may seem daunting—so many pills, so many treatments. Yet, consider this: Andy overcame most of the ADHD problems that had plagued him his entire life; he got off of stimulant medication, and he became the person he had always wanted to be. For him it was well worth the time and effort. Now Andy enjoys a wonderful life, in many ways better than the lives of most people who don't have ADHD. Perhaps it is because he is a true seeker. We predict that he will find more innovative ways to fine-tune his splendid ADHD brain.

CLOSING THOUGHTS

Thriving in modern society requires a lot of mental work. People with ADHD are at a disadvantage in having to overcome symptoms that impair their abilities to work, play, and engage in fulfilling relationships. However, many people with ADHD have the potential to succeed in all areas of their lives by reducing or eliminating symptoms related to the disorder. While medications and standard behavioral therapies have helped many people improve, more can be achieved by integrating standard treatments with complementary approaches that target neurological mechanisms that are critical to optimal brain functioning. Health care providers are encouraged to learn more about these non-drug options in order to offer their patients the widest possible range of treatments. Consumers can play a major role by asking health care professionals to help them try these new methods and by advocating for more research and development of complementary treatments.

REFERENCES

Adler, A.A., &Weiss, M.D. (2004). Clinical implications of new research in attention-deficit/hyperactivity disorder in adults. *Journal of Clinical Psychiatry*, *5*(1), 1–8.

Ahmed, A.H., & Oswald, R.E. (2010). Piracetam defines a new binding site for allosteric modulators of alpha-amino-3-hydroxy-5-methyl-4-isoxazole-propionic acid (AMPA) receptors. *Journal of Medicinal Chemistry, 53*(5), 2197–2203.

Akhondzadeh, S., Naghavi, H.R., Vazirian, M., Shayeganpour, A., Rashidi, H., & Khani, M. (2001). Passionflower in the treatment of generalized anxiety: A pilot double-blind randomized controlled trial with oxazepam. *Journal of Clinical Pharmacology and Therapeutics, 26*(5), 363–367.

American Psychiatric Association. (1994). *Diagnostic and statistical manual of mental disorders* (4th ed.). Washington, DC: American Psychiatric Association.

American Psychiatric Association. (2000). *Diagnostic and statistical manual of mental_disorders* (Text rev.). Washington, DC: American Psychiatric Association.

Antalis, C.J., Stevens, L.J., Campbell, M., Pazdro, R., Ericson, K., & Burgess, J.R. (2006). Omega-3 fatty acid status in attention-deficit/hyperactivity disorder. *Prostaglandins Leukotriens and Essential Fatty Acids, 75*(4–5), 299–308.

Arnold, L. E. (2001). Alternative treatments for adults with attention-deficit hyperactivity disorder (ADHD). *Annals of the New York Academy of Sciences, 931*, 310–341.

Arnold, L.E., Amato, A., Bozzolo, H., Hollway, J., Cook, A., Ramadan, Y., et al. (2007). Acetyl-l-carnitine (ALC) in attention-deficit/ hyperactivity disorder: A multi-site, placebo-controlled pilot trial. *Journal of Child and Adolescent Psychopharmacology, 17*(6), 791–802.

Arnold, L. E., & DiSilvestro, R. A. (2005). Zinc in attention-deficit/ hyperactivity disorder. *Journal of Child and Adolescent Psychopharmacology, 15*(4), 619–627.

Arns, M., de Ridder, S., Strehl, U., Breteler, M., & Coenen, A. (2009). Efficacy of neurofeedback treatment in ADHD: The effects on inattention, impulsivity, and hyperactivity: A meta-analysis. *Clinical EEG and Neuroscience, 40*(3), 180–189.

Ayachi, S., El Abed, A., Dhifi, W., & Marzouk, B. (2007). Chlorophylls, proteins and fatty acids amounts of *arthrospira platensis* growing under saline conditions. *Pakistan Journal of Biological Sciences, 10*(14), 2286–2291.

Baranov, V.B. (1994). *Experimental trials of herbal adaptogen effect on the quality of operation activity, mental and professional work capacity.* Contract 93-11-615 Stage 2 Phase I. Moscow: Russian Federation Ministry of Health Institute of Medical and Biological Problems (IMBP).

Barkley, R.A. (2009). Deficient emotional self-regulation: A core component of attention-deficit/hyperactivity disorder. *Journal of ADHD and Related Disorders, 1*(2), 5–37.

Bateman, B., Warner, J.O., Hutchinson, E., Dean, T., Rowlandson, P., Gant, C., et al. (2004). The effects of a double-blind, placebo-controlled, artificial food colourings and benzoate preservative challenge on hyperactivity in a general population sample of preschool children. *Archives of Disease in Childhood, 89*(6), 506–511.

Beauchaine, T.P. (2001). Vagal tone, development, and Gray's motivational theory: Toward an integrated model of autonomic nervous system functioning in psychopathology. *Developmental Psychopathology, 13*(2), 183-214.

Beauchaine, T. P., Katkin, E. S., Strassberg, Z., & Snarr, J. (2001).

Disinhibitory psychopathology in male adolescents: Discriminating conduct disorder from attention-deficit/hyperactivity disorder through concurrent assessment of multiple autonomic states. *Journal of Abnormal Psychology, 110*(4), 610–624.

Bendz, L.M., & Scates, A.C. (2010). Melatonin treatment for insomnia in pediatric patients with attention-deficit/hyperactivity disorder. *Annals of Pharmacotherapy, 44*(1), 185–191.

Benjamin, J., Li, L., Patterson, C., Greenberg, B.D., Murphy, D.L., & Hamer, D.H. (1996). Population and familial association between the D4 dopamine receptor gene and measures of novelty seeking. *Nature Genetics, 12*(1), 81–84.

Bernardi, L., Porta, C., Gabutti, A., Spicuzza, L., & Sleight, P. (2001). Modulatory effects of respiration. *Autonomic Neuroscience, 90*(1–2), 47–56.

Bilici, M., Yildirim, F., Kandil, S., Bekaroglu, M., Yildirmis, S., Deger, O., et al. (2004). Double-blind, placebo-controlled study of zinc sulfate in the treatment of attention deficit hyperactivity disorder. *Progress in Neuro-Psychopharmacology and Biological Psychiatry, 28*(1), 181–190.

Blum, K., Chen A.L., Braverman, E.R., Comings, D.E., Chen, T.J., Arcuri, V., et al. (2008). Attention-deficit/hyperactivity disorder and reward deficiency syndrome. *Journal of Neuropsychiatric Disease and Treatment, 4*(5), 893–918.

Blumenthal, M. (Ed.). (2003). *The ABC clinical guide to herbs.* Austin, TX: American Botanical Council.

Bouchard, M.F., Bellinger, D.C., Wright, R.O., & Weisskopf, M.G. (2010). Attention-deficit/hyperactivity disorder and urinary metabolites of organophosphate pesticides. *Pediatrics, 125*(6), e1270–1277.

Bourre, J.M. (2006). Effects of nutrients (in food) on the structure and function of the nervous system: Update on dietary requirements for brain. Part 1: Micronutrients. *Journal of Nutrition, Health and Aging, 10*(5), 377–385.

Bradberry S., & Vale, A. (2009). Dimercaptosuccinic acid (succimer; DMSA) in inorganic lead poisoning. *Clinical Toxicology (Philaelphia), 47*(7), 617–631.

Bradley, R.T., Atkinson, M., Tomasino, D., Rees, R.A., & Galvin, P. (2007). *Facilitating emotional self-regulation in preschool children: Efficacy of the Early HeartSmarts program in promoting social, emotional and cognitive development*. Institute of HeartMath: Boulder Creek, CO. Available online at www.heartmath.org.

Bradley, R.T., McCraty, R., Atkinson, M., Arguelles, L., & Rees, R.A. (2007). Reducing test anxiety and improving test performance in America's schools: Results from the TestEdge National Demonstration Study. Boulder Creek, CO: Institute of HeartMath. Available online at www.heartmath.org.

Bratman, D., & Girman, A.M. (2003). *Mosby's handbook of herbs and supplements and their therapeutic uses*. St. Louis, MO: Mosby.

Brekhman, I.I., & Dardymov, I.V. (1969). New substances of plant origin which increase non-specific resistance. *Annual Review of Pharmacology and Toxicology, 9*, 419–430.

Brown, R.P., Gerberg, P.L. (2004). *The Rhodiola revolution*. New York: Rodale Press.

Brown, R P., & Gerbarg, P.L. (2005a). Sudarshan Kriya yogic breathing in the treatment of stress, anxiety, and depression: Part I. Neurophysiologic model. *Journal of Alternative and Complementary Medicine, 11*(1), 189–201.

Brown, R.P., & Gerbarg, P.L. (2005b). Sudarshan Kriya yogic breathing in the treatment of stress, anxiety, and depression: Part II. Clinical applications and guidelines. *Journal of Alternative and Complementary Medicine, 11*(4), 711–717.

Brown, R.P., & Gerbarg, P.L. (2012). *The healing power of the breath: Simple techniques to reduce stress and anxiety, enhance concentration, and balance your emotions*. Boston, MA: Shambhala.

Brown, R.P., Gerbarg, P.L., & Bottiglieri, T. (2000). S-adenosylmethionine (SAMe) in the clincial practice of psychiatry, neurology, and internal medicine. *Clinical Practice of Alternative Medicine, 1*(4), 230–241.

Brown, R.P., Gerbarg, P.L., & Muskin, P.R. (2009). *How to use herbs nutrients and yoga in mental health care*. New York, NY: Norton.

Bruner, A.B., Joffe, A., Duggan, A.K., Casella, J.F., & Brandt, J. (1996). Randomised study of cognitive effects of iron supplementation in non-anaemic iron-deficient adolescent girls. *Lancet, 348*(9033), 992–996.

Burke, M.G. (2010). The impact of screen media on children. *Psychiatric Times, 27*(10), 40–47.

Bussing, R., & Lall, A. (2010). Keys to success in ADHD treatment. *Psychiatric Times, 27*(10), 4–49.

Chen, C.S., Burton, M., Greenberger, E., & Dmitrieva, J. (1999). Population migration and the variation of dopamine D4 receptor (DRD4) allele frequencies around the globe. *Evolution and Human Behavior, 20*(5), 309–324.

Christakis, D.A., Zimmerman, F.J., DiGiuseppe, D.L., & McCarty, C.A. (2004). Early television exposure and subsequent attentional problems in children. *Pediatrics, 113*, 708–713.

Church, D., Hawk. C., Books. A., Toukolehto. O., Wren, M., Dinter, I., et al. (in press). *Psychological trauma in veterans using EFT (Emotional Freedom Techniques): A randomized controlled trial.* Retrieved December 29, 2010 from http://veterans.house. gov/Media/file/111/7-21-10/Churchsubmission.pdf.

Conners, C.K. (1997). *Conners Rating Scale—Revised.* North Tonawanda, NY: Multi-Health Systems.

Cortese, S., Faraone, S.V., Konofal, E., & Lecendreux, M. (2009). Sleep in children with attention-deficit/hyperactivity disorder: Meta-analysis of subjective and objective studies. *Journal of the American Academy of Child and Adolescent Psychiatry, 48*(9), 894–908.

Craig, A.D. (2003). Interoception: The sense of the physiological condition of the body. *Current Opinion in Neurobiology, 13*(4), 500–505.

Critchley, H.D. (2005). Neural mechanisms of autonomic, affective, and cognitive integration. *Journal of Comparative Neurology, 493*(1), 154–166.

Cubillo, A., Halari, R., Ecker, C., Giampietro, V., Taylor, E., & Rubia, K. (2010). Reduced activation and inter-regional functional connectivity of fronto-striatal networks in adults with childhood attention-deficit hyperactivity disorder (ADHD) and persisting symptoms during tasks of motor inhibition and cognitive switching. *Psychiatry Research, 44*(10), 629–639.

Curl, C.L., Fenske, R.A., & Elgetun, K. (2003). Organophosphorous pesticide exposure of urban and suburban children with organic and conventional diets. *Environmental Health Perspectives, 111*(3), 377–382.

Dahl, J.J., & Falk, K. (2008). Ayurvedic herbal formula as an antidote to 9/11 toxicity. *Alternative Therapies, 14*(1), 24–28.

Dalley, J.W., Theobald, D.E., Bouger, P., Chudasama, Y., Cardinal, R.N., & Robbins T.W. (2004). Cortical cholinergic function and deficits in visual attentional performance in rats following 192 IgG-saporin-induced lesions of the medial prefrontal cortex. *Cerebral Cortex, 14*(8), 922–932.

Du Paul, G.J., Power, T.J., Anastopoulos, A.D., Reid, R, McGoey, K., & Ikeda, M. (1997). Teacher ratings of ADHD symptoms: Factor structure and normative data. *Psychological Assessment, 9*, 436–444.

Ebstein, R.P., Novick, O., Umansky, R., Priel, B., Osher, Y., Blaine, D., et al. (1996). Dopamine D_4 receptor (D_4DR) exon III polymorphism associated with the human personality trait of novelty seeking. *Nature Genetics, 12*(1), 78–80.

Eisenberg, J., Ben-Daniel, N., Mei-Tal, G., & Wertman, E. (2004). An autonomic nervous system biofeedback modality for the treatment of attention deficit hyperactivity disorder: An open pilot study. *Israeli Journal of Psychiatry and Related Science, 41*(1), 45–53.

Ernst, E., Pittler, M.H., & Wider, B. (Ed.). (2006). *The desktop guide to complementary and alternative medicine: An evidence-based approach* (2nd ed.). Mosby: London.

Eubig, P.A., Aguiar, A., & Schantz, S.L. (2010). Lead and PCBs as risk factors for attention-deficit/hyperactivity disorder. *Environmental Health Perspectives, 118*(12), 1654–1667.

Fehmi, L.G., & McKnight, J.T. (2001). Attention and neurofeedback synchrony training: Clinical results and their significance. *Journal of Neurotherapy, 5*(1–2), 45–61.

Fuchs, T., Birbaumer, N., Lutzenberger, W., Gruzelier, J.H., & Kaiser, J. (2003). Neurofeedback treatment for attention-deficit/hyperactivity disorder in children: A comparison with methlyphenidate. *Applied Psychophysiology and Biofeedback*, *28*(1), 1–12.

Feuerstein, G. (1998). *The yoga tradition: Its history, literature, philosophy, and practice.* Prescott, AZ: Hohm Press.

Furmanowa, M., Skopinska-Rozewska, E., Rogala, E., & Malgorzata, H. (1998). *Rhodiola rosea* in vitro culture: Phytochemical analysis and antioxidant action. *Acta Societis Botanicorum Poloniae*, *76*(1), 69–73.

Gastpar, M., Singer, A., & Zeller, K. (2005). Efficacy and tolerability of hypericum extract STW3 in long-term treatment with a once-daily dosage in comparison with sertraline. *Pharmacopsychiatry*, *38*(2), 78–86.

Gerbarg, P.L. (2007). Yoga and neuro-psychoanalysis. In F.S. Anderson (Ed.), *Bodies in treatment: The unspoken dimension* (pp. 132–133). Hillsdale, NJ: Analytic Press.

Gevensleben, H., Holl, B., Albrecht, B., Schlamp, D., Kratz, O., Studer, P., et al. (2009). Distinct EEG effects related to neurofeedback training in children with ADHD: A randomized controlled trial. *International Journal of Psychophysiology, 74*(2), 149–157.

Gevensleben, H., Holl, B., Albrecht, B., Schlamp, D., Kratz, O., Studer, P., et al. (2010). Neurofeedback training in children with ADHD: 6-month follow-up of a randomised controlled trial. *European Child and Adolescent Psychiatry*, *19*(9), 715–724.

Glieck, J. (1988). *Chaos: The making of science.* New York: Penguin.

Gouliaev, A.H., & Senning, A. (1994). Piracetam and other structurally related nootropics. *Brain Research: Brain Research Review*, *19*(2), 180–222.

Greenburg, L.M., & Kindischi, R.N. (1999). *TOVA test of variable attention: Clinical guide.* Los Alamitos, CA: Universal Attention Disorders.

Gustafsson, P.A., Birberg-Thornberg, U., Duchen, K., Landgren, M., Malmberg, K., Pelling, H., et al. (2010). EPA supplementation improves teacher rated behaviour and oppositional symptoms in children with ADHD. *Acta Paediatrica, 99*(10), 1540–1549.

Haffner, J., Roos, J., Goldstein, N., Parzer, P., & Resch, F. (2006). [The effectiveness of body-oriented methods of therapy in the treatment of attention-deficit hyperactivity disorder (ADHD): Results of a controlled pilot study]. *Z Kinder Jugendpsychiatr Psychother*, *34*(1), 37–47.

Hallowell, E., & Ratey, J. (1995). *Driven to distraction: Recognizing and coping with attention deficit disorder from childhood through adulthood*. New York, NY: Simon & Schuster.

Hallowell, E., & Ratey, J. (2005). *Delivered from distraction: Getting the most out of life with attention deficit disorder*. New York: Ballantine Books.

Harkness, R., & Bratman, S. (2003). *Mosby's handbook of drug–herb and drug–supplement interactions*. St. Louis, MO: Mosby.

Hartmann, T. (2003). *The Edison gene: ADHD and the gift of the hunter child*. Rochester, VT: Park Street Press.

Herrero, M., Vicente, M.J., Cifuentes, A., & Ibáñez, E. (2007). Characterization by high-performance liquid chromatography/electrospray ionization quadrupole time-of-flight mass spectrometry of the lipid fraction of Spirulina platensis pressurized ethanol extract. *Rapid Communications in Mass Spectrometry, 21*(11), 1729–1738.

Hoebert, M., van der Heijden, K.B., van Geijlswijk, I.M., & Smits, M.G. (2009). Long-term follow-up of melatonin treatment in children with ADHD and chronic sleep onset insomnia. *Journal of Pineal Research, 47*(1), 1–7.

Hölzel, B. K., Carmody, J., Vangel, M., Congleton, C., Yerramsetti, S. M., Gard, T., et al. (2011). Mindfulness practice leads to increases in regional brain gray matter density. *Psychiatry Research, 191*(1), 36–43.

Hutchinson, D.O., Frith, R.W., Shaw, N.A., Judson, J.A., & Cant, B.R. (1991). A comparison between electroencephalography and somatosensory evoked potentials for outcome prediction following severe head injury. *Electroencephalography and Clinical Neurophysiology, 78*(3), 228–233.

Iulu, F., Dolotov O.V., Kondrakhin, A., Dubynina, E.V., Grivennikov, I.A., & Kovalev, G.I. (2009). [Effects of nootropic drugs on hippocampal and cortical BDNF levels in mice with different exploratory behavior efficacy]. *Eksp Klin Farmakol, 72*(6), 3–6.

Jacobson, M.F., & Kobylewski, S. (2010). Color us worried: Why synthetic food dyes should be banned. *Nutrition Action Healthletter,* September 2010, 10–11.

Jensen, P. S., & Kenny, D. T. (2004). The effects of yoga on the attention and behavior of boys with attention-deficit/ hyperactivity disorder (ADHD). *Journal of Attention Disorders, 7*(4), 205–216.

Johnson, M., Ostlund, S., Fransson, G., Kadesjo, B., & Gillberg, C. (2009). Omega-3/omega-6 fatty acids for attention deficit hyperactivity disorder: A randomized placebo-controlled trial in children and adolescents. *Journal of Attention Disorders, 12*, 394–401.

Kennedy, D.O., Little,W., & Scholey, A.B. (2004). Attenuation of laboratory-induced stress in humans after acute administration of *Melissa officinalis* (lemon balm). *Psychosomatic Medicine, 66*(4), 607–613.

Kiddie, J.Y., Weiss, M.D., Kitts, D.D., Levy-Milne, R., & Wasdell, M.B. (2010). Nutritional status of children with attention deficit hyperactivity disorder: A pilot study. *International Journal of pediatrics,* in press.

Klawansky, S., Yeung, A., Berkey, C., Shah, N., Phan, H., & Chalmers, T.C. (1995). Meta-analysis of randomized controlled trials of cranial electrostimulation: Efficacy in treating selected psychological and physiological conditions. *Journal of Nervous and Mental Disease, 183*(7), 478–484.

Klinkenberg, I., Sambeth, A., & Blokland, A. (2010). Acetylcholine and attention. *Behavioural Brain Research,* in press.

König, S., & Joller, P. (2006). Influence of a food supplement on the behaviour of children with attention deficit disorders (ADD/ADHD). *Päediatrie,* January 2006, 33–36.

Konofal, E., Lecendreux, M., Arnulf, I., & Mouren, M.C. (2004). Iron deficiency in children with attention-deficit/hyperactivity disorder. *Archives of Pediatric and Adolescent Medicine, 158*(12), 1113–1115.

Konofal, E., Lecendreux, M., Deron, J., Marchand, M., Cortese, S.,

Zaïm, M., et al. (2008). Effects of iron supplementation on attention deficit hyperactivity disorder in children. *Pediatric Neurology, 38*(1), 20–26.

Krummel, D.A., Seligson, F.H., & Guthrie, H.A. (1996). Hyperactivity: Is candy causal? *Critical Review of Food Science and Nutrition, 36*(1–2), 31–47.

Krystal, A.D., & Ressler, I. (2002). The use of valerian in neuropsychiatry. *CNS Spectrum, 6*(10), 841–847.

Kuehn, B.M. (2010). Increased risk of ADHD associated with early exposure to pesticides, PCBs. *Journal of the American Medical Association, 304*(1), 27–28.

Kuntsi, J., McLoughlin, G., & Asherson, P. (2006). Attention deficit hyperactivity disorder. *NeuroMolecular Medicine, 8*(4), 461–484.

Kurkin, V.A., & Zapesochnaya, G.G. (1986). Chemical composition and pharmacological properties of *Rhodiola rosea*. *Chemical and Pharmaceutical Journal* (Moscow), *20*(10), 1231–1244.

Lake, J., & Spiegel, D. (2007). *Complementary and alternative treatments in mental health care*. Washington, DC: American Psychiatric Association.

Larsen, S. (2006). *The healing power of neurofeedback: The revolutionary lens technique for restoring optimal brain functioning*. Rochester, VT: Healing Arts Press.

Larsen, S., Harrington, K., & Hicks, S. (2006). The LENS (low energy neurofeedback system): A clinical outcomes study on one hundred patients at Stone Mountain Center, New York: Investigations in neuromodulation, neurofeedback and applied neuroscience. *Journal of Neurotherapy, 10*(2), 69–78.

Lazar, S. W., Kerr, C.E., Wasserman, R.H., Gray, J R., Greve, D.N., Treadway, M.T., et al. (2005). Meditation experience is associated with increased cortical thickness. *NeuroReport, 16*(17), 1893–1897.

Leins, U., Goth, G., Hinterberger, T., Klinger, C., Rumpf, N., & Strehl, U. (2007). Neurofeedback for children with ADHD: A comparison of SCP and theta/beta protocols. *Applied Psychophysiology and Biofeedback, 32*(2), 73–88.

Leisman, G., Melillo, R., Thum, S.l., Ransom, M.A., Orlando, M., Tice, C., et al. (2010). The effect of hemisphere specific remediation strategies on the academic performance outcome of children with ADD/ADHD. *International Journal of Adolescent Medicine and Health, 22*(2), 275–283.

Lévesque, J., Beauregard, M., & Mensour, B. (2006). Effect of neurofeedback training on the neural substrates of selective attention in children with attention-deficit/hyperactivity disorder: A functional magnetic resonance imaging study. *Neuroscience Letters, 394*(3), 216–221.

Linden, M., Habib, T., & Radojevic, V. (1996). A controlled study of the effects of EEG biofeedback on cognition and behavior of children with attention deficit disorder and learning disabilities. *Biofeedback & Self-Regulation, 21*(1), 35–49.

Liss, B., & Liss, S. (1996). Physiological and therapeutic effects of high frequency electrical pulses. *Integrative Physiological and Behavioral Science, 31*(2), 88–95.

Lloyd, A., Brett, D., & Wesnes, K. (2010). Coherence training in children with attention-deficit hyperactivity disorder: Cognitive functions and behavioral changes. *Alternative Therapies, 16*(4), 34–42.

Lobaugh, N.J., Karaskov, V., Rombough, V., Rovet, J., Bryson, S., Greenbaum, R., et al. (2001). Piracetam therapy does not enhance cognitive functioning in children with Down syndrome. *Archives of Pediatric and Adolescent Medicine, 155*(4), 442–448.

Loo, S., & Barkley, R. (2005). Clinical utility of EEG in attention deficit hyperactivity disorder. *Applied Neuropsychology, 12*(2), 64–76.

Lubar, J.F., Swartwood, M.O., Swartwood, J.N., & O'Donnell, P.H. (1995). Evaluation of the effectiveness of EEG neurofeedback training for ADHD in a clinical setting as measured by changes in T.O.V.A., scores, behavioral ratings, and WISC-R performance. *Biofeedback & Self-Regulation, 20*(1), 83–99.

Lyon, M.R., Cline, J.C., Totosy de Zepetnek, J., Shan, J.J., Pang, P., & Benishin, C. (2001). Effect of the herbal extract combination *Panax quinquefolium* and *Ginkgo biloba* on attention-deficit hyperactivity disorder: A pilot study. *Journal of Psychiatry and Neuroscience, 26*(3), 221–228.

Mizuno, T., Kuno, R., Nitta, A., Nabeshima, T., Zhang, G., Kawanoku-chi, J., et al. (2005). Protective effects of nicergoline against neuronal cell death induced by activated microglia and astrocytes. *Brain Research, 1066*(1–2), 78–85.

Molina, B.S., Hinshaw, S.P, Swanson, J.M., Arnold, L.E., Vitiello, B., Jensen, P.S., et al. (2009). The MTA at 8 years: Prospective follow-up of children treated for combined-type ADHD in a multisite study. *Journal of the American Academy of Child and Adolescent Psychiatry, 48*(5), 484–500.

Monastra, V.J. (2008). Quantitative electroencephalography and attention-deficit/hyperactivity disorder: Implications for clinical practice. *Current Psychiatry Reports, 10*(5), 432–438.

Monastra, V.J., Monastra, D.M., & George, S.F. (2002) The effects of stimulant therapy, EEG biofeedback, and parenting style on the primary symptoms of attention-deficit/hyperactivity disorder. *Applied Psychophysiology and Biofeedback, 27*(4), 231–249.

Muller, S.F., & Klement, S. (2006). A combination of valerian and lemon balm is effective in the treatment of restlessness and dyssomnia in children. *Phytomedicine, 13*(6), 383–387.

Murdock, M. (1987). *Spinning inward: Using guided imagery with children for learning, creativity, and relaxation.* Boston, MA: Shambhala.

Murray, D.W., Arnold, L.E., Swanson, J., Wells, K., Burns, K., Jensen, P., et al. (2008). A clinical review of outcomes of the multimodal treatment study of children with attention-deficit/hyperactivity disorder (MTA). *Current Psychiatry Reports, 10*(5), 424–431.

Nash, J.K. (2000). Treatment of attention deficit hyperactivity disorder with neurotherapy. *Clinical Electroencephalograhy, 31*(1), 30–37.

Negi, K.S., Singh, Y.D., Kushwaha, K.P., et al. (2000). Clinical evaluation of memory enhancing properties of Memory Plus in children with attention deficit hyperactivity disorder. [Abstract]. *International Journal of Psychiatry, 42.*

Nettleton, J.A. (1991). Omega-3 fatty acids: Comparison of plant and seafood sources in human nutrition. *Journal of the American Dietetic Association, 91*(3), 331–337.

Niederhofer, H. (2010). Ginkgo biloba treating patients with attention-deficit disorder. *Phytotherapy Research, 24*(1), 26–27.

Noggle, J. J., & Khalsa, S.B.S. (2010). Group randomized, controlled evaluation of yoga for adolescent mental health within a high school curriculum [Abstract #20]. *International Journal of Yoga Therapy, 20*(S1), 28.

Oades, R.D., Lasky-Su, J., Christiansen, H., Faraone, S.V., Sonuga-Barke, E.J., Banaschewski, T., et al. (2008). The influence of serotonin and other genes on impulsive behavioral aggression and cognitive impulsivity in children with attention-deficit/hyperactivity disorder (ADHD): Findings from a family-based association test (FBAT) analysis. *Behavioral and Brain Function, 4*, 48–62.

Ochs, L. (2006). Low energy neurofeedback system (LENS): Theory, background, and introduction. *Journal of Neurotherapy, 10*(2–3), 5–39.

Office of Dietary Supplements National Institute of Health. Retrieved December 21, 2010 from http://ods.od.nih.gov/factsheets/vitamina/.

Overcash, S.J. (2005). The effect of ROSHI protocol and cranial electrotherapy stimulation on a nine-year-old anxious, dyslexic male with attention deficit disorder: A case study. *Journal of Neurotherapy, 9*(2), 63–77.

Panossian, A., & Wikman, G. (2009). Evidence-based efficacy of adaptogens in fatigue, and molecular mechanisms related to their stress-protective activity. *Current Clinical Pharmacology, 4*(3), 198–219.

Peck, H.L., Kehle, T.J., & Bray, M.A. (2005). Yoga as an intervention for children with attention problems. *School Psychology Review, 34*(3), 415–424.

Petkov, V.D., Yonkov, D., Mosharoff, A., Kambourova, T., Alova, L., Petkov, V.V., et al. (1986). Effects of alcohol aqueous extract from *Rhodiola rosea* L. roots on learning and memory. *Acta Physiologica Pharmacologica Bulgariga, 12*(1), 3–16.

Porges, S.W. (2001). The polyvagal theory: Phylogenetic substrates of a social nervous system. *International Journal of Psychophysiology, 42*(2), 123–146.

Raghuraj P., Ramakrishnan A.G., Nagendra H.R., & Telles S. (1998).

Effect of two selected yogic breathing techniques on heart rate variability. *Indian Journal of Physiology and Pharmacology, 42*(4), 467–472.

Ramirez, P.M., Desantis, D., & Opler, L.A. (2001). EEG biofeedback treatment of ADD: A viable alternative to traditional medical intervention? *Annals of the New York Academy of Sciences, 931,* 342–358.

Robbins, J. (2000). *A symphony in the brain: The evolution of the new brain wave biofeedback.* New York, NY: Atlantic Monthly Press.

Rokem, A., Landau, A.N., Garg, D., Prinzmetal, W., Silver, M.A. (2010). Cholinergic enhancement increases the effects of voluntary attention but does not affect involuntary attention. *Neuropsychopharmacology, 35*(13), 2538–2544.

Routtenberg, A. (1978). The reward system of the brain. *Scientific American, 239*(5), 154–164.

Roy, A., Bellinge, D., Hu, H., Schwartz, J., Ettinger, A.S., Wright, R.O., et al. (2009). Lead exposure and behavior among young children in Chennai, India. *Environmental Health Perspectives, 117*

American Journal of Epidemiology, 171(5), 593–601.

Salehi, B., Imani, R., Mohammadi, M.R., Fallah, J., Mohammadi, M., Ghanizadeh, A., et al. (2010). Ginkgo biloba for attention-deficit/ hyperactivity disorder in children and adolescents: A double blind, randomized controlled trial. *Progress in Neuropsychopharmacology and Biological Psychiatry, 34*(1), 76–80.

Sarang, S.P., & Telles, S. (2006). Changes in P300 following two yoga-based relaxation techniques. *International Journal of Neuroscience, 116*(12), 1419–1430.

Sarang, S.P., & Telles, S. (2007). Immediate effect of two yoga-based relaxation techniques on performance in a letter-cancellation task. *Perceptual and Motor Skills, 105*(2),379–385.

Schoenthaler, S. J., & Bier, I. D. (1999). Vitamin-mineral intake and intelligence: A macrolevel analysis of randomized controlled trials. *Journal of Alternative and Complementary Medicine, 5*(2), 125–134.

Shaffer, R.J., Jacokes, L.E., Cassily, J.F., Greenspan, S.I., Tuchman,

R.F., & Stemmer P.J., Jr. (2001). Effect of interactive metronome training on children with ADHD. *American Journal of Occupational Therapy*, *55*(2), 155–162.

Shekim, W.O., Antun, F., Hanna, G.L., McCracken, J.T., & Hess, E.B. (1990). S-adenosyl-L-methionine (SAM) in adults with ADHD, residual state: Preliminary results from an open trial. *Psychopharmacology Bulletin*, *26*(2), 249–253.

Sherlin, L., Arns, M. , Lubar, J. & Sokhadze, E. (2010). A position paper on neurofeedback for the treatment of ADHD. *Journal of Neurotherapy*, *14*(2), 66–78.

Shevstov, V.A., Zholus, B.I., Shervarly, V.I., Vol'skij, V.B., Korovin, Y.P., Khristich, M.P., et al. (2003). A randomized trial of two different doses of a SHR-5 *Rhodiola rosea* extract versus placebo and control of capacity for mental work. *Phytomedicine*, *10*(2–3), 95–105.

Slovacek, S. P., Tucker, S. A., & Pantoja, L. (2003). *A study of the Yoga Ed Program at The Accelerated School*. Program Evaluation and Research Collaborative, Charter College of Education, Los Angeles, CA. Available online at www.calstatela.edu/academic/ccoe/c_perc/c_perc.

Song, H.S., & Lehrer, P. M. (2003). The effects of specific respiratory rates on heart rate and heart rate variability. *Applied Psychophysiology and Biofeedback, 28*(1), 13–23.

Southworth, S. (1999). A study of the effects of cranial electrical stimulation on attention and concentration. *Integrative Physiological and Behavioral Science*, *34*(1), 43–53.

Spasov, A.A., Mandrikov, V.B., & Mironova, I.A. (2000). The effect of the preparation rodakson on the psychophysiological and physical adaptation of students to an academic load. *Eksp Klin Farmakol*, *63*(1), 76–78.

Spasov, A.A., Wikman, G.K., Mandrikov, V.B., Mironova, I.A., & Neumoin, V.V. (2000). A double-blind, placebo-controlled pilot study of the stimulating and adaptogenic effect of *Rhodiola rosea* SHR-5 extract on the fatigue of students caused by stress during an examination period with a repeated low-dose regimen. *Phytomedicine*, *7*(2),85–89.

Stergiakouli, E., & Thapar, A. (2010). Fitting the pieces together:

Current research on the genetic basis of attention-deficit/hyperactivity disorder (ADHD). *Neuropsychiatric Disease and Treatment, 7*(6), 551–560.

Stevens, L., Zhang, W., Peck, L., Luczek, T., Grevstad, N., & Mahon, A. (2003). EFA supplementation in children with inattention, hyperactivity, and other disruptive behaviors. *Lipids, 38*, 1007–1021.

Stevenson, J., Sonuga-Barke, E., McCann, D., Grimshaw, K., Parker, K.M., Rose-Zerilli, M.J., et al. (2010). The roles of histamine degradation gene polymorphisms in moderating the effects of food additives on children's ADHD symptoms. *American Journal of Psychiatry, 167*(9), 1108–1115.

Streeter, C.C., Whitfield, T.H., Owen, L., Rein, T., Karri, S.K., Yakhkind, A. (2010). Effects of yoga versus walking on mood, anxiety, and brain GABA levels: A randomized controlled MRS study. *Journal of Alternative and Complementary Medicine, 16*(11), 1145–1152.

Strehl, U., Leins, U., Goth, G., Klinger, C., Hinterberger, T., & Birbaumer, N. (2006). Self-regulation of slow cortical potentials: A new treatment for children with attention-deficit/hyperactivity disorder. *Pediatrics, 118*(5), e1530–1540.

Subramanya, P., & Telles, S. (2009). Effect of two yoga-based relaxation techniques on memory scores and state anxiety. *BioPsychoSocial Medicine, 3*, 8.

Sumar, S. (1998). *Yoga for the special child: A therapeutic approach for infants and children with Down syndrome, cerebral palsy and learning disabilities*. Special Yoga Publications.

Swanson, J., Arnold, L.E., Kraemer, H., Hechtman, L., Molina B., Hinshaw, S., et al. (2008a). Evidence, interpretation, and qualification from multiple reports of long-term outcomes in the Multimodal Treatment Study of Children with ADHD (MTA): Part I. Executive summary. *Journal of Attention Disorders, 12*(1), 4–14.

Swanson, J., Arnold, L.E., Kraemer, H., Hechtman, L., Molina, B., Hinshaw, S., et al. (2008b). Evidence, interpretation, and qualification from multiple reports of long-term outcomes in the Multimodal Treatment Study of Children with ADHD (MTA): Part II. Supporting details. *Journal of Attention Disorders, 12*(1), 15–43.

Szegedi, A., Kohnen, R., Dienel, A., & Kieser, M. (2005). Acute treatment of moderate to severe depression with hypericum extract WS 5570 (St John's wort): Randomised controlled double blind non-inferiority trial versus paroxetine. *British Medical Journal*, *330*(7490), 503.

Tallal, P., Chase, C., Russell, G., & Schmitt, R. L. (1986). Evaluation of the efficacy of piracetam in treating information processing, reading and writing disorders in dyslexic children. *International Journal of Psychophysiology*, *4*(1), 41–52.

Telles, S., Gaur, V., & Balkrishna, A. (2009). Effect of a yoga practice session and a yoga theory session on state anxiety. *Perceptual and Motor Skills*, *109*(3), 924–930.

Telles, S., Raghuraj, P., Arankall, D., & Naveen, K.V. (2008). Immediate effect of high-frequency yoga breathing on attention. *Indian Journal of Medical Sciences*, *62*(1), 20–22.

Tenenbaum, S., Paul, J.C., Sparrow, E.P., Dodd, D.K., & Green, L. (2002). An experimental comparison of Pycnogenol and methylphenidate in adults with attention-deficit/hyperactivity disorder (ADHD). *Journal of Attention Disorders*, *6*(2), 49–60.

Thayer, J. F., & Brosschot, J. F. (2005). Psychosomatics and psychopathology: Looking up and down from the brain. *Psychoneuroendocrinology*, *30*(10), 1050–1058.

Torrioli, M.G., Vernacotola, S., Mariotti, P., Bianchi, E., Calvani, M., et al. (1999). Double-blind, placebo-controlled study of L-acetylcarnitine for the treatment of hyperactive behavior in fragile X syndrome. *American Journal of Medical Genetics*, *87*(4), 366–368.

Trebaticka, J., Kopasova, S., Hradecna, Z., Cinovsky, K., Skodacek, I., Suba, J., et al. (2006). Treatment of ADHD with French maritime pine bark extract, Pycnogenol. *European Child and Adolescent Psychiatry*, *15*(6), 329–335.

Van der Heijden, K.B., Smits M.G., Van Someren, E.J., Ridderinkhof, K.R., & Gunning, W.B. (2007). Effect of melatonin on sleep, behavior, and cognition in ADHD and chronic sleep-onset insomnia. *Journal of the American Academy of Child and Adolescent Psychiatry*, *46*(2), 233–241.

Van Veen, M.M., Kooij, J.J., Boonstra, A.M., Gordijn, M.C., & Van

Someren, E.J. (2010). Delayed circadian rhythm in adults with attention-deficit/hyperactivity disorder and chronic sleep-onset insomnia. *Biological Psychiatry, 67*(11), 1091–1096.

Vaschillo, E.G., Vaschillo, B., & Lehrer, P.M. (2006). Characteristics of resonance in heart rate variability stimulated by biofeedback. *Applied Psychophysiology and Biofeedback31*(2), 129–142.

Vasiliev, V. (2006). *Let every breath: Secrets of the Russian breath masters*. Toronto, CA: Russian Martial Art.

Vasiliev, V., Viktorinova, A., Trebaticka, J., Paduchova, Z., Ursinyova, M., Uhnakova, I., et al. (2009). Natural polyphenols modify trace element status and improve clinical symptoms of attention-deficit hyperactivity disorder. Biomed Pharmacother, in press.

Weber, W., Vander Stoep, A., McCarty, R.L., Weiss, N.S., Biederman, J., & McClellan, J. (2008). *Hypericum perforatum* (St. John's wort) for attention-deficit/hyperactivity disorder in children and adolescents: A randomized controlled trial. *Journal of the American Medical Association, 299*(22), 2633–2641.

Weintraub, A. (2004). *Yoga for depression*. New York: Broadway Books.

Weisler, R.H., & Goodman, D.W. (2008). Assessment and diagnosis of adult ADHD: Clinical challenges and opportunities for improving patient care. *Primary Psychiatry, 15*(11), 53–64.

Weiss, M.D. (2010). The unique aspects of assessment of ADHD. *Primary Psychiatry, 17*(5), 21–25.

Weiss, M.D., & Salpekar, J. (2010) Sleep problems in the child with Attention-Deficit Hyperactivity Disorder. *CNS Drugs, 24*(10), 811–828.

Willatts, P., Forsyth, J.S., DiModugno, M.K., Varma, S., & Colvin, M. (1998). Effect of long-chain polyunsaturated fatty acids in infant formula on problem solving at 10 months of age. *Lancet, 352*(9129), 688–691.

Williams, N. (2010). *Yoga therapy for every special child*. Philadelphia, PA: Singing Dragon.

Wilsher, C.R., Bennett, D., Chase, C.H., Conners, C.K., DiIanni, M., Feagans, L., et al. (1987). Piracetam and dyslexia: Effects on reading tests. *Journal of Clinical Psychopharmacology*, 7(4), 230–237.

Wu, X., Zhu, D., Jiang, X., Okagaki, P., Mearow, K., Zhu, G., et al. (2004). AMPA protects cultured neurons against glutamate excitotoxicity through a phosphatidylinositol 3-kinase-dependent activation in extracellular signal-regulated kinase to upregulate BDNF gene expression. *Journal of Neurochemistry*, *90*(4), 807–818.

Zoler, M.L. (2010). Prevalence of ADHD in U.S. reached 9.5% in 2007–2008. *Clinical Psychiatry News, 38*(12), 16.

Zs-Nagy, I. (2002). Pharmacological interventions against aging through the cell plasma membrane: A review of the experimental results obtained in animals and humans. *Annals of the New York Academy of Sciences*, *959*, 308–320; discussion 463–465.

Zylowska, L., Ackerman, D. L., Yang, M.H., Futrell, J.L., Horton, N.L., Hale, T.S., et al. (2008). Mindfulness meditation training in adults and adolescents with ADHD. *Journal of Attention Disorders*, *11*(6), 737–746.

INDEX

In this index, *f* denotes *figure* and *t* denotes *table*.